Dorset Libraries
Withdrawn Stock

GOTHAM WRITERS' WORKSHOP:
writing movies

A PRACTICAL GUIDE FROM NEW YORK'S
ACCLAIMED CREATIVE WRITING SCHOOL

GOTHAM WRITERS' WORKSHOP:
writing movies

A PRACTICAL GUIDE FROM NEW YORK'S ACCLAIMED CREATIVE WRITING SCHOOL

WRITTEN BY GOTHAM WRITERS' WORKSHOP FACULTY
EDITED BY ALEXANDER STEELE

A & C Black • London

1 3 5 7 9 10 8 6 4 2

Published 2008

A & C Black Publishers Limited
38 Soho Square
London W1D 3HB
www.acblack.com
ISBN 978–1–408–10130–8

First published 2006 by Bloomsbury USA, New York

A CIP catalogue record for this book is available from the British Library

This book is produced using paper made from wood grown in managed,
sustainable forests. It is natural, renewable and recyclable. The logging and
manufacturing processes conform to the environmental regulations of the country
of origin.

Printed and bound in Great Britain by
Caligraving Ltd, Thetford, Norfolk

How to Use this Book

You shouldn't just read your way through this book, but write your way through it as well. After all, you're reading this book because you want to write a screenplay.

In every chapter, you'll find two kinds of writing assignments. The assignments labeled *Take a Shot* will help you deepen your understanding of what you're learning through film analysis or by flexing your muscles with a writing exercise. The assignments labeled *Stepping-Stone* will give you one or more tasks designed to help you develop your own screenplay. If you have a screenplay idea you're burning to write, go ahead and use the stepping-stones on that idea. If you're not sure what you want to write about, you can just pick an idea and run with it, or you can save the stepping-stones for when you're ready. The stepping stones are not a paint-by-numbers method for writing a great screenplay (such a thing does not exist) but they will certainly lead you in the right direction.

Throughout the book, we will be using five movies to illustrate most of our points: *Die Hard*, *Thelma & Louise*, *Tootsie*, *Sideways*, and *The Shawshank Redemption*. To reap the maximum benefit from this book you should watch or re-watch these movies.

You should also visit the Web site for this book: www.Writing Movies.info. There you will find the screenplays for the five movies cited above, along with other helpful material.

Contents

CHAPTER 1

Screenwriting: Inventing a Myth

BY ALEXANDER STEELE

In his heyday, Charlie Chaplin was the most famous person on the planet. When a certain evil dictator stormed to power in Germany in the 1930s, people asked him why he had a mustache like Chaplin's. Not the other way around. Soon the precarious state of the world was translated to movie audiences in a scene from Chaplin's *The Great Dictator* that showed a maniacal tyrant (played by Charlie) dancing a kind of ballet with a globe of the earth, tossing it, twirling it, finally destroying it.

Movies are the contemporary mythology. They turn our past, present, and future into lore, giving us the stories we live by.

Movies are watched by presidents and prisoners and everyone in between. No wonder their influence is so immense. When Clark Gable peeled off his shirt in *It Happened One Night,* revealing a bare chest, sales of undershirts plummeted. When Marlon Brando staggered about in a torn T-shirt in *A Streetcar Named Desire*, sales of T-shirts skyrocketed. If you don't think movies have a huge impact on our consciousness, ask anyone in the fashion industry. Their influence extends to tourism, politics, lingo, morality, even religion. From New York City to Istanbul to Kuala Lumpur.

If you're reading this, chances are you're among those who want to join the rank of modern-day Homers and write a movie. In our classes at Gotham Writers' Workshop, we've encountered thousands of people with the same worthy ambition and we've helped many of them achieve this goal. If you hope to break into

1

the movie business, you'll need some combination of imagination, talent, skill, determination, and persistence. Maybe a little luck. Most important, you'll need to write one or more screenplays of outstanding quality. Complete screenplays. Not just ideas to be pitched in plush offices or five-page "treatments" to be developed by established screenwriters. To make it, you need complete screenplays. Of outstanding quality.

This book will help you get there. The focus of this book is on writing scripts for feature films—movies that run 90–120 minutes and are designed to be seen without commercial interruption. If you're more interested in writing television movies or short films, some things will be a little different, but most of the craft will be the same. The same is true for animated films, but know that scripts for animated films are almost always developed in-house by a producing organization. If you have not been hired to write your script, then you are a creating a *spec screenplay*, something you are writing on your own volition in the hope that someone somewhere will buy it. Spec is short for "speculation," such as "speculating in the gold market."

A Visual Medium

> *If God could do the tricks we do, he'd be a happy man.*
> —Eli Cross, a megalomaniacal movie
> director in *The Stunt Man*

Film is a visual medium. That's the first thing you need to know. In prose, it's all about the words. In film, the image dominates. When you think of a movie, you see an image in your mind.

A woman swimming in moonlight jerked underwater by an unseen force. (*Jaws*)

A bumbling detective covering his privates with a guitar as he investigates a nudist colony. (*A Shot in the Dark*)

A lounge singer in a slit dress slithering across a grand piano. (*The Fabulous Baker Boys*)

A girl with fire-colored hair racing through streets to save her boyfriend's life. (*Run Lola Run*)

A twister spinning a house high above the Kansas plains. (*The Wizard of Oz*)

A Greek hero slashing his sword at the seven heads of a ferociously writhing hydra. (*Jason and the Argonauts*)

A grownup son and his father playing catch on a celestially lit baseball field. (*Field of Dreams*)

Go ahead, think of a favorite movie, right now. What happens?

These images can imprint themselves deeply on our psyches. A personal example. On a Saturday afternoon, when I was around five years old, I gathered around the TV with some older kids to watch a horror movie, *The Tingler*. (Bad idea.) I remember only one thing about that movie, but it's an image I will never shake. A deaf-mute lady was lying in bed when this evil person entered the room with the intention of harming her. Terror overtook the lady's face and although she tried to scream, she couldn't get the scream out. Now, nobody considers *The Tingler* a great horror movie and I might find the whole thing laughable if I watched it today, but let me tell you, that image chilled me to the core. In my mind's eye, I couldn't stop seeing that woman *trying to scream*! The image gave me nightmares for the better part of a year.

Reading prose fiction is largely an internal experience; we slip into the minds of the characters and envision our own pictures from the words. In film the reverse is true. We experience a movie from the outside in. We ride along with the visuals and they lead us toward our inner thoughts and sensations and emotions.

There is a famous writer's maxim: *Show, don't tell.* This applies double—make that triple—to screenwriting. Watch a good movie. Turn off the sound. You can probably follow the general flow of the story perfectly well, even if it's a movie you've never seen before. If you want to go a step further in your visual education, watch a silent movie. Audiences were held spellbound by movies for several decades when they were completely silent. You'll find no scarier moment in film than the unmasking of the phantom's grotesque face in *Phantom of the Opera*. No moment more heartrending than the teenage Joan staring at her death pyre in *The Passion of Joan of Arc*. Nothing funnier than the sight of Buster Keaton madly fleeing bees, bullets, boulders, and a mob of brides in *Seven Chances*.

Even if you never plan to direct a movie, never intend to know the difference between an f-stop and a long lens, as a screenwriter you need to think in terms of telling a story visually. It may help to compare movies to the stage. In the early days of filmmaking, movies were essentially filmed plays and that was mind-blowing enough for a while because the whole phenomenon of motion pictures was startlingly new. But soon filmmakers began to discover all kinds of tricks for telling stories in a more cinematic way. Here are probably the three most important tricks:

Cutting through space and time. Movies possess the godlike power to travel anywhere in the blink of an eye.

In luxurious headquarters at Cairo, a military officer receives a mission, lights a pipe for his superior, blows out the match. Then, hundreds of miles away, we see a flaming sunrise in the desert. Daylight then reveals the same officer, riding a camel across the sand, enroute to his new assignment. (*Lawrence of Arabia*)

Moving the field of vision. The camera can show whatever it wants to show.

Two outlaws come to the ledge of a towering canyon. Far below, we see a river rushing over murderous rocks. In the distance, we see a posse of lawmen riding toward them in pursuit. Then we see the rising panic on the outlaws' faces. (*Butch Cassidy and the Sundance Kid*)

Special effects. Nothing falls outside the reach of movie magic, and computer graphics have only expanded the possibilities.

Three men in sunglasses fire their guns at a hero in black, who holds up his hand. The spiraling bullets stop in midair, then tumble to the ground. The hero flies horizontally at one of the foes, disappearing inside his chest, causing him to become distorted, then emit lightning-like charges, then explode into pieces. (*The Matrix*)

When movies gained the power of sound, a whole new dimension was added. Suddenly there was dialogue, of course, but you could also enhance the story with aural elements. You could hear the gunshots and the rushing water and even "hear" the profound silence of the desert. Even so, visuals remain the most dominant element in movies. In fact, whenever you're deciding how to portray a moment in your script, go first for the visual, following it up with sound effects or dialogue. And, really, the art of film is the way these three elements—visual, aural, verbal—merge to tell a story, a story that seeps inside the viewers and makes them *feel something*.

Take a Shot

Think of three movie images that have made a strong impact on you. Write a paragraph on each, describing your memory of the image and why it affected you so deeply.

The Blueprint

> *Audiences don't know somebody sits down and writes a picture; they think the actors make it up as they go along.*
>
> —Joe Gillis, a down-on-his-luck screenwriter
>   in *Sunset Boulevard*

It may not seem like the writer has much to do with any of this. I've just told you that movies are about images, not words, and yet the writer works only with words. This is why the director is usually considered the mastermind of a movie and why it's called Frank Capra's *It Happened One Night.* Who the hell knows who wrote it? Screenwriters are often considered pretty low on the totem pole in the motion picture business. The studio mogul Jack Warner referred to them as "schmucks with Underwoods" and, believe it or not, I've heard of screenwriters not being invited to the premiere of their own movie. Except for those that double as directors, the names of screenwriters are virtually unknown to the general public. But let's set the record straight.

It all starts with the screenplay. The screenwriter is the one who invents the myth. Frank Capra was a brilliant director but *It Happened One Night* would not be the masterpiece it is without a script written with equal brilliance by a guy namcd Robert Riskin. Let's take that further and say that no great movie has ever been made from a screenplay that wasn't also great. That's why we call this book *Writing Movies,* not *Writing Screenplays.*

A screenplay is the blueprint for the movie. Everything will spring from what is set down in the screenplay. Here's a scene as it might appear in a script:

```
INT. MOTEL ROOM - NIGHT

The  room  is  dowdy.  Jeff  stares  at  the  window,
watching rain mournfully tap the glass.

                    JEFF
          I'm sorry.

Amanda  slips  off  her  wedding  ring  and  sets  it  on
the table.

                    AMANDA
          Me too.
```

Though this is certainly not a scene of genius, it does convey everything that will happen—visual, aural, verbal—with the elegant economy of a blueprint. (Yes, indeed, visuals and sound are included in a screenplay.) The intent of the scene is clear, and yet there is also room for others to fill out the scene with their own creativity and expertise. In a sense, the screenwriter is working on two planes at once—the script and the movie that will be.

If and when a movie arises from the screenplay, it will be a tremendously collaborative process. That brief scene in the motel should be pretty simple to put on film, right? Not really. The look of this motel room will have been slaved over by the director of photography, production designer, and let's not forget the folks responsible for the rain. After the actors have been prepared by costume, hair, and makeup people, they will need to delve into their deepest emotions to act this scene. Tears may be involved. And the director will be overseeing all of this, trying to make it come out right and striving to stick close to schedule. In fact, it will take at least several hours, if not longer, to shoot this scene, which will probably be shot at least three ways—closeup on Jeff, closeup on Amanda, master shot with both of them. Later on, the director will work with the editor to decide which takes to use and how to splice them together. Then a sound editor will add in the sound of the rain and the composer might burnish the scene with a little music. Damn! That's a lot of work for maybe fifteen seconds of screen time. No wonder movies usually cost many millions of dollars to make. But those millions of dollars aren't worth a dime unless some screenwriter has created a great story, without which no one will pay a nickel to see this movie.

Screenplays, like most blueprints, are not sacrosanct. Liberties can and should be taken during the creative process. Things come up. A director changes the setting. The actors do a little improvising. Scenes get cut or switched around in the editing stage. For these reasons, a finished movie almost never parallels the final script with exactitude. And yet . . . the first and most fundamental step in this labyrinthine process is a writer just imagining on a blank page.

Ideas

> CHARLIE: *The only idea more overused than serial*
> *killers is multiple personality. On top of that, you explore*
> *the notion that cop and criminal are really two aspects of*
> *the same person. See every cop movie ever made for other*
> *examples of this.*
> DONALD: *Mom called it "psychologically taut."*
> —A conversation between a professional screenwriter
>   and his wannabe brother in *Adaptation*

Before there is a movie, before there is a screenplay, before there is anything, there must be an idea. A glimmer, hint, whisper. Something to get the boulder rolling. Finding the initial idea can be the most daunting part of the process but, fortunately, there is no shortage of places to search.

Your own life
Your own life is, after all, the thing you know best. But you should tread carefully here. Movies require a lot of story juice to keep them pumping and intensifying for two hours or so and that's why movies lean on autobiography far less than fiction, which has more license to be meandering and introspective. First of all, don't even think about telling your whole life story unless it's as fascinating as, say, the life of Napoleon, and even movies on Napoleon tend to focus on an aspect of his life rather than the whole thing. Even if there's an interesting aspect of your life, though, it will still need some help.

One of the more autobiographical movies of recent times is *Almost Famous*, written and directed by Cameron Crowe. As a teenager obsessed with rock music, Crowe got a job writing about a rising rock band on tour for *Rolling Stone* magazine without the editors knowing how young he was. And that's the basis of Crowe's movie. You have to admit, Crowe had a good story. Take an innocent kid, drop him in the midst of high-profile sex, drugs, and rock 'n' roll, add in the pressure of writing for a major magazine and the tension between his assignment and the bonds he forms with the band. Crowe's true story was so strong he didn't have to fabricate very much, but fabricate he did, to make the story all the more dramatic. If you're tempted to write a movie based on your life, ask yourself whether you've got something half as good Crowe's story. If the answer is yes, great, use it . . . and then you still need to make things up. Simply because something really happened doesn't mean it's good enough, yet, for your movie.

A better approach is to use something from your life merely as a starting point. Let's say you're stuck on an airplane next to a big, loud fellow who won't stop jabbering and causes an ungodly odor when he pulls off his shoes, and yet after a few hours you realize that he isn't such a bad guy. It's a good start, but you'll need much more to make a movie. So eventually you manipulate and magnify; for example, it's the holiday season and the plane is grounded by a snowstorm so the two travelers are forced to share a one-bed motel room and then travel by ground together all the long way to their destination. I don't know how John Hughes got the idea for the movie *Planes, Trains and Automobiles* but it could have been something like that. Lost your job? Endured a bad divorce? Struggled with addiction? All kinds of things in your life might prove the inspiration for a movie and—the good news about bad experiences—the more trying the circumstances, the more potency they will have as story material.

You might even draw an idea from a setting or milieu with which you are familiar. Medical school, a modern-day ranch, a Peace Corps stint in Mongolia. Most of us love a backstage peek at life's myriad sideshows. Look at the way *Bull Durham* takes us into the dugout of minor-league baseball or the way *Animal House* throws us into the rowdiest fraternity on campus. What interesting world can you introduce us to?

When it comes right down to it, though, don't worry too much about that old adage: Write what you know. Write what you want to write about.

Something you've seen or heard about

Keep your eyes and ears open. Regardless of where you live—small village or bursting metropolis—you've got a world of material around you.

One night, Sylvester Stallone watched the world heavy-weight champ, Muhammed Ali, take on an unknown contender nicknamed the Bayonne Bleeder (for his ability to absorb punishment). The challenger lost but, against all expectations, he lasted fifteen rounds and in one electrifying moment he even knocked Ali to the canvas. That's how Stallone came to write *Rocky*.

While hitchhiking through West Virginia as a young man, John Sayles heard tell of the bitter wars that erupted in the region when the coal miners first attempted to unionize during the 1920s. Most everyone around there, in turn, had heard these stories from their parents and grandparents. Sayles listened carefully and then transformed what he heard into *Matewan*.

The great writer-director Billy Wilder was watching the movie *Brief Encounter*, a tearjerker about a couple who borrow an apartment for their adulterous trysts. Despite the film's poignancy, Wilder found himself wondering about the fellow who lent the apartment, the person who had to climb into that warmed-up bed at night. This led Wilder straight into *The Apartment*.

History or the news

The pageant of history offers an endless source of story ideas. During World War I, an eccentric Englishman led an army of Arabian Bedouins against the Turkish army and then found his allegiance wavering between his Arab followers and the British army that employed him. It was only a matter of time before a movie captured the saga of *Lawrence of Arabia*. Historical tales don't have to be so epic, though, nor do they need to stick all that close to the historical fact (especially when the facts aren't that well known). *The Lion in Winter* is an intimate drama about a dysfunctional family in 1183 that happens to include King Henry II of England, his wife, Eleanor of Aquitaine, and their less-than-princely sons Richard, Geoffrey, and John.

Looking to more recent times, the news is an evergreen source of ideas. While in grad school, Kimberly Peirce came across an article in an alternative newspaper about a young woman who passed herself off as a man in a small Nebraska town. Fascinated by the tale, Peirce went to the town, interviewed the people who knew Brandon Teena, and cowrote the movie *Boys Don't Cry*. While *Boys Don't Cry* stayed fairly true to the facts, which lent themselves beautifully to a story, you can use the news merely as a starting point. A much-publicized racial incident in Brooklyn inspired Spike Lee to write *Do the Right Thing*, but the story he spun is completely fictional. *Dr. Strangelove* is a ridiculously far-fetched story but it was obviously inspired by the Cold War paranoia that pervaded the headlines in the early 1960s. Truth is, you can flip through a newspaper almost any day of the week—on the front page, in the wedding announcements, among the obituaries—and find the seed of a great story idea.

Adapt something

A high percentage of movies are adapted from works in another medium. A random sampling: *Terms of Endearment* (novel), *Men in Black* (comic book), *Amadeus* (play), *The Untouchables* (TV series), *Friday Night Lights* (nonfiction book), *Dog Day Afternoon* (magazine article), *Lara Croft: Tomb Raider* (video game).

With so many ready-made stories ripe for the picking, why not pick? Here's the rub, though. You cannot adapt anything that is under copyright protection without obtaining the rights, and if the property has achieved any degree of fame or acclaim, you can bet that someone in the movie business already holds the rights to it, rights that were purchased with a nice chunk of change. Pursuing any well-known property is usually a waste of time, and that includes remakes of older or foreign movies. So, if you want to adapt, you'll need to find something no one has yet thought to snatch up, something farther off the beaten path.

You might keep a lookout for short stories. Virtually all short stories these days make their first appearance in little-known literary magazines, of which there are hundreds. Most of the stories in these magazines won't be appropriate for movie adaptation but some of them will be, and chances are good that no one in the movie business will have heard of the story you want. You track down the author, which shouldn't be that hard, and you arrange to buy the rights for a modest fee. A few movies adapted from short stories: *Rear Window, Sunset Boulevard, Memento, Blade Runner, In the Bedroom, Brokeback Mountain.*

If a work is old enough, usually more than a hundred years old, then the property will be in the public domain, meaning it's fair game to anyone. Classic stories can be problematic, however, because the movie people have probably already thought of it and they may even be developing a new version on their own. You'll have a better chance by updating a classic, perhaps even giving it a new twist. *Apocalypse Now* is Joseph Conrad's *Heart of Darkness* set in Vietnam. *After Hours* is very much like Lewis Carroll's *Alice in Wonderland* set in contemporay New York City. *O Brother, Where Art Thou* is, more or less, Homer's *The Odyssey* set in the Depression-era South.

If you keep an open mind, you might find something to adapt in the most unlikely of places. Amy Fox, whom you will meet in chapter 10, wrote a one-act play about three people hanging out on a New York City rooftop. Even though she also wrote screenplays, Amy never considered the play a movie idea. However, someone who saw the play in a tiny off-off-Broadway theater, namely Ismail Merchant of the legendary Merchant/Ivory production company, did see movie potential in the story. He bought the rights, hired Amy to write the screenplay, and a few years later the story emerged on the screen as *Heights.*

If you choose to write an adaptation, you have a headstart on your story but don't think you can just type out the original in screenplay format. You will need to transform the source material into a movie, a process that requires you to follow most of the steps you would take if you were working on something brand new. It's really no less difficult than starting from scratch.

Imagination

Oh, yes, you can also just spin a story out of pure imagination. Who knows what gave someone the idea of making a movie about a gigantic ape who falls in love with a beautiful actress, and is shipped from a remote island to New York City, eventually climbing the Empire State Building with her clutched in his massive hand? Maybe someone just thought it up. Doesn't matter. *King Kong* was a fabulous idea.

Regardless of where your initial idea comes from, you'll need to apply your powers of imagination to tease out the best possible story. Often it's a matter of playing the game of "What If?" What if a guy lent out his apartment for adulterous trysts? How can I maximize the drama there? Let's say he's an ambitious fellow who lends out his apartment to executives in the corporation where he works, lured by the hope of advancement. All right, interesting, somewhat plausible. And let's say he's actually a romantic at heart so the whole arrangement is a bit icky to him. And that means he should have a romantic yearning of his own so let's give him a crush on a woman who works at the corporation. These things happen. And then . . . what if his crush is having an affair with one of the executives to whom he's lending his apartment? Yes, good. And what if he doesn't discover this until after the executive has given him a coveted promotion? Even better. And what if . . . The best storytellers are masters of this game.

Premise

This story's gonna grab people. It's about this guy, he's crazy about this girl, but he likes to wear dresses. Should he tell her? Should he not tell her? He's torn, Georgie. This is drama.

—The enthusiastic but minimally talented
writer-director title character in *Ed Wood*

It will help if you translate your idea into a *premise*—a brief encapsulation of what the movie will be about. It's good to have a premise before you actually start writing. You're free to tinker with your premise throughout the writing process, but it'll go easier if you have one at the outset.

It also helps to keep your premise brief. Brief, meaning you can put it down in no more than three sentences. This will force you to focus your idea. You'll have to do this anyway when it comes time to market your script because then your premise will be turned into a one- or two-sentence pitch, known as a *logline*. We're using the terms *premise* and *logline* as pretty much the same thing, the only real difference being that a logline will be perfectly composed to attract the most interest with the fewest words. For now though, don't worry about perfect wording so much as just crystallizing the idea. Here's a sample premise:

> *Vertigo* – A private investigator is hired to shadow a mysterious woman with suicidal tendencies and he becomes obsessed with her. When he is unable (due to his vertigo) to stop her from plunging to her death, his obsession only intensifies. He finds another woman who looks strikingly like the first and attempts to transform her into the dead woman in appearance and spirit.

There is no formula for a perfect story but here are some elements you would be wise to include:

- Interesting characters
- Intense conflict
- Visual opportunity
- Emotional power

Take another look at that *Vertigo* premise and notice how well the premise offers promise on all of those things. Even without Hitchcock aboard, that would be a good point from which to start writing a movie.

You're also looking for a premise that has *appeal*, that sounds like something people would be drawn to. When you're playing around with a premise, see if you can picture it up on the screen, see if you can picture an audience full of people transported by the movie they're watching. You might even envision the poster for the movie. A great way to test your premise is simply to tell it to some people. What's the reaction? An absent nod? A quick glint in the eye? A great premise often delivers an instant buzz. It's okay if some people aren't grabbed by your premise—no movie appeals to everyone—but if nobody is catching a buzz from your premise, then it may be lacking in electrical charge.

While playing around with your premise, it'll help to figure out what kind of movie you're aiming for. Let me give you three key things to consider.

High/Low Concept

Movies can be roughly grouped into high-concept and low-concept stories. High-concept means unusual or startling or flashy or eye-catching. Here's one for you:

> *Speed* – A psychopath wires a city bus so it'll explode if the speed dips below 50 mph. With the bus careening through the city streets unable to stop or slow down, the full load of terrified passengers seems doomed. But a bomb squad specialist boards the bus and, with the help of a smart-aleck gal who drives well, he tries to bring the bus to safety.

No, it's not very likely to happen, but high-concept stories usually aim for escapism over verisimilitude and such escapism is one of the thrilling pleasures of movies. Eventually, you'll have to find ways to make the story somewhat plausible, in its own way, but when starting out you can banish all boundaries from your imagination. Indeed, many high-concept stories bend reality altogether, as in *Field of Dreams, Splash,* or *The Ring.* Here's one of the more bizarre high-concepts to come down the pike:

> *Being John Malkovich* – A struggling puppeteer takes a job at an office, where he discovers a passageway that turns out to be a portal into the head of the actor John Malkovich. He goes into business with the icy woman on whom he has a crush, selling tickets—twenty dollars for fifteen minutes inside Malkovich. Eventually Malkovich catches on to the scheme and he's mad as hell about it.

The low-concept premise isn't nearly as exciting on first sight. You won't find threats of mass destruction or weird warps on reality here. A low-concept story derives its drama from events that are more reminiscent of real life. The secret weapon of these movies is their ability to show who and how we really are. Here's one for you:

> *Lost in Translation* – An aging American movie star is feeling lost in Tokyo while he is there to make some big bucks shooting a whiskey commercial. He befriends a twenty-something American woman who feels lost in her marriage to a hotshot photographer. The two hang out, helping each other cope with life's disappointments.

Other movies that qualify as low-concept include *American Beauty, The Fabulous Baker Boys, The Graduate,* and lowest of the low concepts, *My Dinner with Andre.*

You don't have to aim all the way high or low; some premises hover somewhere in between. *Vertigo,* for example. It's got enough weirdness to be kind of high, but it's kind of low in that the focus is mainly on fascinating human interaction.

Neither high or low (or medium) is better than the other, but whichever way you go, look for a premise that offers the most *oomph* in whatever direction you're pursuing. If you want heart-pounding action, it's tough to beat a bus wired to explode if it dips below a designated speed. If you want lost souls, make them wander jet-lagged through a land where they don't speak the language.

Hollywood/Indie

Movies also can be grouped into what we will call the "Hollywood" and "indie" styles.

Technically, "Hollywood" refers to movies developed under the auspices of one of the Hollywood studios, and "indie" refers to movies developed independently of the studio system. (The indie movement is said to have begun in the early 1980s, but movies in the indie style have been around a long time, both in America and abroad.) In reality, an indie-style movie may be developed by a major studio, and a Hollywood-style movie may be developed outside the studios. Everyone is in bed with everyone else in the movie business, so we're talking "styles" here as opposed to the actual point of origin.

Hollywood movies are expected to do boffo box office across the world, from Sioux City to Singapore. It's always been this way but blockbuster lust was born in the mid-1970s when *Jaws* devoured audiences in unprecedented numbers. To attract those vast audiences, Hollywood movies tend to have some or all of these qualities:

- Mass appeal (not too intellectual or downbeat)

- Roles suitable for major stars (attractive lead characters with showoff scenes)

- A high-concept premise (easier to market)

- Glamour or spectacle (requiring a large budget)

Prime examples: *Titanic, E.T., A Beautiful Mind*

An indie-style movie is also expected to reap profit (no producer is in the business to lose money), but these movies are made
on a relatively low budget and, thus, they can turn a profit without
everyone in the world seeing them. This gives them more artistic
freedom. They may have one or more of the first three elements
listed above, but they don't have to. In fact, they are geared for a
more select audience that likes things darker, grittier, stranger, or
more subtle than what is normally found in mainstream movies.
Prime examples: *sex, lies and videotape, Being John Malkovich, American Splendor*

Neither the Hollywood nor the indie style can lay a greater claim
to quality. Both camps have produced their share of masterpieces
and turkeys. They're just different, that's all. But it'll help if you
have a sense of which style you're working with so that you will stay
on track with your chosen style. For example, if you're writing a
spectacular tale of love and intrigue set against the backdrop of a
doomed luxury liner, then you better not have one of your leads
turn into a sniveling coward because few movie stars will play that
and, even if they did, the masses don't like movie stars acting that
way. Conversely, if you're writing about a subtle relationship between a disenchanted man and women who meet in Tokyo and
hang out but never leap into a romance, then you should stay away
from expensive stunts and special effects and give it enough edge
to satisfy the indie audience.

Genre

Movies are grouped by genres—the type of story it is. You'll see
movie genres categorized in different ways, but here are the genres most commonly seen and referred to:

ACTION/ADVENTURE : Chases, fights, derring-do: *Jaws, Lethal
Weapon, Speed*

COMEDY : Predominantly funny: *Some Like It Hot, The Graduate, Planes, Trains and Automobiles*

COMEDY/DRAMA : A mix of funny and serious: *The Apartment, Terms of Endearment, Lost in Translation*

CRIME : Criminals and their crimes: *White Heat, The Godfather, The Usual Suspects*

DRAMA : Predominantly serious: *Casablanca, To Kill a Mockingbird, Million Dollar Baby*

EPIC : A grand adventure against a sweeping backdrop: *Gone with the Wind, Lawrence of Arabia, Titanic*

FANTASY : Set in a magical world: *Lost Horizon, The Princess Bride, Lord of the Rings*

FILM NOIR : Moody, dark, corrupted: *Out of the Past, Touch of Evil, Body Heat*

HORROR : A supernatural or scream-inducing menace: *Frankenstein, The Exorcist, The Ring*

MUSICAL : Partly told with song: *The Wizard of Oz, West Side Story, Chicago*

PERIOD : A bygone time and place: *Tom Jones, The Sting, Remains of the Day*

ROMANTIC COMEDY : Charming romance that ends happily: *The Philadelphia Story, Breakfast at Tiffany's, When Harry Met Sally . . .*

SCIENCE FICTION : Space, the future, or some kind of scientific twist: *Star Wars, Blade Runner, The Matrix*

THRILLER : Driven by suspense, largely psychological: *Vertigo, Fatal Attraction, Memento*

WAR : About war: *Paths of Glory, Apocalypse Now, Saving Private Ryan*

WESTERN : Cowboys, horses, six-shooters: *Stagecoach, High
Noon, Unforgiven*

Trends change in regard to genres. Action/adventure and science fiction have loomed large in the past few decades (better
blockbuster potential) while epics, film noir, musicals, and west-
erns haven't been in serious vogue for some time. But what goes
around comes around. And then there are all manner of subgenres, such as: coming of age, buddy, road, sports, caper, detective,
courtroom, prison, espionage, ensemble, biography, and mockumentary.

Genre is about expectation. When the general public selects a
movie to see, they pay attention to the genre. Even if they don't
know the genre names, the genre is clearly signaled to them in all
the promotional material for the movie—posters, commercials,
previews, Web sites—and they pick a movie based on those clues.

You need to know what genre you're working with because you
need to deliver on the expectations of that genre. A movie can follow the conventions of its genre without slavishly imitating other
films in the genre or sacrificing uniqueness, but it's important that
a movie play to the most fundamental expectations of the genre.
In a romantic comedy, a couple better meet in a cute way and they
better end up together. If, say, the woman dies of disease at the
end, we will never forgive her for ruining our viewing experience.
So, study the genre you're working in. Staying true to genre is even
more important to Hollywood movies than indies, where the audience is a bit more willing to have their expectations thwarted.

Can a movie mix genres? Yes, as a matter of fact, and this is a
great way to bring a fresh take on the familiar. Comedy/drama is
so common as to deserve a genre of its own, but other genres can
blend, too. *Butch Cassidy and the Sundance Kid* derives its distinctive
flavor from its status as a western/comedy. You get horses and
guns aplenty, but you also get moments like the one in which
Butch and Sundance are surrounded by banditos in Bolivia and
Butch says, "Kid, there's something I think I ought to tell you—

I've never shot anybody before." *Alien* is really a cross between science fiction and horror. The setting—a transport vehicle in outer space in the future—is a science-fiction environment, but the story is about the crew of the vehicle fighting for their lives against a badass creature, a convention of the horror movie. The merging of genres in *Alien* was reflected in the terrific promotional line for this movie: "In space no one can hear you scream."

How to Choose a Premise

Here's a big question many screenwriters wrestle with: Is my idea original enough?

You may come up with a premise that is totally unique, as *King Kong* was when it was first made in 1933. But hundreds of movies have appeared since then, which means that the chances of coming up with a never-before-seen story have grown rather slim. That's okay. True originality doesn't come from the core idea as much as it comes from the way the story is told. If you're working on an idea that is somewhat familiar, look for a way to spruce it up with a new spin or a fresh vision. *Dr. Strangelove* and *Fail-Safe* both appeared at the height of the Cold War and they have the same general premise: The United States inadvertently launches a nuclear missile toward Moscow that can't be called back. *Dr. Strangelove* is a rip-roaring black comedy while *Fail-Safe* is deadly serious. Years later, *WarGames* used a very similar premise, this time putting teenagers at the center of the action. All three of these movies could be called "original." If you've got time someday, count off all the movie variations on the *Romeo and Juliet* story.

Here's another question screenwriters wrestle with when writing specs: Should my choice of a premise be determined by what has the best chance of selling?

Yes and no. Mostly no.

If you analyze which spec screenplays sell, you'll find that the majority of the sales are for high-concept Hollywood-style scripts. Yes, that's true. However, if you analyze how most screenwriters

break into the business, you'll find that most of them do so by im-
pressing people with their talent, very likely by submitting a script
that doesn't actually sell but gets them into the arena where it's
possible for them to work as screenwriters. We'll get into this tricky
concept more in our final chapter, but for now you need to know
that if you're serious about breaking into the screenwriting game,
you'll have your best shot by first demonstrating your potential.

The surest way for you to show off your talent is to write the kind
of movie you feel the most kinship with. If you revel in the dark
sensuality of film noir, wander that way. If you like the skewed universe of quirky indies, put on your hippest hat and go for it. Dazzling your readers and outshining the competition will win the day
much more than a patently commercial script executed with mere
competence. And you don't need to worry about current trends. If
tsunami movies are all the rage now, the trend will ebb before
you've finished writing your script, let alone had time to market it,
a time-consuming process in its own right if you're not seriously
connected.

Write a story that appeals to you, *deeply* appeals to you. Only
then will you have the enthusiasm and inspiration it takes to come
up with something wonderful.

Persistence of Vision

> *This man creates for a living! He puts food on your*
> *table and on mine! Thank him for it! Thank him, you*
> *ungrateful sonofabitch! Thank him or you're fired!*
> —Jack Lipnik, a rabidly passionate
> producer in *Barton Fink*

Here's how a lot of people come to screenwriting. They see a
movie that Hollywood has obviously poured many millions of dollars into and, well before the smoke clears and the final credits
roll, they realize that, hey, this movie sucks. So they make the

assumption that they can write something better—maybe not brilliant, but certainly better than *that*. And this leads to the perfectly reasonable assumption that they have what it takes to become a professional screenwriter.

There is, however, a fallacy in this notion. It's true that many of the movies we see do, in fact, suck, but it's seldom the fault of the writers. The vast majority of professional screenwriters are highly skilled at their trade. Here's what invariably happens with those movies that suck, and the bigger the budget the more likely it is to happen. A screenwriter sells a script that is quite good, or the screenwriter is hired to write a script and he does a damn fine job with it. Movie executives are usually savvy enough to hire and buy from the best writers. But then executives give notes to the writer in the hope of making the movie more likable, more accessible, more of what they hope will be a worldwide runaway box-office phenomenon. The notes may go something like this: "Give the hero a dog to make him more sympathetic." Or: "How about if the lady doctor moonlights as a stripper?" Or: "Hey, why don't we set the whole thing in outer space?" The screenwriters do their best not to ruin the script but often it's a losing a battle, and frequently the script goes through several sets of writers, all of whom are good but somewhat helpless in the face of the pressure being imposed upon them. Directors, star actors, or marketing people sometimes help drag the script further away from its original vision, and then there are focus groups and preview cards. The upshot: A terrific screenplay is turned into a movie that, to some people, sucks.

Here's the point. You won't break in by writing something no better, or even a little better, than the lamest of the movies you pull off the shelf at the video store. Once you've sidled your way into the screenwriting elite, you might get away with that and be well paid for it. Until then, however, you have to be good. Really good. You have to write scripts as great as those that the pros write before their material is made more "commercial." You have to write screenplays that are stellar.

And that's not so easy.

If you thumb through a screenplay, it may not seem so difficult to write. They run to only a hundred pages or so and there's really not all that many words on each page. Lots of white space. You don't even need to fuss much over grammar or create sentences worthy of F. Scott Fitzgerald. It looks a damn sight easier than writing a novel. Ah, but you see, the very thing that makes screenplays look so easy is what makes them so challenging. You have to tell a story with depth and breadth that flies like the wind, every word and image perfectly hitting the mark, and holds the readers enthralled all the way through, eventually leaving them overcome with wonder and emotion. In not that many pages. With lots of white space. Good screenplays are marvels of economy and precision.

Relax, though, you've come to the right place. The chapters that follow are written by members of the Gotham Writers' Workshop faculty, each one an experienced screenwriter and teacher. These fine people are going to teach you all of the fundamental elements of screenwriting craft. By craft, we mean the time-tested principles for good screenwriting that have been developed over the years. You can spend a lifetime mastering screenwriting craft, but it's a teachable thing and the moment you start learning it, your writing will improve. Good writing, of any kind, originates from a solid working knowledge of craft; regardless of how inspired or talented you feel, you just won't get that far down the boulevard without it. It's impossible to locate the line where craft turns into artistry, but these two things are undeniably linked and it may well be that artistry is nothing more than craft soaring into flight.

Is what we have here any different than what you will find elsewhere? You'll see all kinds of screenwriting advice out there, coming from the leading screenwriting gurus, not to mention more books, teachers, consultants, and Web sites than you can shake an Oscar at. Much of it is good stuff, and much of it is mirrored in this book. I don't know that we've got it down better (our hope), but I can say with assurance that we have crystallized screenwriting craft into advice that is sound, clear, practical, comprehensive, and flexible.

That flexibility, by the way, is important. Most great films defy some aspect of the conventional advice, and nowadays we're all so jaded by overexposure to stories coming at us in every direction that it helps to tell stories in a new way, to bend or break or flaunt a few rules. But here's the twist: You can disobey the rules much more effectively if you know them in the first place.

Allow me to summon the example of Orson Welles. At the age of twenty-five, Welles wrote, directed, and starred in his first movie, *Citizen Kane*. It may or may not be the greatest movie ever, as is often claimed, but it's certainly one of the most revolutionary. So much in the screenplay was new or at least unfamiliar—son-of-a-bitch protagonist, fragmented chronology, faux newsreel within the movie, telling the story from multiple points of view—and we're not even talking about the directorial flourishes, such as the moment when the camera rises to a rooftop, soars through a neon sign, then dives through a skylight into a nightclub. *Citizen Kane* expanded the possibilities of how you tell a story on film, just as Picasso's *Guernica* revolutionized painting and the Beatles's *Sgt. Pepper's Lonely Hearts Club Band* revolutionized recorded popular music.

Welles, however, knew what he was doing. Though young, he was far from a novice at storytelling, having already written, directed, and starred in numerous high-level radio and stage productions. To help himself make the leap into cinema, Welles viewed John Ford's *Stagecoach*, a good old-fashioned western, countless times, analyzing the mechanics of telling a film story. And you know what? He still needed help with the screenplay of *Citizen Kane*, which he cowrote with the very experienced Herman Mankiewicz. Welles was nothing if not daring and didn't blanch at trying something never done before, but the guy took craft very seriously. You need to do the same, regardless of whether you're out to write a B-movie slasher or something so cutting-edge it'll be the buzz of the Sundance festival. Orson Welles wasn't a know-it-all. He was a *student*, a human sponge who absorbed everything around him then let it rain down in a fresh way. That's how you innovate.

The very best way to learn screenwriting craft (surpassing even this book) is to study movies. If you're not already a film buff, turn into one by the next full moon. Watch movies frequently, and though you shouldn't stop viewing them for pleasure, you should also start analyzing them in terms of screenwriting craft. Talk to any successful screenwriter and you'll find yourself in conversation with a movie zealot, someone who can recite the final scene of *Casablanca* verbatim or explain how the addition of voice-over affects our perception of the protagonist in *Blade Runner*. You should also read screenplays to see how professionals capture a movie on the page. It's quite easy to find screenplays of movies on the Internet at no charge. Help yourself. You'll learn the most from studying films that are good or great, but there's also something to be picked up from watching mediocre or bad films, so feel free to screen Ed Wood's *Plan 9 from Outer Space* and ask yourself why it's often dubbed the worst movie ever made.

Being a movie-lover alone won't make you a screenwriter, of course. At some point you have to strap yourself into a chair and log in hundreds of hours of actual writing. There's no high as splendid as the act of creation, so this is a time to treasure. But it's also work. Hard work. Screenwriters don't spend their days lounging poolside with movie stars; they spend their days slaving away on their scripts.

If you're serious about screenwriting, you need to set aside serious time for it. Carve out blocks of time when you can zero in on your writing with an absolute minimum of distractions. Shoot for at least five hours a week, which you can divvy up any way you like. More than five is even better. Make a schedule and stick to it. As best you can. Life will interfere. It always does. But the folks who turn out great scripts tend to be the ones who guard their writing time as ferociously as a mother bear guards her young. It's okay if you don't always produce decent material in these sessions. Floundering is a time-honored practice among writers and you're welcome to flounder all you like. (Writing is a bit different than other jobs in this respect.) The important thing is that you develop the discipline to sit down and write, consistently, even when you're not in the mood for it. Eventually good stuff will come.

It can be lonely. Though it would be nice, you probably won't have a super-cool mentor like Morpheus (from *The Matrix*) standing beside you, assuring you that when the time is right you'll be able to control the bullets with your mind. You'll be on your own. If you can't handle the long hours flying solo, find a partner, which will at least give you an Abbott to play off your Costello. Collaboration seldom works for prose, but it can work perfectly well for screenplays, provided you find someone with whom you're comfortable. (Hint: Get the best person possible, preferably someone smarter than yourself.)

In addition to your "hard" time at the keyboard or pad of paper, you should also utilize "soft" time, meaning the invaluable practice of letting your mind meander through your story as you go about your daily life—driving to work, folding the laundry, standing in church as you recite your wedding vows. Great notions often come about this way, and you may find that soft time is the perfect method for solving a problem that's making you crazy at your computer. Carry a notebook with you wherever you go. There's no telling when a good thought might materialize; if you don't set it down it may just vanish back into the ether whence it came. One of the very best times to think is while lying in bed before drifting off to sleep. If you can manage to work straight into your dreamscape, all the better, for what are movies if not dreams printed on celluloid? So keep another notebook by your bedside.

You'll find the writing process that works best for you, but let me fast-forward through a good methodology. You spend time gathering and focusing ideas, perhaps accompanied by some research. Then you do some outlining of your story. When it comes time to write a first draft, it's good to push through it quickly, not slowing down to tinker or second-guess yourself. And then . . . you go through a series of rewrites until you've made your script as great as you can possibly make it. Voilà—you've got a screenplay.

On a larger scale, developing as a screenwriter is also a process.

It's quite likely that the very first screenplay you write won't be a work of genius, won't even be good enough to get you in the game. If you're a first-timer bothered by this notion, then dismiss the thought—we writers usually need to believe we're creating something the world can't live without every time we expend the sweat and passion that writing requires. (So . . . sure, a few screenwriters have struck gold their first time in the hills.) Just know that regardless of where you are now—clueless, promising, experienced— your work will grow better and better through the simple act of sailing onward.

If you're somewhat new to this world, from here on you'll be absorbing a tremendous amount of information. It may seem like too much at times. You may feel as if your head is about to explode, even without the assistance of special effects. Fear not. That is usually the first step. If you keep at it with patience and persistence, you will come to know the art and craft of screenwriting without even thinking about it, just as Neo (in *The Matrix*) learned to effortlessly control hyperreality with his mind. Think of it this way: When we view movies, we are actually seeing thousands of still images linked together (projected at a rate of twenty-four per second), but our eyes are tricked into seeing these stills as a continuous flow of motion. There's a lovely term for this phenomenon: persistence of vision. Eventually everything you learn will blur together in your mind as a wondrous and flowing whole. Really, it will.

Five Movies

Throughout this book we'll be focusing on five movies—*Die Hard*, *Thelma & Louise*, *Tootsie*, *Sideways*, and *The Shawshank Redemption*. Many of you will already know these movies. (Be warned that we will be giving away crucial story points, so if you haven't seen one of these films, you may want to watch it before reading the subsequent chapters.) As a bonus feature, you can download the screenplays for these movies at www.WritingMovies.info.

You might even want to watch the movies with the screenplays it hand. The scripts are close enough to the finished product so you won't get lost, but there are enough minor differences to illustrate how a screenplay evolves during the filming and editing process. These are all excellent films and each one springs from an expertly written screenplay. In your personal study, you may choose to pay the most attention to the one that most closely resembles the kind of movie you like or seek to write.

Here is a quick preview of these five movies:

Die Hard (1988)
Written by Jeb Stuart and Steven de Souza (based on the novel *Nothing Lasts Forever* by Roderick Thorp)
Directed by John McTiernan
Starring Bruce Willis, Bonnie Bedelia, Alan Rickman, and Reginald VelJohnson

Die Hard is a classic action/adventure and a prime example of the big-budget Hollywood movie. A hero matches wits, fists, and weapons with the villains, a story that's been going since the days of ancient myth and is frequently echoed in the genres of action/adventure, science fiction, horror, and, of course, the western. Hollywood puts out plenty of popcorn movies but *Die Hard* towers above most of them in terms of excitement and execution. It's a high-concept movie, though its concept has became so imitated that many a script has been pitched as *Die Hard* on an airplane or *Die Hard* on a cruise ship or *Die Hard* at a writing school.

Thelma & Louise (1992)
Written by Callie Khouri
Directed by Ridley Scott

Starring Susan Sarandon, Geena Davis, Harvey Keitel,
Brad Pitt, and Michael Madsen

Thelma & Louise attracted a lot of attention when it roared onto
the scene because it turned the outlaw tale upside down by using
women as the leads and infusing the action with an undercurrent
of feminism. It even made the cover of *Time* magazine. Genre-wise,
it's an interesting mix. Let's call it drama/action/adventure with
the subgenres of buddy/road movie thrown in. Most unique of all,
it's an exhilarating tragedy. At the risk of offering false hope: The
writer is a woman, this was her first screenplay, and they made it
pretty much the way she wrote it, none of which is exactly the
norm for a Hollywood movie.

Tootsie (1982)
Written by Larry Gelbart, Murray Schisgal, and Don
McGuire
Directed by Sydney Pollack
Starring Dustin Hoffman, Jessica Lange, Teri Garr,
Charles Durning, Sydney Pollack, and Bill Murray

Tootsie is one of the funniest movies ever made, provoking laughs
in practically every scene. You could make a case that it's a romantic comedy, but let's call it a comedy because the romance
takes a while to develop. The high-concept story has a lot of old-
fashioned farce in it, including cross-dressing, quick changes, and
slamming doors, but it also manages to go deeper, taking a
man/woman through a believable and heartfelt transformation.
By all reports, the making of this movie was as frantic as the story,
with a parade of writers, last-minute changes, and a temperamen-
tal star, but somehow the final product emerged as pure comic
perfection.

Sideways (2004)
Written by Alexander Payne and Jim Taylor (based on
the novel *Sideways* by Rex Pickett)

Directed by Alexander Payne
Starring Paul Giamatti, Thomas Haden Church, Virginia Madsen, and Sandra Oh

Sideways is our indie example. True, this movie found a much larger audience than is typical for such films, but it stays very true to the indie spirit, a low-budget, low-concept movie that follows complex (not to mention outrageously flawed) characters through the nooks and crannies of their existence. If you turned off the sound and put subtitles at the bottom of the screen, you would have no trouble believing this was a French film. Thanks to his successful track record, the director could have cast major stars but he chose to go with lesser-knowns. *Sideways* is a true comedy/drama, always balancing itself between absurdity and heartbreak, much like your life and mine.

The Shawshank Redemption (1994)
Written and directed by Frank Darabont (based on the novella "Rita Hayworth and the Shawshank Redemption" by Stephen King)
Starring Tim Robbins, Morgan Freeman, Jr., Bob Gunton, James Whitmore, and Gil Bellows

The Shawshank Redemption is a prison drama about a man who is beaten, raped, abused, and frequently thrown into "the hole." The sky is usually as gray as the stone walls, and the only female companionship comes from the posters on a wall. The film is bleak and slow and long. No wonder it fared poorly at the box office. Then . . . through word of mouth, TV, and video rentals, *The Shawshank Redemption* turned into one of the most beloved movies of our time, becoming almost a religious experience for many of its devotees. This movie breaks all kinds of rules, relating to both craft and appeal, which just goes to show that the only real rule is that a movie should move its audience.

*   *   *

Each of these movies has attained the status of modern myth. If you wish to invent your own myth, be it spectacular or quiet, we shall try to guide you into the flickering light.

Stepping-Stone: Premise

Brainstorm three rough ideas that might lead to a good movie. Even if you already have an idea in mind, go ahead and think up two others, just to see what happens. Then pick the most promising idea and translate it into a premise of no more than three sentences. Your premise may change as you develop your story, but this will give you a point of origin.

CHAPTER 2

Plot: The Path of Action

BY DANIEL NOAH

I love John Carpenter's horror flick, *The Thing* (written by Bill Lancaster). The film opens on the vast emptiness of the Antarctic, nothing but snow and ice, far as the eye can see. A Norwegian helicopter roars out from behind a mountaintop, upsetting the quiet. The chopper is in pursuit of a beautiful husky that's leaping across the boundless white. Then, inexplicably, a guy in the chopper takes a shot at the dog. The husky darts to a nearby American camp, where a group of scientists are posted. The helicopter lands and the Norwegians charge the camp, firing wildly at the husky. Chaos ensues and the Norwegians are killed. Bewildered, the American scientists take in the gentle dog.

The scientists soon realize the dog is not as innocent as it seems. In fact, it's not even a dog. It's an alien species that can mimic the form of any living creature it comes into contact with. And if it mimics you—you die. By the time the scientists figure out what's happening, the "thing" in their camp might have mimicked any one of them. It would look exactly like its victim. Talk like him, move like him, know everything he knows. But this perfect duplicate is far from a man; it's a deadly creature intent on destroying anyone who exposes it. No one can be trusted. Everyone must be feared. Completely isolated, nowhere near civilization, they've got to smoke the creature out from hiding before it kills them all.

The Thing is a horror movie and brain-teaser rolled into one, like H. P. Lovecraft coupled with Agatha Christie. Even as you're

33

clutching your popcorn, bracing for the next shock, your brain is working overtime while you desperately try to piece together who's who, what's what, and, most important . . . what will happen next.

This powerful need to know what will happen next is the stuff of a great plot. Plot is what keeps us on the edge of our seats, mentally alert in anticipation of the twists and turns that surely await us. And a great plot isn't only necessary for a supernatural nail-biter like *The Thing*. Plot is what keeps us watching any kind of movie, regardless of how sensational or how subtle it might be. That's the key thing plot does. It keeps you watching.

So what is a plot?

A plot, literally, is the sequence of events that comprise a story. Those events aren't random, even in the most "lifelike" movies. Although many films reflect real life, good plots have little in common with the way real life actually unfolds. Real life, seen in a purely naturalistic way, is boring. If you don't believe me, get your hands on a copy of Andy Warhol's experimental film *Sleep*, five and half hours of a man—you guessed it—sleeping. What a plot does is reorganize real life, omitting the boring parts, emphasizing the dramatic parts, and artfully arranging events so as to keep an audience riveted for two hours or so. Nonstop.

Let me tell you something: Plot is tough. Possibly the toughest part of writing a screenplay. And possibly the most important, too. I sometimes spend days on end tinkering and experimenting, desperately trying to figure out how to arrange the events of my plot in a way that makes sense. Almost every time I start a new screenplay, I feel so daunted by plot that I convince myself I'm all washed up, finished in this business forever. But then, inevitably, I crack it. All those blurry ideas snap into sudden focus. What seemed so complicated before becomes very, very simple. You'll feel that rush of clarity, too. But it won't come from magic. In fact, it'll come from something closer to the careful and deliberate process of a scientist. There are time-tested principles (ancient, really) to help you get there. I'm now going to walk you through them, step by step.

Major Dramatic Question

At the center of every good movie there is a single driving force around which all other elements gather. It has the rage of a hurricane, the focus of a cougar, the horsepower of a Lamborghini. It's not the movie's star. It's not a special effect. It's not the most awe-inspiring action sequence or the most tearjerking dialogue. It is deceptively simple, so sly and stealthy, you don't even know it's there.

It's a question.

Sure, a good story raises lots of intriguing questions, but there is one question at the white hot center of all the others. This is the "major dramatic question," or MDQ for short. Every good story has its unique MDQ. Think of it as the story's nucleus. It's a centrifugal force that propels the story along its path of action, accelerating it steadily and breathlessly toward a climactic conclusion. And once the MDQ is answered, the story is over.

You want one of these for your story, don't you? Let me show you how to find it. The MDQ is comprised of three primary parts.

Protagonist

Most stories revolve around a single character, known as the *protagonist*. Really, protagonist is just a hifalutin term for the main character. Your protagonist is the primary player, the one whose story it is, whose desires, actions, and predicaments drive the plot. He or she is at the center of the events, the most important person. In *Gone with the Wind*, it's Scarlett O'Hara. In *Raiders of the Lost Ark*, it's Indiana Jones. In *Silence of the Lambs*, it's Clarice Starling. You get the idea.

Why do movies have a protagonist? Because it helps the audience to have a single character whom they can follow and identify with. To share his burdens. To invest in her dreams. We struggle along with Scarlett. We cheer on Indy. We fear for Clarice. It's easier for us to feel something if we're experiencing it alongside a single character, rather than several. Occasionally a film has more than one protagonist, and we'll discuss that later. But most movies have just a single protagonist, and until you're experienced with screenwriting it's best to stick with one.

It's important that you know your protagonist. His deepest thoughts, her most intimate feelings. But the visual nature of movies means that the screenwriter's job is to take all those thoughts and feelings and *externalize* them into forms that can be *seen* and *heard*. Your protagonist's thoughts and feelings must be represented as *action*. And that action needs direction.

Goal

Your protagonist's actions should focus on a single, overarching goal that he or she pursues throughout the story. While the protagonist may act on smaller objectives along the way, that primary goal is the one that keeps him or her pushing forward at all costs. Once that goal is achieved—or not—the story is over. For example, Scarlett O'Hara's goal in *Gone with the Wind* is to win Ashley Wilkes for herself. Indiana Jones's goal in *Raiders of the Lost Ark* is to obtain the legendary Ark of the Covenant. Clarice Starling's goal in *Silence of the Lambs* is to catch the serial killer, Buffalo Bill.

The goal should be something that the protagonist desires fiercely. The whole movie will turn on this goal so it had better be something terribly important. Important enough to drive the protagonist and hold the audience from start to finish.

Put the protagonist and goal together and you form the major dramatic question (MDQ), as such:

Will Scarlett win Ashley?

Will Indiana Jones obtain the Ark of the Covenant?

Will Clarice catch Buffalo Bill?

Notice how simply I stated those goals. A goal should be a model of simplicity.

A clear goal keeps the protagonist—and the story itself—on a directed path. The audience needs to have a sense of what the protagonist is after and to be able to follow how well he or she is progressing in pursuit of the goal. Even a sprawling epic like *Gone with the Wind* always stays connected to Scarlett's one goal of winning Ashley.

The goal should also be tangible, meaning something external and specific. It would be too abstract if Indiana Jones were seeking "to maintain the balance between good and evil." That would be hard to dramatize, hard to capture on film. It would be too broad if Indy's goal were simply "to have a good bout of adventure," or even "to defeat the Nazis." These goals aren't achievable in specific ways. "To obtain the Ark of the Covenant" works much better because it's something we can easily see Indy acting toward in external, specific, concrete ways. We can *watch* the struggle, and Indy's success or failure will be unmistakable. He will either get the Ark or he won't. That's a key point. The MDQ should be a question that can be answered with a firm "yes" or "no."

Though the goal itself should be simple, there may be a world of complexity beneath it. In fact, often there is a deeper desire underlying the goal. Something more abstract and internal. In *Silence of the Lambs*, for example, Clarice's deeper desire is to silence the lambs whose screams haunt her from the night she witnessed their slaughter on her uncle's farm. This is why she is training to be an FBI agent and it's why she wants to catch Buffalo Bill before he takes another victim. The internal desire is often the emotional root of the external goal, signaling what is really at stake for the protagonist. Clarice wouldn't be able to spend the entire movie trying to silence the screams in her mind—no way to show that—but her deeper desire adds depth to her surface goal of catching Buffalo Bill.

Simple, and yet complex.

The MDQ is the thing that keeps us watching, wondering how things will turn out. By the end of the movie, there will be—there *must* be—an answer to the MDQ. A "yes" or a "no." Indy and

Clarice both manage to achieve their goals. Scarlett fails, realizing she will never possess Ashley and that he wasn't the right mate for her anyway. Sometimes, protagonists realize that the goal wasn't really what they needed after all.

Conflict

The protagonist acts to achieve the goal. But he or she should come up against obstacles, opposing forces that block the fulfillment of that goal. When obstacles get in your protagonist's way, there is conflict. Conflict is an essential part of the MDQ equation because it's what makes a story dramatic. Most of us don't want to watch a movie about someone sleeping. Or even achieving the goal without breaking a sweat. If it were easy for Scarlett to win Ashley, or for Indy to obtain the Ark, or for Clarice to catch Buffalo Bill, these movies would be absurdly short and painfully dull.

Just as a protagonist pursues a primary goal through the story, he or she usually acts against a primary obstacle. The primary obstacle often comes in the form of a person, an *antagonist*. Most people think of an antagonist as the bad guy, and often it is. Darth Vader is a classic antagonist whom we love to hate. But the antagonist can also be a perfectly decent person who happens to be at cross-purposes with the protagonist, such as Carl Hanratty, a federal agent on the trail of a counterfeiter in *Catch Me If You Can*. So whether he wears a black cape or a cozy felt hat, the character who most stands in the protagonist's way is the antagonist. The primary obstacle doesn't need to be a single person, or even a person at all. It can take many forms: a beast (*Jaws*), nature (*The Perfect Storm*), machinery (*2001*), an empire (*Star Wars*), or even a whole world (*The Matrix*). All of these are the primary obstacles that block protagonists from achieving their goals.

Though there is only one goal, there may be a multitude of obstacles. In fact, the more obstacles, the better. Many of these obstacles will come from an antagonist but some may emerge from elsewhere. Not only does Scarlett need to contend with the fact that Ashley is happily married to Melanie, but she's got the Civil War, a dying way of life, a plantation, starvation, and three husbands to deal with. In the context of the story, these are all obstacles to Scarlett's primary goal of winning Ashley.

Conflict comes in two forms—external and internal. External conflicts come from obstacles exterior to the protagonist, like the antagonist. Internal conflicts refer to struggles within the protagonist's own mind. Movies need external conflicts because they are easier to portray on screen, but the richest characters have both external and internal conflicts. In addition to Clarice's external obstacles to catching Buffalo Bill—discovering his identity, soliciting information from Hannibal Lecter, deciphering clues, tracking him down—Clarice must overcome her fears of the dark side of human nature, as well as her insecurities about being a woman in a man's job and of being a "country rube." These internal conflicts give the story more psychological depth.

Conflict is the most indispensable element of a good story. It's what happens when the unstoppable force meets the immovable object. A crashing together of contrary intentions that rivets us and keeps our eyes locked on the screen. Remember this: Movies are not about casual events in a life. They are about the most crucial, challenging, earthshaking events.

MDQ Illustrated

Let's take a look at the MDQ of *Die Hard*.

The protagonist of *Die Hard* is John McClane, a New York City cop who has come out to L.A. for the Christmas holidays to visit his estranged wife. He arrives at the corporate high rise where his wife is attending a lavish Christmas party hosted by her employer.

Quick, what's McClane's goal in *Die Hard*? Did you say: To reconcile with his wife? Bzžz. Wrong guess. Read on.

Soon after McClane arrives, a group of terrorists seize the building, taking everyone inside hostage. Everyone except for

McClane, who slips into a stairwell undetected. It's now up to him, and him alone, to save the hostages. Because he's the only one who knows. Because he's the only one who can. But most of all, because *his wife* is one of them. That is McClane's goal: to free the hostages.

Thus, the MDQ of *Die Hard* is: Will McClane free the hostages?

While McClane certainly came to L.A. to reconcile with his wife, the need to stop the terrorists takes precedence. That's what McClane will be doing throughout the movie—trying to stop the terrorists in order to free the hostages. He will free them or not by the end of the story. That's how you know a goal when you see it. It's the thing the protagonist is in pursuit of for the majority of the movie.

Is there conflict for McClane? Plenty. The terrorists are led by Hans Gruber, the mastermind of a brilliant plan to distract the authorities with the hostages long enough to break into the company vault and make off with millions in untraceable bonds. Hans is the primary obstacle, *the antagonist.* But there are many other obstacles as well. In addition to Hans, there is the entire team of terrorists, who are well equipped, well trained, and ruthless. McClane has no way to call for help. When he finally gets help, the authorities only make things worse. And McClane is without shoes, which is no small obstacle on a battlefield. (There are even more, but you get the idea.) These are all external conflicts. There's some internal conflict, too, namely McClane's need to keep his spirits up while he wages a war he can't possibly win.

Is there a deeper desire underlying McClane's goal? In a sense, yes. McClane's desire to reconcile with his wife is actually a subplot (which you'll learn about in a later chapter), but this yearning also does work as a kind of deeper desire under McClane's primary goal. There is a sense that if he can save the hostages he might be able to eventually work things out with his wife. This underlying desire adds poignancy to McClane's mission and it's part of what makes this story so powerful.

Let me also say this: It's best if your MDQ can be answered in a compressed amount of time. Some stories need to sprawl over years, or decades, but most unfold in a short amount of time—weeks or days. This compression of time adds a level of tension to the plot. *Die Hard*, for example, occurs in a single night.

Three-Act Structure

Once you've pinned down the MDQ of your screenplay, it's time to figure out how it will play out over the course of the movie. In other words, you need to determine the plot. The most significant element of plotting is figuring out the structure. The structure is the overall shape, or architecture, of the story. As you begin to design your screenplay, you must apply a kind of dramatic structural engineering that will help hold everything together.

Screenplay structure begins with the simplest of concepts, so absolute, so rooted in universal truth, it's downright philosophical. Call it the Rule of Three. Most everything in life can be broken into three parts: the beginning, the middle, the end. Your experience of reading this book fits this model: You buy the book, you read it, you begin writing a brilliant screenplay. A day consists of three parts: morning, afternoon, night. Life itself even follows the Rule of Three: you're born, you live, you die. Beginning, middle, end. One, two, three.

This empirical law of nature is the basic tenet of all storytelling. Aristotle introduced this concept more than five thousand years ago in his treatise on tragic drama, *The Poetics*. He writes the following about works of drama:

> . . . they should be based on a single action, one that is a complete whole in itself, with a beginning, middle, and end, so as to enable the work to produce its own proper pleasure with all the organic unity of a living creature.

In other words, the idea of beginning, middle, and end is innate to our experience of living, and so it is the most organic format for us to use in stories. The idea of beginning, middle, and end can be found in any mode of storytelling, from campfire tales to Greek mythology to movies.

In screenwriting, we formalize the beginning, middle, and end into something called *acts*. Most every screenplay has three of them—Act I, Act II, Act III. These acts have specific functions. Act I is where the story is set up. Act II is where the conflict escalates. Act III is where the story climaxes and resolves. Everyone in the movie business talks about screenplays in terms of the three acts, so you need to become well versed in this concept.

Let's give it a visual. The acts look like this:

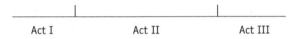

Act I   Act II   Act III

Now, these acts aren't like the acts in a play, which are clearly marked by blackouts and intermissions. The act breaks in movies are invisible to the audience. But that invisibility doesn't make the acts unimportant. Quite the contrary; the audience expects the three-act structure to be there. They might not know it, but they feel it. They crave the progression of story that a three-act structure delivers. Never forget that movies are designed to be watched in a prescribed period of time, unlike the experience of reading a book, which can be set down, picked up, set down again. A film owns its audience, and with that ownership comes the responsibility of holding interest. This is why the structure in screenplays is emphasized so much more than in novels. The viewer's interest must be hooked for every moment of a film's running time. Without the three acts, people would grow restless.

Before we move on, it's crucial that you understand how screenplays relate to time. One page of a screenplay equals approximately one minute of screen time. The average length of a feature screenplay runs between 90 and 120 pages, which equates to the average running time of a feature film, 90 to 120 minutes.

The length of the acts breaks down roughly like so:

Act I: 30 pages

Act II: 60 pages

Act III: 30 pages

(It has become fairly common now for third acts to be a bit shorter than first acts. So, really, you can think of Act III as running 15 to 30 minutes.)

30, 60, 30. That's a lot easier to think about than a clean 120. But that's still three amorphous blocks of screen time that need to be filled. Fear not: Just as morning, afternoon, and night are determined by the position of the sun, certain events define each act and help them shift from one phase to the next.

Major Events

Remember, plot is a sequence of events. But what is an event? Simple enough. An event is when something happens. A baby is born. A car breaks down. You stub your toe. Events.

In drama, an event effects change. A change in circumstance, in feeling, in knowledge, in perception. A character enters a scene with a goal in mind. Faces some obstacle, large or small. Struggles with the obstacle, then either overcomes it, or doesn't. The result of the conflict sparks a change, creating a new situation. In the next scene, the character acts against a new obstacle based on the new situation, and another change occurs. Then another. And another. And so it goes on. Each event—each change—is a link on a chain that will comprise your plot. The entire movie should be linked through direct cause and effect this way.

So really your plot may look more like this:

ooooooooooo|oooooooooooooooooooooooooooooooooo|ooooooooooo
Act I   Act II   Act III

Mostly you will use two kinds of events, events that effect either a negative or a positive change. An example of a negative event would be: A woman on the hunt for her husband's killer is suddenly blamed for the crime. An example of a positive event would be: A boxer learns he's getting a shot at the title. If the event is totally neutral, with no real positive or negative change, it's probably not worth including in the screenplay.

Each link on the chain is an event, and each event is a change. But some of those events are especially important. These major events represent *radical change*. These radical changes are what really get your plot going and what cause one act to spring into the next. Working with these major events will also make it easier for you to plot your story because they act as guideposts that help steer your protagonist along his or her path of action.

Warning: I'm now going to introduce some fancy technical terms for the major events. These terms aren't standardized; different screenwriters and gurus have their own vocabulary. But the terms I'm using are perfectly acceptable and they're known to most people in the business. It's also going to sound like I'm giving you a formula because I'm going to tell you exactly where specific events should fall in your story. It is a formula, and it isn't. After all, anyone can follow directions. It's the *way* you follow them that will make your story distinctive. The specific placement of these major events is to ensure that you keep your story tightening and tensing before the audience tunes out. While these are time-honored principles, they are not to be followed slavishly. And, by all means, whenever I mention a page number on which something should happen, factor in a grace margin of ten pages or so. This is not an exact science.

Full disclosure: Some screenwriters consider these terms and concepts anathema to good writing. And sometimes the writer's intuition is more important than any technique that can be learned from a screenwriting book. But the fact is, most screenwriters consider these concepts essential. Whether they consciously follow these schemas or if they work from the hip, one cannot deny that an overwhelming majority of movies follow most, if not all, of these principles. And once you learn all this stuff, you're free to forget about it, as many experienced screenwriters do.

Okay, ready? A movie usually has five major events: *inciting incident, plot point 1, midpoint, plot point 2,* and *climax.*

Here's another chart that shows you approximately where these major events fall in the three act structure.

```
Inciting Incident  Plot Point 1      Midpoint        Plot Point 2        Climax
      |              |                 |                 |                  |
  oooOooouuuooooO|ooouuuooonnnnoOoooooooonnnooooO|oooooooooooooOoo
          Act I                      Act II                      Act III
```

These events usually fall approximately on these pages in a screenplay:

Inciting incident: page 10

Plot point 1: page 30

Midpoint: page 60

Plot point 2: page 90

Climax: a few pages from the end

Sometimes these events are easy to spot in a movie, sometimes they're a little more slippery. Occasionally, they're not there at all (but only very occasionally). And it's even possible for knowledgeable people to disagree on which events are which in a given movie. As I warned, this is not an exact science.

Now let's take all of this out of theory and see how it works in an actual movie.

Plot Illustrated

I'm going to illustrate plot by breaking down *Die Hard*. If you're not a fan of action flicks, relax. Everything I'm about to say applies to the vast majority of films, but the classic nature of *Die Hard*'s plot lends itself to a very clear analysis of the fundamental plot principles.

Lights down. Let's go.

Act I

Most screenplays begin with a brief *lead-in*, lasting around ten pages. In these pages we meet the protagonist. We learn a little about the kind of person he is, what makes him tick. We are also introduced to the world in which the story is set. And we're shown any other key elements of the story we need to know before the plot gets revved up.

In the lead-in of *Die Hard*, we meet the protagonist, John Mc-Clane. He's a wisecracking New York cop who's in Los Angeles for the holidays in hope of reconciling with his estranged wife, Holly, an executive at the Nakatomi Corporation. He meets up with Holly at a private Christmas party in Nakatomi Plaza, a sleek, modern high rise.

McClane couldn't be more out of place here, dressed down and strapped with a gun, as well-tailored "California eccentrics" swarm around in revelry. At the party, we meet several key supporting players, including Holly's boss, Mr. Takagi. We also learn that the operations of the entire building are controlled by a computer, and that the partygoers are the only inhabitants in the otherwise empty high rise.

McClane and Holly talk. It's clear that they love each other and share a desire to patch things up. But there are unresolved issues over Holly's decision to move across the country for this job. It's easy to see how different their two worlds are, and the chasm they must somehow bridge if they are to save their marriage.

That's the big stuff we learn in the lead-in. But there are even more details, little kernels which will pop later in the story, from Holly reverting to her maiden name, to McClane removing his shoes in order to follow his plane-mate's advice to relieve stress by making "fists with his toes," to the Rolex given to Holly as a company gift. These tidbits may seem inconsequential in the moment, but in a well-plotted screenplay nothing is arbitrary. Every single thing is included for a reason.

The lead-in culminates with the first major event, the *inciting incident*. The inciting incident is the event that sets the story into motion, that will lead the protagonist toward the pursuit of the goal. This is often the first appearance or hint of the primary opposing force. The normal course of the protagonist's life is almost always disrupted here, for better or worse.

In *Die Hard*, the inciting incident occurs when Hans Gruber and his band of terrorists invade the building, locking it down, seizing control of the computer system, and cutting off all outside communication. (This happens 18 minutes into the movie, a little later than usual, but we get an ominous glimpse of the terrorists approaching at 14 minutes.) Hans and his men burst into the party and take everyone in the building hostage. There's no way to call for help (this is pre–cell phones), and no route to escape. Hans Gruber is in total control.

Except over McClane, who has slipped unseen into a stairwell. He is now the only free person who knows what's happening in Nakatomi Plaza, as well as being the only person in a position to do anything about it.

McClane lies low, trying to keep out of sight long enough to figure out what to do. After giving a speech to the hostages, Hans takes Takagi into an empty office. He demands that Takagi reveal the computer code that will unlock a vault containing 640 million dollars' worth of bonds. McClane creeps near and watches from hiding.

At the end of Act I comes the next major event, *plot point 1*. Plot point 1 is usually an even more drastic event than the inciting incident. This is the event that makes the pursuit of the goal mandatory

or absolutely irresistible for the protagonist. The goal may first surface here, or the idea of it may have existed before, but here it becomes essential. The inciting incident and plot point 1 are usually
closely related, working like a one-two punch to solidify the goal;
once plot point 1 hits, the protagonist cannot walk away from that
damned goal.

In *Die Hard*, plot point 1 occurs when Takagi refuses to disclose
the code and Hans shoots him in the head. (It happens 31 min-
utes into the movie.) This simple action changes everything.
McClane now knows that he's dealing with cold-blooded killers.
Clearly the hostages are in serious danger. Before this moment,
McClane could have decided to wait things out in hiding. Now he
knows he must take action or people will die, maybe even Holly.
McClane has his goal and we have our major dramatic question:
Will McClane free the hostages?

Plot point 1 appears right at the end of Act I, but don't think of
it as an ending so much as a springboard into the next act.

Act II

If Act I consists of setting up the conflict, then Act II is where that
conflict plays out and escalates. From here on, it's all about the
protagonist fighting against the obstacles to achieve the goal. It's
the longest act, and you'll need plenty of conflict to sustain it.

Hans has his tech specialist set about breaking the computer
code, a complex routine that requires going through seven com-
puterized locks.

McClane's first priority is to alert the authorities to the situation
in the building. He trips the fire alarm, but the trucks are called
back when Hans calls it off as a false alarm.

Now Hans knows there's a rogue loose in the building whom he
is going to have to deal with. McClane's cover is blown. Hans sends
a man after McClane, whom McClane promptly kills. Finding a
CB radio on the dead man, McClane calls a police dispatcher.
McClane can't get the dispatcher to understand the situation, but,

nevertheless, she sends a squad car to investigate. As McClane waits for the cavalry, Hans, having listened in on his distress call, directs his men to search the building and smoke McClane out.

Notice how every event in a well-plotted story is part of a chain of cause and effect. McClane trips the fire alarm, which causes Hans to send a man after McClane, which allows McClane to get hold of a CB radio and call the police, which results in Hans launching a manhunt. Also notice how the events are alternating between negative and positive for McClane.

With several terrorists in pursuit, McClane slyly evades them, climbing down an elevator shaft and crawling through an air duct. Soon two of the bad guys catch up with him, but McClane kills them both.

A lone policeman comes to the building but, after talking to a terrorist posing as the security guard, he decides nothing is wrong and heads out. McClane's plan to alert the authorities is failing.

Now, then. Act II is usually divided by a major event called the *midpoint*. Falling smack-dab in the middle of the act, the midpoint is not only the center of Act II, it's also the center of the entire story. By virtue of where the midpoint falls—dead in the middle—it needs to accomplish a bit more than a simple negative or positive change for the protagonist (though it usually does that, too). Often the midpoint brings about a shift in tone, or a slightly new vibe. You don't want a story to feel static; you want it to feel like it's evolving, and that's what happens here. Also the midpoint is usually a knockout moment, a spike of energy to adrenalize the story so the middle doesn't sag, but actually peaks. Most midpoints tend to be extremely memorable, something that people consider one of the best parts of the movie.

Here's the midpoint of *Die Hard*. Seeing the cop drive away, McClane hurls the dead body of one of the terrorists from a window and onto the hood of the patrol car. (This happens 57 minutes into the movie.) Needless to say, this catches the cop's attention and he calls in reinforcements, just as McClane wanted him to.

This represents a positive change; McClane achieves his objective of getting help from the outside. The larger significance of this midpoint is that it alters the playing field to pull a radical new set of factors into the world of the story. Until this point, the characters and the action have remained fairly isolated. It's almost as if the inhabitants of Nakatomi Plaza have been the only people in the city. But now the grounds of the plaza will be swarming with cops, FBI agents, and television crews broadcasting the story. Suddenly the building seems to have become the center of activity in all of Los Angeles. It's a whole new dynamic. A new vibe. Plus, the body landing on the cop car in *Die Hard* is one of the movie's most talked-about scenes.

Even so, McClane is still the only one inside the damn building who can do anything. He begins to carry on radio conversations with Powell, the cop who first investigated the building, feeding him information, and he even has a few radio talks with Hans, trying to antagonize him into losing his cool.

McClane also notices a bunch of detonators and a plastic explosive in the bag of one of the dead terrorists. What are those for? McClane doesn't know, but he realizes this doesn't bode well for the safety of the hostages. This is a good moment to point out that the conflict should continually escalate throughout Act II, the obstacles growing increasingly more formidable. The fact that the terrorists have explosives ratchets up the stakes.

Soon a police SWAT team attempts to charge the building, but the terrorists hold them at bay with their weapons, including a missile launcher. To prevent the cops from getting shot, McClane ends the siege by tossing the plastique down an elevator shaft, causing a massive explosion.

Then, in a beautiful scene of cat and mouse, McClane and Hans meet face to face and engage in a complex game of deception. (McClane has never actually seen Hans, and Hans takes advantage of this fact by pretending to be a hostage on the run.) Neither succeeds in killing the other, but Hans wins the round when McClane is forced to leave the detonators (the only ones) behind while fleeing a terrorist who gets the best of McClane by spraying him (and his bare feet) with shattered glass. It's worth noting that this first meeting between the protagonist and antagonist isn't about physical force, as you might expect from an action film. Instead, it's a battle of wits between two extremely cunning players. And it's riveting.

As we approach the end of Act II, we hit *plot point 2*. At plot point 2, the stakes usually escalate to the highest level yet, and this pushes the protagonist toward a final confrontation with the primary obstacle. Whatever is going to happen is going to happen imminently and decisively.

Plot point 2 is usually (though not always) a major victory for the opposing force and a major setback for the protagonist. In fact, plot point 2 usually brings the protagonist to his or her lowest point in the story. It's often a crossroads, a do-or-die moment, when the protagonist must choose to either back down or plunge ahead with renewed strength. Protagonists will always choose the latter path.

Plot point 2 in *Die Hard* occurs when the FBI cuts the power to the building, which opens the seventh and final lock on the vault, something Hans had known would happen all along. (It happens 103 minutes into the movie, which is later than usual, but *Die Hard* runs a little over two hours.) Hans is at the final stage of his plan, which we discover means more than just making off with the loot. He's planning on ushering the hostages to the roof and blowing them sky high. Hence the need for the explosives and the detonators. The authorities will assume that the terrorists also perished in the explosion, leaving the bad guys to flee in peace. With the vault open, it's now a countdown to mass death. (A ticking clock is always a great device for holding an audience.)

At the same time, McClane reaches his lowest point. He doesn't yet know about the open vault and evil escape plan but he senses doom, telling Powell over the radio, "I'm getting a bad feeling up here." He's on the ropes. Exhausted, pulling shards of glass from his bloody feet, he instructs Powell to tell Holly that he loves her, and to apologize for all the mistakes he made in their marriage. Knowing he will probably die soon, McClane is forced to face the failure of his marriage and his failure to free the hostages. He is very close to giving up. But he doesn't give up. That ain't McClane's style. Might as well go down swinging and hope for that lucky punch.

Just as plot point 1 springs us into Act II, plot point 2 springs us into Act III.

Act III

The first part of Act III usually contains a compressed series of events that escalate to the final confrontation.

When McClane sees explosives wired to the roof of the building, he realizes what Hans plans to do with them. The hostages are now being evacuated to the roof. Time is short. At this same moment, Hans finally discovers that Holly is McClane's wife, a fact that previously eluded him due to Holly using her maiden name. Hans seizes Holly as insurance should McClane get in the way of his plan's final stage.

In a spectacular sequence, McClane clears the hostages off the roof. He saves their lives but almost loses his own as an explosion forces him to dive off the edge of the rooftop. He dangles from a fire hose, which he uses to smash through a window and reenter the building just seconds before falling to certain death.

The hostages are safe. All, that is, but one: Holly. McClane knows that this is his last and only chance to take Hans down and save his wife.

Which brings us to the *climax*. This is it. The big showdown. The final confrontation with the primary obstacle. Your hero has won and lost some battles, but this is the one by which he will win or lose the war itself. Whatever happens here is the be-all and end-all of the story. There will be no more chances. The MDQ will be answered. The goal will be won or lost forever. And know that the protagonist must take the final action himself. It wouldn't be right if it were the police or FBI who ultimately saved the day. It must be McClane.

In *Die Hard*, the climax occurs when McClane invades the vault, interrupting Hans's getaway. At gunpoint, McClane pretends to surrender, dropping the machine gun he carries. With Hans off his guard, McClane grabs a handgun duct-taped to his back and shoots Hans in the chest. Hans crashes through a window and stops his fall only by grabbing onto Holly's wrist. Both Holly and Hans are about to plunge forty stories down. McClane unclasps the watch on Holly's wrist, the very thing Hans clings to, and Hans plummets downward to a violent death.

McClane has saved the hostages, including Holly. The MDQ has been answered with a heroic "yes." McClane wins.

There's still one final piece to a plot, the *resolution*, which gives us a glimpse of the story's aftermath. Often it speaks to that deeper desire underlying the protagonist's goal, hinting at what is to come for the protagonist.

In *Die Hard*, the resolution comes when McClane and Holly drive off merrily together in the limo. We sense they now know that if Hans Gruber and his band of terrorists couldn't keep them apart, petty marital problems don't stand a chance.

The Subtle Plot

To show you how prevalent these plot principles are, let's analyze them in relation to a movie that couldn't be more different from *Die Hard*. That would be *Sideways*.

Die Hard is a classic Hollywood film, filled with slam-bang action, heroes, and villains, and the whole nine yards. *Sideways* is a subtle, nuanced, character-driven, indie film. To illustrate the difference, *Die Hard* features a scene in which the hero picks glass out of his bleeding feet while battling terrorists; *Sideways* features an entire scene in which the hero clips his toenails. Most indie films (not to mention foreign films) fall into the second category. These movies still usually follow the basic plot principles but everything is, well, more subtle.

Take, for example, the protagonist's goal. Previously, I told you
that goals should be clear and tangible, with often a more abstract,
deeper desire underneath them. Subtle movies often do away with
the external goal and use something more internal and vague as
the primary goal. In other words, the deeper desire becomes the
protagonist's goal. While external goals lead to plot-driven stories,
internal goals lead to character-driven stories. *Die Hard* is a good
example of the former, and *Sideways* is a good example of the latter.

The protagonist of *Sideways* is Miles, a middle-aged school-
teacher and unpublished novelist whose wife has divorced him.
He's a man whose train has left the station without him aboard.
The two things that mean the most to him, his writing career and
his love life, are in shambles.

The goal in *Sideways* is not nearly as easy to pinpoint as in *Die
Hard*. In fact, I had to really dig to figure out what it was. Miles
needs some kind of success in order to get out of this dark period
in his life. A publishing deal, a romance—anything. There are
probably many ways to state what Miles's goal might be. Let's go
with: to pull himself out of his rut. So the MDQ of *Sideways* is: Will
Miles pull himself out of his rut?

The primary obstacle is also fairly abstract. It's not a person or
a beast or an empire. The primary obstacle is failure itself. Being
very much a character-driven movie, much of the failure is actually
inside Miles's mind; it's not so much external events that cause his
failure as his own self-sabotaging and fear. You could safely say that
Miles's worst enemy is Miles. He doesn't even pursue his goal
along a straightforward path of action. The desire is there, but he's
afraid to go after it. In fact, Miles spends most of the movie side-
stepping any situation that might put him face to face with failure.

But even when the goal is mostly internal and indirectly pur-
sued, you still have to find ways to give the protagonist tangible
objects of desire. Otherwise you would have nothing to show,
nothing for the protagonist to *do*. There are a number of external
expressions of Miles's goal of pulling himself out of his rut. His
book is still being considered by a single publisher. And he's

attracted to Maya, a waitress he knows from one of his favorite restaurants. If either of these situations were to end well for Miles, it might bring him out of his rut. Even though he doesn't pursue these objectives with the singular focus and tenacity as, say, John McClane, Miles isn't sleeping for five and a half hours, either. He's actively engaged in external goals and conflicts, just in more subtle ways.

Now let's look at how the MDQ is played out through the major events. Yes, *Sideways* does have major events, even if they are more difficult to spot.

In the lead-in to *Sideways*, we meet Miles and his best friend, Jack, as they set out for a weeklong getaway to wine country, their last hurrah before Jack's coming wedding. You could say the inciting incident is simply when Miles and Jack set off on the trip, as claimed by one of my colleagues in chapter 8 (see, I told you knowledgeable people can disagree on this stuff). But I'm going to take a leap and say that the inciting incident is when Miles sees an old photo of himself as a child in his mother's room. Gazing upon his younger self, he is struck by how far he is from fulfilling his dreams—and how close he is to failure. (This happens 15 minutes in.) But, truth be told, a strong argument could be made that *Sideways* has no distinct inciting incident. Remember, none of this is an exact science.

Plot point 1 arrives when Miles learns that his ex-wife is getting remarried (which happens 35 minutes in). This represents a enormous setback, as Miles has harbored hopes of a reconciliation. He can no longer live in denial, foolishly thinking he'll get his wife back. Though he doesn't exactly spring into action, it's clear that he must find something soon to get his life back on track.

Moving into Act II, Jack drags Miles into a complex web of lies as he pretends to be single in order to woo Stephanie, a woman he meets at a winery. Stephanie has a friend, Maya, whom Miles gets paired with. Despite Miles's discomfort with Jack's charade, Miles is attracted to Maya.

The midpoint arrives at the end of their double date. As Jack and Stephanie disappear into Stephanie's bedroom, Miles manages to edge haltingly toward making a connection with Maya. (This happens 60 minutes in.) Getting in good with Maya, a woman he is attracted to, is a big deal, a boon to Miles's goal of pulling himself out of his rut. It puts him on the upswing, giving him the nerve to go after Maya through the rest of the act. Also, true to midpoint form, Miles's Pinot Noir monologue here is one of the most talked-about moments in the movie.

Quick digression. It's also in this sequence that Miles mentions that's he's saving a vintage bottle of wine, a Cheval Blanc, for a "special occasion." Though this information in itself isn't a major event, it is nonetheless an important setup for an event to occur later. I point this out to illustrate the deliberate way that specific information is dispensed, at carefully chosen moments, to lay the groundwork for later payoffs.

In *Sideways*, plot point 2 is a typically huge blow to the protagonist. Since Maya has now dumped Miles upon learning of Jack's charade, Miles's only hope is his book. He finally works up the guts to call his agent for a status report. His agent gently informs Miles that the final publisher has turned him down. (This happens 90 minutes in.) That's it for Miles. His ex-wife is getting married, Maya has dumped him, and his book is dead. There is no getting around his failure. Though Miles doesn't handle this moment well (he freaks out and guzzles the contents of a spit bucket), he doesn't fold up and die either. He stays on his feet.

Now we move into Act III. Following a few more adventures, Miles and Jack head back for the wedding. There, Miles finally has a face-to-face encounter with his ex-wife. She announces to Miles that she is pregnant with her new husband's child. It's a crushing blow, the biggest reminder yet of Miles's failure, and it seems like the final nail in his coffin. But then Miles takes a surprising stand against his failure.

The climax of *Sideways* is so subtle, you could blink and miss it. It arrives in a seemingly mundane scene when Miles finally drinks that Cheval Blanc '61. He drinks it all alone, without ceremony, from a

Styrofoam cup in a greasy burger joint. Miles has given up on that special occasion to open this bottle. He's accepting his failure, letting go and moving on. It's here that Miles actually does achieve his goal of pulling himself out of his rut. Failure has been defeated, in a sense, because he's taken away its power to drag him down.

In the resolution, Miles receives a call from Maya, and the film ends with a hint that they may get together after all. Sometimes, letting go of broken dreams makes room for new ones.

See, everything is there. It's all just a little more subtle.

Take a Shot

Watch a movie. Any movie will do, but you want to watch it on DVD or tape. Try to identify the following: major dramatic question, inciting incident, plot point 1, midpoint, plot point 2, climax. You may not spot these things right away. You will do best by watching the movie straight through, then re-watching it to analyze how the plot fits together. (You can test yourself against our answers if you use one of the movies listed at www.WritingMovies.info)

Variations

It is advisable to stick with the tried-and-true principles of plot until you've completed a few screenplays. Even Warhol began as a realistic sketch artist before he moved on to all those soup cans and experimental movies. Once you know and understand the "rules," you can break them better. And it's good to break them. In fact, the greatest films, those written and directed by the true masters, are the ones most likely to flaunt the rules of conventional plot. Watch a movie like *2001* or *Vertigo* or *The Godfather* and you'll see plot rules broken left and right. Since it's usually enlightening to study the exceptions, let's look at some ways in which films use variations on the basics.

Multiple Protagonists

Some movies have more than one protagonist. For example, in *Thelma & Louise* we would be hard-pressed to claim that either Thelma or Louise is more central than the other. Together, they comprise "dual protagonists," that is, two protagonists who function as a single unit in pursuit of a common goal. Thelma and Louise share the common goal of trying to reach the border of Mexico before the cops catch up with them. (*Thelma & Louise*, by the way, is a good example of a goal that is not achieved.)

Dual-protagonist movies often fall into the "buddy" subgenre. Famous buddy films would include *Butch Cassidy and the Sundance Kid, Lethal Weapon, Dumb and Dumber*, and all those classic Bob Hope–Bing Crosby "road" movies. You might consider *Sideways* a buddy film, but in this case Miles is the clear protagonist; Miles and Jack definitely don't share a common goal.

Some films go beyond two characters to feature a team of protagonists who all work together toward a common goal. With team protagonists, though, there's almost always a lead protagonist around whom the others gather. For example, while Luke Skywalker is the clear lead of *Star Wars*, Han Solo, Princess Leia, Chewbacca, the Droids, and Obi-Wan are all key characters who work with Luke to overcome the Empire. Some movies offer a variation on the typical team-protagonist setup. In *Alien*, for example, a team of characters share the common goal of survival as a really crabby alien invades their spacecraft and picks them off one by one. Only late in the film does Lieutenant Ripley emerge, almost by default, as the lead protagonist.

Then we have "split protagonists," where two characters have equal weight and equal claim on our affections, but are operating at cross-purposes with each other. *Terms of Endearment* is split equally between Aurora (the mother) and Emma (the daughter). *Heat* is equally split between Hanna (the cop) and McCauley (the crook).

What about the love story? The love story is unique in that it's a pinch of the dual protagonist, a splash of the split. It's dual in that the love story usually features two characters in pursuit of a shared goal (to be together), who often work against a common obstacle to that togetherness. But it's split in that the two characters often confront the obstacle at separate angles, perhaps even clashing with each other in the process. For example, in *When Harry Met Sally* . . . , both Harry and Sally are protagonists who share the goal of finding love, but each must first let go of a specific idea of love in order to recognize they have found it in each other. Not every love story, however, features two protagonists. In movies like *Moonstruck* and *The Philadelphia Story*, one of the romantic partners is the obvious lead.

Multiple Plots

If you think a multiple-protagonist plot is complicated, try one of these.

Some films contain a multitude of characters, each with equal weight, pursuing his or her own goals in separate plots. These are known as "multiple plot" or "ensemble" films. Together, the various stories form a kind of collage. The writer-director Robert Altman is the master of the ensemble movie, which he has perfected in such films as *M*A*S*H*, *Nashville*, and *Short Cuts*. Other notable examples of this kind of film would include *American Graffiti*, *Do the Right Thing*, and *Magnolia*.

Usually there is some overarching element that ties the plots together. For example, in *Nashville*, all the characters are attending a country-music festival in Nashville (a shared event). We meet a gallery of Bed-Stuy, Brooklyn denizens in *Do the Right Thing* on the hottest day of the year (a shared experience). *Magnolia* features a mosaic of stories about characters all haunted by their pasts (a shared theme).

Shifting Goals

Though I've told you that a protagonist must have one primary goal, there are great movies out there in which the goal seems to reveal itself in the first act, only to shift later in the story.

For example, in *Tootsie*, the protagonist, Michael Dorsey, masquerades as a woman, Dorothy Michaels, in order to get work as an actor. His initial goal seems to be to find work. But he achieves this goal at the end of Act I when, as Dorothy, he lands a plum role on a major soap opera. His goal then seems to be to get close to Julie (the actress he falls for). So it seems this movie has violated the golden rule of one driving goal for the protagonist. Has it? Well, yes and no.

If you look closely, you'll see that *Tootsie* is held together by a single goal: to maintain the masquerade. He must maintain the masquerade for the duration of his contract. If he fails to do this, he will ruin his reputation, his agent's reputation, shatter his friend Sandy's ego, and also do a little damage to his own actor's ego. Also, for most of the movie, maintaining the masquerade is the best way for him to get close to Julie. So, this is what Michael is doing in every scene: maintaining the masquerade. Only at the end does Michael realize he can no longer sustain the masquerade and keep his sanity, and so he unmasks on national television. Viewed in this light, Michael ultimately fails to achieve his goal, but he gives up on it for a good reason.

There may be plots where it's necessary for the protagonist's immediate goal to shift, as it does in *Tootsie*, but the plot will still work better if there is some kind of overarching goal that remains constant throughout the movie. This may be a concrete goal, like maintaining the masquerade, or a more abstract goal, like Miles's desire to pull himself out of a rut. The ongoing goal will keep your protagonist on a clear path.

Defying Chronology

Then there are plots that defy chronology in their unfolding. *Pulp Fiction*, for example, begins in one time period, then abruptly shifts back, then ahead, then back again. Part of the fun of the film is piecing together what's happening when, and in what order. The "meta-structure" even defies death itself as the character of Vince Vega is "resurrected" after his own demise. And how about *Memento*, which unfolds backwards, beginning at the end of a mystery and then backtracking through ten-minute increments to see how it all began? The effect is one that reflects the experience of the protagonist, who has no short-term memory; like him, we have no idea what happened before the moment we're in. Then there's *Run Lola Run*, which challenges its heroine to race across town in time to save her boyfriend from thugs—but when she fails, the movie "rewinds" to "start over" and give her two more chances to play it differently. Sort of like the three lives of a video game. Interestingly, even these nonchronological structures still have a clear beginning, middle, and end. They just do it in their own way.

The Shawshank *Exception*

The Shawshank Redemption is one of those movies that breaks almost every rule in the book.

A young banker named Andy Dufresne is convicted of the murder of his wife and her lover and sentenced to life in Shawshank Prison. Though we're initially unsure whether Andy committed the crime, we're certain that he's a good man to whom we want to see no harm come. Andy befriends Red, a seasoned con, and the two form an unbreakable bond as they endure their sentences. After almost twenty years together, Red discovers that Andy has been methodically and patiently tunneling to freedom since he arrived at the prison. Ultimately, Andy breaks out, Red is granted parole, and the two friends reunite on a beach in Mexico.

For starters, who's the protagonist? Andy is clearly at the center of the movie. Yet, most of the events are seen through the eyes of Red. Andy and Red aren't dual protagonists, because they don't pursue a shared goal. They're not split, because they're not on either side of a conflict. In fact, Andy is the protagonist of the film, while Red serves as a witness; something called the witness character. Red narrates the story and observes it, but it is Andy's actions, not Red's, that drive the plot. Andy's struggle is the heart of the film.

And what exactly is Andy's goal? In a sense, there are two goals—the one we *think* Andy is pursuing, and later, the one we *discover* he was secretly in pursuit of the whole time. At first, we believe Andy's goal is to maintain hope (an internal goal). However, at the story's end, we realize that Andy's goal was actually to break out of Shawshank (an external goal). But there is a strong relationship between these goals, as the tunneling probably helped Andy maintain hope, and he needed that hope to stay steadfast with the tunneling.

Even the major events defy easy analysis. The midpoint is easy enough (playing Mozart) and you can probably spot plot point 2 (Tommy's murder), but where the heck is plot point 1? Upon first viewing, in the context of Andy's goal of maintaining hope, plot point 1 seems to be when Andy offers the fearsome Captain Hadley free tax advice, garnering himself special privileges with the prison staff. But looking back with the knowledge that Andy was secretly hatching an escape plan, we realize that the seemingly innocuous moment in which Andy gets Red to agree to obtain a mini–rock hammer is, in fact, plot point 1, a giant step toward Andy's secret goal of breaking out.

Another irregularity of *The Shawshank Redemption* is how the climax is revealed. We don't actually see Andy's dramatic break as it occurs. Instead, we experience the discovery of the event along with Red and the antagonist, Warden Norton, when the warden sends a rock whizzing through the poster. Then we're finally shown the climactic break-out in flashback.

And get this: *The Shawshank Redemption* breaks the holiest of holy rules. It has four acts! As soon as Andy is free, his goal is achieved, but the movie is far from over. It continues to track Red through his parole and release, sticking with him as he follows Andy's clues to join him on the beach in Mexico. In a sense, this is a sort of Act IV in which, at the end of the story, Red really does take on the role of protagonist. So, there's another rule broken— the protagonist shifts.

These rules were not broken by accident; they were broken for strong dramatic reasons. In the final analysis, it's not fidelity to the "rules" that make a film great. Greatness comes when a film finds its true path.

Outlines

For your movie to work, you've got to get the structure and the plot just right. That's why most screenwriters don't just dive in, blindly typing their screenplays from page one. We plan out our stories in advance, using outlines. If a screenplay is a blueprint, think of an outline as a blueprint for the blueprint.

Each writer's process is different. I know a few screenwriters who never work with outlines. But most of us consider outlines essential. I'd estimate that fully half the work I do on a script takes place at the outline stage. Hell, I've even been known to spend more time on my outline than I do writing the screenplay itself! By starting with an outline, you are more or less trying out your ideas to assess how they might translate into a movie. Looking at your outline, you can ask yourself certain key questions. Will my story work in a three-act structure? Does the inciting incident spark the MDQ? Does the midpoint alter the playing field? Are things flowing right? Do I have a strong enough climax? If the plot isn't working right off (and it never does), it's a lot easier to experiment with it in outline form than it is in a screenplay, where you would have to rewrite a disproportionate amount of material to accommodate a single change.

An outline acts like a road map. You can refer to it as you write your screenplay to help you stay on track, to remember where you're going, and to keep your eye on the big picture of your story. For most writers, that's a lot easier than making it up as you go.

There is no right way to outline. You can scribble it on napkins, sort it out on index cards, write it in pig Latin. Whatever works. No one sees your outline but you. That said, there are three common types of outlines used by screenwriters.

Chart of major events: This is often the first outline you'll do. It's quite short, a few lines citing the five major events, the guideposts of your plot. (See page 66.)

Beat sheet: This is where you literally plot out each event, or "beat," of your story. Not just the major events, but every event. Everything that happens, in order, from start to finish. (See chapter 5 and page 174.)

Treatment: This is where you write out a prose version of your story, as long or short as you like. One page, twenty pages, it's up to you. Some writers feel this is a good way to get on the pulse of their screenplay. It can also be a great way to get your story into a readable shape in order to elicit feedback from a few trusted friends.

Here's how I do it. Invariably, I start with the outline of major events. Although it covers only five points, this is actually one of the most crucial stages of my entire process. If the major events don't do what they're supposed to, nothing I subsequently write will hold up. I sometimes spend days getting these five events in order. As soon as I'm satisfied with the major events, I move on to the beat sheet. This is one of the longest and most involved parts of my writing process. I've spent weeks at this stage, tinkering and reorganizing until I've worked out the order of events for the whole movie. Then, if I'm working with producers who need to sign off on my choices, I'll write up a treatment for them, usually around ten pages. If I'm working on a spec script, occasionally I'll write a much shorter treatment so that friends can give me feedback, but most of the time I just skip the treatment and go straight to the screenplay. (Getting to know your characters will help with all of this and that's something you'll learn about in the next chapter.)

Your outlines will guide you along your path of action. Follow them as you work. But don't feel that you must stick to them. Things change as you write. New ideas pop up, old ones fail you. Stay open to inspiration; always be on the lookout for something better. The outline is only the road map, not the journey itself. It works a lot like a real-life road trip. Before you leave, you plan your course: make it to Atlanta by six o'clock, hit Birmingham by noon the next day, New Orleans by nightfall. A solid plan, and yet who knows what a spontaneous detour might reveal? Maybe you scrap the idea of making it to New Orleans by nightfall and visit Black Bayou Lagoon, and there's a tavern there where you shoot darts with the locals, eat the best seafood gumbo you've ever tasted, then meet up with someone who turns out to be a lifelong friend. It's what you do along the path that matters most. Sometimes the best plan is to fold up the map and listen to your instincts.

Stepping-Stone: Major Dramatic Question

Work up the major dramatic question of your movie by identifying the protagonist and his or her goal. Then list as many obstacles as you can think of. Try to include both external and internal obstacles. And see if you can identify a primary obstacle. You may not use all of these obstacles, but your list will help you determine whether your story has enough potential conflict.

Then list ideas for at least five scenes that would show the protagonist in pursuit of the goal. Your scene ideas may or may not end up in your screenplay, but this will get you thinking in the right direction.

Chart Of Major Events

Early in the process, you will probably want to make an outline that charts the major events in your story. This will ensure that your story has enough turning points and escalation, and it will serve as a guide to follow on your early drafts. An easy way to do this is to figure out the five major events of your story and write them down in their simplest form. It won't make sense to anyone except you, but that's okay. Here's how it might look for *Die Hard*:

> *Inciting incident*: Terrorists storm the building
>
> *Plot point 1*: Terrorists kill the head of the corporation
>
> *Midpoint*: McClane captures attention of the cops
>
> *Plot point 2*: Terrorists open the vault
>
> *Climax*: McClane faces off with the terrorist leader

If you want to take this just a bit further, you can make a *story map* (a Gotham Writers' Workshop invention). The story map includes the five major events and gives just a hint of how these events are connected. This will help you get a general sense of the story's progression. Here's how a story map might look for *Die Hard*:

ACT I
John McClane, a wisecracking New York City cop, has come to L.A. to visit his estranged wife. They attend a Christmas party for the Nakatomi Corporation, where his wife is an executive.

Inciting incident: A team of European terrorists storm the building.

The terrorists take everyone in the building hostage, except Mc-Clane, who lurks unseen. Hans Gruber, the suave terrorist leader, requests that Mr. Takagi, the president, reveal the codes for a vault containing millions in bonds.

Plot point 1: When Takagi refuses, Gruber shoots him in the head. McClane realizes the terrorists are killers and he must stop them.

ACT II
McClane repeatedly tries to signal to authorities what is going on, without success. Meanwhile, the terrorists get wind of McClane's presence and come after him.

Midpoint: McClane heaves the body of a dead terrorist from a window onto a cop car. Realizing something is up, the cop calls for reinforcements.

The LAPD and FBI swarm the building, but the terrorists prevent them from entering. McClane continues fighting the terrorists from within. The terrorists succeed in cracking six of the seven locks on the vault.

Plot point 2: When the FBI cuts off the building's power, the seventh lock releases, opening the vault. After seizing the money, the terrorists can move to the final stage of the plan—masking their escape with a massive explosion that will kill all the hostages. McClane, still the only non-hostage in the building, is exhausted and injured, not sure how much steam he's got left.

ACT III
When Gruber learns that one of the hostages is McClane's wife, he seizes her as protection against McClane.

Climax: McClane confronts Gruber in the vault. He manages to save his wife and send Gruber hurtling out a high window to his death.

The terrorist threat is over, the hostages safe, and McClane is reunited with his wife.

Stepping-Stone: Story Map

List the five major events of your movie in their simplest form.

Then, using the five major events as guideposts, create a story map. Your story map doesn't have to look exactly like the one above, but you should keep it brief and focused. Try to make it fit on one page. The major events may well change during the writing process, but this will give you a good starting point.

CHAPTER 3

Characters: The Lifeblood

BY PAUL ZIMMERMAN

Enid, the teenage protagonist of Terry Zwigoff's *Ghost World* (written by Zwigoff and Daniel Clowes), knows what she hates, which is just about everything. She feels totally out of place in a world of soulless materialism. That's why while working at the concession stand of a multiplex, she tells a customer that his popcorn is "smothered in delicious yellow chemical sludge." That's why when her friend suggests they dress up like yuppies to help themselves get an apartment, she goes home and dyes her hair green. That's why she decides not to sell a blouse to a lady at a yard sale because she doesn't like her attitude. That's why she finds herself gravitating toward a geeky, middle-aged record collector named Seymour. Underneath all the rebellion, though, is a confused and sensitive girl who has a crush on a popular guy, wants to be an artist, and needs to find a reason to exist. It's not that she's unwilling to like something, even love it; she just doesn't know where to turn in life.

Throughout the movie, an elderly gentleman waits at a bus stop that has been out of service for years. At the end of the film, after Enid's life has crumbled to pieces, Enid also waits at the ghostly bus stop. Miraculously, a bus arrives. Enid boards it and the bus rumbles off into the night. Where is she going? It's never explained. When I first saw this movie, I wondered where Enid traveled to. Then I found myself wondering what she is doing now, right now. Years after seeing the movie, I still find myself wondering what has become of Enid. Is she living the bohemian life in

New York City? Did she meet up with a guy and settle down in Phoenix? Is she hooked on heroin or living a happy life?

That's the thing about great characters. We think about them as if they were real people, sometimes thinking of them as friends or enemies or lovers. We identify with their struggles, too. I don't have to be a teenage girl (and I'm not) to feel powerfully connected to Enid's alienation and desire.

Characters are the lifeblood of a story. The plot may be the thing that keeps us watching from moment to moment, but we experience movies through the experience of the characters. It is the characters—be they humans, hobbits, rabbits, or aliens—that reach out of the screen and pull us in. It is the characters that make a movie come to life.

When writing, you are creating parts intended to be given flesh and voice by actors. Actors can add a tremendous stamp to characters, for better or worse, but the best characters are well drawn in the script. Even on paper, they give the semblance of having a life of their own. Should you think of specific actors while writing parts? Certainly it's okay to do this, might even help guide you, and the more your parts are attractive to actors, the better. But don't pigeonhole too much; it's better to let the actor in mind help you find the character, rather than writing a part right only for one actor. Allow the characters to come to life on their own terms.

The Protagonist

When people tell you about a movie, they're likely to start with the phrase "It's about a guy who . . ." That guy (or gal or whatever) is the protagonist. The protagonist is the heart of the story, the element that pumps the story full of excitement and emotion. If you don't have a terrific protagonist, you won't have a terrific story. In a sense, the protagonist *is* your story. Ideally, you're looking to create a protagonist who will join the ranks of such wonderful characters as George Bailey, Rick Blaine, Ellen Ripley, Erin Brockovich, Virgil Tibbs, Spartacus, Rocky, Neo, Frodo, and Holly Golightly.

Let's look at the three key things that make for a great protagonist, the three *A*'s. You can be sure that movie stars look for these three things when they read scripts, searching for juicy roles to play.

Action

Almost by definition a protagonist is an active character. The story is driven by their pursuit of a single goal, and so, rather than accept their condition and let others call the shots, they take decisive measures of their own. They don't simply react; they initiate the action. That's part of what makes them exciting to watch.

Michael Dorsey in *Tootsie*, for example, doesn't just meekly accept his agent's admonition that no one will cast him anymore. He gussies himself up as Dorothy Michaels, talks his/her way into the audition, and wins a role he is not even remotely right for.

John McClane in *Die Hard* doesn't cower in hiding and wait for the authorities when he realizes that terrorists have taken over the building. He wages a guerrilla campaign of his own to get them out.

Andy Dufresne in *The Shawshank Redemption* doesn't bow to a system that discourages anything but a robotic acceptance of authority. He finds dozens of small ways to maintain his humanity while slowly and patiently executing a spectacular plan of escape.

When Louise of *Thelma & Louise* shoots a would-be rapist, she and Thelma don't turn themselves in and hope for the best. They hit the road for Mexico. Whatever it takes to break free—robbing a store or locking a cop in a trunk—they're not afraid to do it.

Protagonists may be in a passive state when the story begins, but once roused they will fight to achieve their goal. There will be setbacks, times when they feel like giving up, but they will soldier on to the bitter end. They will take action.

Okay, occasionally a protagonist stays passive for a good part of the story. In such movies, though, it is almost always just a matter of time before they get moving and take matters into their own hands. Part of the tension, and fun, is waiting for them to do so. Benjamin in *The Graduate* is adrift for half the movie, directionless, easy prey for Mrs. Robinson's manipulations. But as soon as he sets his sights on Mrs. Robinson's daughter, he becomes a whirlwind of action.

In rare instances, usually in very character-driven movies, you'll see a protagonist who stays relatively passive throughout. Miles in *Sideways* fits this bill. He's a dreamer, someone who wants to break away from being a loser, but he doesn't do all that much to pursue his goal. He often lets others dictate the action. He might even be described as passive-aggressive, doing such things as telling Jack he's on the way while he takes his time showering and reading a book. When he does take steps, he's likely to take them backwards, as when he calls his ex-wife while on a date with Maya. Most of the time he simply avoids any kind of real action, grabbing a nap or drinking himself into stupor. Why is it okay to have a character this passive? Well, it's real. Most people in real life are more likely to behave like this than as a typical movie hero, so most of us can relate, on some level, to a passive protagonist. If you're writing an extremely realistic movie and you have the skill to maintain the dramatic tension in this manner, this may be the way to go.

Otherwise, get your protagonist off the sofa and into action.

Arc

Another mark of protagonists is their ability to change. In pursuing their goals, protagonists meet obstacles that force them to adjust and adapt, and, in turn, they grow or transform in some way. This progression is called an *arc*. In most cases, the protagonist changes for the better, evolving into some version of a stronger, wiser, more sensitive human being. Occasionally, the protagonist can go the other direction, such as Jimmy in *Mystic River* or Hank in *A Simple Plan*, who start out as solid family men and end up as ruthless murderers. The protagonist's arc works hand in hand with the events of the plot and is a big part of what makes the story an emotionally rewarding experience.

John McClane, like most protagonists in action films, doesn't have a vast or complicated character arc but, after all the carnage, it is clear that he now has it within himself to make the compromises it will take to get back with his wife and family.

Michael Dorsey may or may not be as fussy an actor by the end of the movie, but he is certainly a changed man in regard to his treatment of women. Having lived as one, he is now able to see them as human, not just sex objects or acting disciples.

Sideways presents a more subtle case. There are no massive changes in store for Miles; he's not going to get hit by lightning and turn suddenly into Cary Grant. But there is a feeling at the end of the film that he has found some kind of tenuous inner balance. It's a small thing, but when he receives the ambiguous phone call from Maya, we sense that he is ready to approach her again with a somewhat cleaner slate, a less paralyzing sense of his own inadequacy. For a character like Miles, that's not an insignificant distance to have traveled.

Of course, the protagonist doesn't change all at once. It is an ongoing process, an evolution. It doesn't happen randomly either, but rather is a direct result of the events of the story. As the story develops externally, the protagonist is going through a simultaneous internal progression.

In *Thelma & Louise*, Thelma has an especially dramatic arc. She goes through roughly four major phases:

- Caged, naïve, timid

- Freed, but careless

- Understanding her ability and worth, taking charge

- Fully alive, at peace, fearless

These phases play out through the story something like this: At the beginning, Thelma is a traditional housewife, stuck at home, thoroughly under the thumb of her jerk of a husband. She isn't stupid; she gets what a dud she's married to, but she seems to have passively, if not happily, accepted the situation. This is about to change. Leaving with Louise for the weekend without Darryl's permission is her first act of liberation. Still, she frets that Darryl's "gonna shit," and, nervous about venturing into great wide world of "psycho killers, bears, and snakes," she overpacks absurdly for the two-day trip, hauling along most of her wardrobe, a clock, a lantern, fingernail scissors, and, of course, a gun.

Once she's on the road, Thelma starts to come alive. She's exhilarated, but not really grounded. She's like a kid, a little out of control, not really thinking about the circumstances, content to let Louise manage things. She drinks too much and allows herself to be maneuvered into the bad business with Harlan. That sobers her up a bit, but she still lusts for fun and ends up experiencing her first orgasm with the studly hitchhiker, J. D.

When J. D. steals their bankroll, Thelma is forced to sober up even more. Growing instantly more mature, she starts to take some control of the situation. Most significantly, she expertly robs a convenience store to get them more money. She gains a new confidence and realizes she's got a "knack" for outlaw behavior and, whereas before she was more or less a passenger on Louise's ride, she's now making all the decisions. She also realizes that she is "not goin' back. No matter what happens."

Finally, Thelma arrives at a place of true peace. Driving through the splendor of the desert, she says, "I feel awake . . . wide awake. I don't remember ever feeling this awake." She's come fully alive, and is now fully free. So alive and free, in fact, that she'd rather drive off a cliff than go back to the prison that inevitably awaits her. When they're surrounded by cops and perched on the edge of the canyon, it is Thelma who broaches the unthinkable, and advises Louise to just keep driving. Thelma has made a 180-degree turn. She gone from being a trapped woman with no real life to someone who is completely independent and spectacularly alive. Her journey can be viewed in the vast distance between her first line of dialogue ("I still have to ask Darryl if I can go") and her last ("Hit it").

Note that the protagonist's change shouldn't come totally out of nowhere. Seeds must be planted. In the very first scene, we see that Thelma isn't thrilled by Darryl, that she has some hankering to break free. This is a journey the character needs to take, in some way *wants* to take. It's almost as if she's been waiting for the events of the story to occur.

The most common exceptions to the rule of protagonist change are the heroes of ongoing action series, such as James Bond, Indiana Jones, or Lara Croft. They tend to be unalterable icons; they are who they are. Besides, if, say, James Bond were suddenly to become more sensitive to violence, there would be no sequels.

Andy in *The Shawshank Redemption* offers a more complex exception. It can't really be said that when he leaves Shawshank Andy is significantly different from when he entered prison. Shortly after he arrives, we see that he's smart, surprisingly tough, and patient. Presumably these traits deepen over the years, but they don't really change. But, in a sense, Andy still has an arc. He doesn't change, but our *perception* of him evolves. Let's call it an "arc of perception." Like Red, we don't think he'll survive at first, but we soon learn that he's made of sterner stuff. We see him maintain his dignity and humanity in the face of repeated physical and psychological assaults by the warden, the guards, and the prisoners, but it is not until near the end of the story, when his escape plan is finally revealed, that we learn just *how* smart, *how* tough, and *how* patient he really is. His character is taken to another level: We knew he was good, we just had had no idea he was *this* good. In certain stories, this kind of arc can be extremely rewarding for an audience.

It's essential that you figure out the arc of your protagonist and then make sure there is a direct relationship between that arc and the overall structure of the plot. Changes in the plot should feed changes in the protagonist, which should, in turn, feed changes in the plot. The interweaving of plot and character in this way is what makes for a great story.

Appeal

The protagonist is our guide through the movie, and if the guide is bad company, we are probably not going to stay on board for the entire trip. So there needs to be a reason why these characters deserve our attention, why we bond with them or at least stick with them for the duration of the story. A protagonist must appeal to us in some way, but the screenwriter has a great latitude in determining what that way might be.

Some protagonists are easy to root for.

Andy Dufresne is nothing short of an inspirational person. Through sheer intelligence, patience, bravery, and fortitude he manages to maintain his dignity, placate the guards (at least sometimes), and make the prison a more endurable place. Though always self-effacing, he serves as a beacon of light to all around him.

John McClane is just as much of a hero as Andy, albeit less of a boy scout. Not only can he vanquish single-handedly a building full of terrorists, but he's also highly likable—down to earth and funny, an unpretentious working stiff trying to get back into the good graces of his family.

And who wouldn't love Thelma and Louise? They are strong, funny, decent women in open rebellion against a system designed to keep them in their place. They are just finding themselves and beginning to exert their individuality.

The term *protagonist* is often used synonymously with *hero*. Sometimes the comparison is apt, sometimes not. Protagonists don't have to be all that likable or good. Their appeal can come from other places. They can be seriously flawed, and test us.

Michael Dorsey is really kind of a pain in the ass. He's an irritating perfectionist, a hectoring know-it-all who is unwilling to compromise even it's in his best interest. He's also a crude womanizer, peppering various guests at his birthday party with hackneyed pickup lines. So why should we bother with him? Michael may be a pain, but he is a committed pain. He has real talent and passion for the craft of acting. He's not greedy, either. He shows little apparent concern for money, or even fame. All he hungers for is a good role to play, and the opportunity to do it right. And he shows incredible daring when he assumes the identity of a woman, Dorothy, to pursue his goal. We may not like Michael, but it's impossible for us not to respect and admire him. That makes him appealing. His identity as Dorothy—who is generous, warm, wise—also increases his appeal.

Miles Raymond is even more difficult to like than Michael, certainly harder to admire. He's a sad, self-pitying, deceitful, drunken, morose loser. We're not even sure he's a good writer. For heaven's sake, the guy even steals money from his mother. The only thing that Miles can claim bragging rights to is his knowledge of wine, but, except for a limited subculture of oenophiles, it's hard to imagine the rest of us bonding with this miserable guy just because he can discern hints of vanilla and apple in a glass of Sauvignon Blanc.

So, yes, Miles is a bit of a hard case. Some viewers find him irredeemably unpleasant, and so are never able to fully embrace *Sideways*. But I believe that, if the viewer hangs in there with him, Miles reaches deeper inside of us than many more sympathetic protagonists. The character hasn't been sugarcoated or given movie-star charisma, and this very rawness, this reality, pulls us in. Miles has an unbearable sense that life is passing him by and leaving him nothing. A lot of us can relate to that, I think. Fear is a constant threat, paralyzing him, leading to self-defeating behavior. In all fairness, though, Miles does have his good qualities—he shows some actual charm with Maya, and remains a loyal friend to Jack. Most importantly, Miles is not a complete victim. Hope clings for life inside him, battered though it may be. The tension between his fragile hope and his paralyzing fear gives Miles poignancy, humanity, and, yes, in the end, appeal.

A protagonist can even be someone who is downright bad, even despicable. Characters from whom we would cower in real life can, on screen, turn into deliciously guilty pleasures. But they've got to be imbued with some kind of appeal that will make us willingly follow them through their dark journeys.

Henry Hill, the protagonist of *Goodfellas,* is a thief, cheat, drug dealer, and adulterer. Basically, he's an unscrupulous hood. But Henry is still pretty hard to dislike. He treats folks okay, for the most part, and he's got an infectious zest for his work that is fun to witness. His likability is also bolstered by the "others are worse" principle; for all his criminality, Henry is not a particularly violent man, while his cronies are one of two kinds of murderer, crazed or cold-blooded. In that crowd, Henry's a prince.

Bridget Gregory, the protagonist in *The Last Seduction,* is thoroughly evil. She's larcenous, deceitful, manipulative, cold as ice, murderous, but . . . we love her. As Shakespeare showed in *Richard III,* a villain can be a magnetic protagonist. Like Richard, Bridget seems to relish her dastardly deeds, and she executes them with brilliance; no matter how dire the circumstance, she's always thinking three moves ahead. A high level of competence is always appealing. She also happens to be the sexiest person on screen, as well as the funniest, coolest, and toughest, all very appealing qualities. It may disturb us to identify with such a morally objectionable character, but in the end it's entirely satisfying to watch her spin her web of deceit.

It's nice when we like protagonists, but if we don't, we should at least respect or identify or sympathize with them, and barring that, we should at least find them fascinating or great fun.

The Other Characters

One great character does not a movie make. Though you may put the most effort into creating your protagonist, the story won't come fully alive unless the other characters are also engaging and interesting. Think of it this way: Every character, just like every real person, is the star of his or her own personal movie, even if the writer has decided otherwise. These characters have their own business to attend to, and, in their minds, they have not been created simply to carry baggage for the star. So, let me offer a few words on behalf of the other characters.

Main Relationship Character

In most movies, the protagonist has one primary relationship in the story. This "main relationship character" (MRC) is usually either a romantic interest or an ally (friend or mentor). This is the person with whom the protagonist will have the most dealings. It is usually a large part, and often the actor playing these roles will get costar billing with the protagonist.

Some notable romantic MRCs would include Rhett Butler in *Gone with the Wind*, Mary Jensen in *There's Something About Mary*, Susie Diamond in *The Fabulous Baker Boys*, and Ilsa Lund in *Casablanca*. Holly McClane, from *Die Hard*, would fit in this category.

Some notable ally MRC's would include Sam in the *Lord of the Rings* trilogy, Ned Logan in *Unforgiven*, Rebecca in *Ghost World*, and Tyler Durden in *Fight Club*. Red stands as a great example of this in *Shawshank*, as does Jack in *Sideways*. Thelma and Louise pretty much fulfill this role for each other.

Very often the protagonist has both a romance and an ally, but usually one of those relationships is more central than the other. In *Tootsie*, for example, Julie, the romantic interest, has more screen time than Michael's ally, his roommate Jeff. In *Sideways*, on the other hand, Jack is a larger role than Maya.

The MRC is key to the protagonist's journey. The romantic ones may provide the story's central conflict, or the romance may be more of a sideline, albeit an important one. Ally MRCs usually serve to assist protagonists with their quests and help spur them onward. Whatever their plot function, the MRC invariably will have a major impact on the emotional development of the protagonist. The MRC will often be a catalyst in the protagonist's transformation, as Julie is to Michael. Having to deal with this impossibly beautiful woman in a nonsexual way, Michael is forced to see beneath her physical appearance, and finally come to understand that an attractive woman is not there merely to be hit upon. Sometimes the MRC is used to reveal some aspect of the protagonist through a telling contrast. As compared to brash Jack, Miles appears all the more fearful of life; later, we see that Miles is actually the saner of the two.

The dynamic between the protagonist and the MRC is what gives the story much of its juice. When you think of *Gone with the Wind*, you think of the sparks between Scarlett and Rhett, and when you think of *Lord of the Rings*, you think of the exceptional bond between Frodo and Sam. So you need to put almost as much effort into creating a great MRC as you do for your protagonist. Not only that, you want to get some real chemistry going between these two characters.

Often the MRC is actually a flashier character than the protagonist, something that is certainly true of Mary Jensen and Tyler Durden. This can be a helpful technique if your protagonist is intended to be a bit on the ordinary or passive side. The MRC can be around to give a kick in the pants to your protagonist. Following moody Miles through *Sideways* would be unbearable if we didn't have the riotous Jack aboard for the ride. In some cases, it may seem to the casual observer that the MRC is actually the star of the show, a mistake that could perhaps be made for *There's Something About Mary* or *Fight Club*. You can always spot the true protagonist, though, by determining whose goal the story is centered around and who is undergoing the biggest transformation.

Antagonist

The antagonist is the character that presents the strongest obstacle to the protagonist's goal. The antagonist may or may not have as much screen time as the MRC (often they don't), but they exert a powerful influence on the story. It's vital to have an antagonist who can provide as great an opposition as possible. The more formidable the foe, the better the game. A seemingly invincible antagonist will also help cast the protagonist as the underdog, and thus make us root for him or her all the more.

Very often the antagonist is, simply, the bad guy. He may have various and complex motivations, but basically, well . . . he's bad. Hans Gruber in *Die Hard* is a perfect example. Other leading members of the evil club would be Max Cady in *Cape Fear*, Noah Cross in *Chinatown*, Commodus in *Gladiator*, and Frank Booth in *Blue Velvet*.

But just as the protagonist is not necessarily the good guy, so, too, the antagonist is not necessarily a villain, just the chief character working in opposition to the protagonist. Joanna Kramer, in *Kramer vs. Kramer*, and Tracy Flick, in *Election*, for example, aren't exactly nice, but they're hardly spiritual cousins to the Wicked Witch of the West. They're just operating counter to the interests of the protagonists. And antagonists such as Carl Hanratty in *Catch Me If You Can* and Sam Gerard in *The Fugitive* are, in fact, pretty good guys who end up befriending and even helping their respective protagonists. Hal in *Thelma & Louise* could be considered the primary antagonist, as he is the main guy pursuing the women for most of the movie, but he is sympathetic to his quarry, and his actions are clearly fueled by an honorable desire to help Thelma and Louise. (Simply being evil, by the way, does not qualify a character to be the antagonist. Hannibal Lector, in *The Silence of the Lambs*, is a terrifying character, whose malevolence saturates the entire movie, but he's *not* the antagonist. Clarice Starling's goal is to save a kidnapped girl from the clutches of the serial killer Buffalo Bill, and so Buffalo Bill is the antagonist. For all his evilness, Hannibal actually functions as a kind of twisted ally to Clarice.)

Some movies have no single antagonist, but rather a generalized opposing power. In war movies, for example, like *Saving Private Ryan*, *M*A*S*H*, or *The Thin Red Line*, the real adversary is often either "The Enemy" (the Germans or Japanese, etc.), or the very concept of war (the insanity of violence, the stupidity of the war makers, etc.). Usually, though, we feel the opposition more strongly if it's been given a human face. In *Shawshank*, for example, Andy's antagonist is the entire penal system, including the courts, the guards, the administrators, and even some fellow prisoners. But the opposition coalesces into the character of Warden

Norton, who becomes the focal point of all that is keeping Andy down. When it comes time for your protagonist to face his enemy, it's good to give that enemy a face.

In some cases, no antagonist is needed. Michael Dorsey in *Tootsie* has enough problems maintaining his identity as a woman. And sometimes the antagonist can be a force inside the mind of the protagonist. Who in *Sideways* is a bigger obstacle to Miles than Miles himself? When Miles has his first date with Maya, they bond immediately over the wine, and this lovely woman, remarkably, seems interested in him. So what does Miles do? He drinks way too much, starts to babble, crosses to the "dark side," leaves the table, and makes a pathetic phone call to his ex-wife. The evening could have been perfect, but Miles just can't enjoy it, can't *let* himself enjoy it. And the only one standing in his way is himself.

Minor Characters

Don't neglect the smaller parts. You don't want to make them too fascinating or they'll upstage the story, but you don't want them to be cardboard cutouts, either. The livelier each character is, the livelier the movie. Remember, even these guys see themselves as stars of their own stories.

Tootsie has so many wonderful characters, it's hard for anyone to steal the show, but Sandy comes close at times. She has a wild energy that springs from her outsized insecurities. Her scenes are both funny and sad, and always a little dangerous. This woman might melt down at any moment. Darryl, Thelma's husband in *Thelma & Louise*, comes close to being a little too cartoonish perhaps, but he lends terrific comic relief whenever we see him. Unduly proud of his moussed hair and lofty position as regional manager of a carpet store, he makes it a true pleasure to dislike him, and he gives us a powerful interest in rooting for Thelma's emancipation. Even the really small parts can shine for their brief moments in the spotlight. Take, for example, Theo, the computer expert on the terrorist team in *Die Hard*. He's cheerful, brilliant, cool-headed, and utterly amoral, and we get all this in probably less than two minutes of total screen time.

If you watch these movies, you can tell that the actors playing these parts had a ball with them. That's a great thing to think about. If you give the actors, in parts large or small, something they can make the most of, you'll have a much richer screenplay. Whenever you see a really good movie, you'll find that *all* the characters are given some real blood.

More Arcs

Change isn't reserved only for protagonists. It's possible that other characters may have their own arcs, internal progressions that result in change. Usually they're not quite as extensive or developed as a protagonist arc, but they can be. More often than not, when supporting characters change, it's a result of their interaction with the protagonist. In that way, the relationships among the characters are made more dynamic.

Red's arc in *Shawshank* is actually the true character arc of the story. Through Andy's inspiration, Red goes from being without hope to having hope, from merely existing to truly living, from dully speaking by rote to the parole board to speaking from the heart, and thus both literally and metaphorically freeing himself. Similarly, Julie in *Tootsie* is changed through her interaction with Michael (or, more precisely, Dorothy). She is first seen as an essentially passive dreamboat, aware of her history of being victimized by men, but not willing to deal with the problem. Under Dorothy's tutelage, she grows into someone far more ready to stick up for herself. Eventually, she dumps the controlling Ron and there is the implication that she may, heaven help her, end up with Michael. The relationship between Michael and Julie is especially dynamic because they change each other.

Minor characters can have their arcs, too. Darryl, in *Thelma & Louise* first appears as a strutting, would-be big shot, preening in the mirror and belittling his wife. But even dumb Darryl is shaken by the sensational events of the story. When last we see him, he's sitting comatose in his chair. If he manages to get another wife, will he treat her any better? Well, maybe.

You can also use the "arc of perception" on supporting characters. It's probably more common to do this with a supporting character than with a protagonist. Jack in *Sideways* is a brilliant example. At first, Jack seems just a bit of a babe hound. That he's looking to get some action before his wedding is not exactly honorable, but it's also not unique in the annals of male misbehavior. We get a warning signal when he seems to be developing an actual relationship with Stephanie, not telling her about the wedding and overtly leading her on, but still he could be taken as a guy who's just getting in over his head. But when, after he's had his face bashed in and has had to go to the hospital as a result of his shenanigans, he *still* can't stop himself from putting the moves on the zaftig waitress, we finally get it—this guy is truly, deeply disturbed. Jack was, of course, a total psycho at the beginning of the movie; we just didn't realize it until the end. It's like that sometimes with people in real life, isn't it? You know them, but you don't really *know* them.

Not all of your characters should change, but if you can effect a change with one or two characters beyond your protagonist, you will have a more dynamic story. Take a good look at the potential for change in each of your characters.

Orchestrating the Cast

You need to give some thought to the cast of characters. Who will be the characters in your story? How many characters do you need? How prominent a role will each one play? Screenplays are compressed, so you need to be careful in your selections. There is no room for characters who don't enhance the story in some way. Everyone needs to carry his or her weight. You'll start with your protagonist and his or her journey. Once you understand that, you begin building around it. Start considering the other major characters. Who should help the protagonist? Who should hinder the protagonist? Is there a love interest? If the main plot isn't romantic, the romance may be in a subplot (a subject covered in a later chapter).

Very often the major characters of a movie fall neatly into the roles we've discussed—protagonist, romantic interest, ally, or antagonist. Certainly *Die Hard* fits this mold: McClane (protagonist), Holly (romantic interest), Al (ally), Hans (antagonist). That's a classic arrangement for a cast, but don't feel locked in to this model. Every story has it's own needs, its own chemistry. If your story doesn't need a romantic interest or ally or even an antagonist, don't try to shoehorn one in there. As a rule, you usually don't want more than three or four major characters. There just isn't time for more.

It's important to have the *right* number of characters. Too few, and the story can begin to feel claustrophobic. Too many, and the focus can get diffused, and you might not do justice to everyone. Look to consolidate; if two characters are fulfilling the same role in the story, you might consider combining them. The size of the cast will depend largely on the scope of the story. There is something epic about *Die Hard*, with hostages and the FBI and TV crews involved. All of Los Angeles seems to become part of the saga, so it makes sense that *Die Hard* contains a whole symphony of supporting characters. Beyond the major four, you have Argyle, Takagi, Ellis, Karl, Theo, the deputy police chief, Johnson and Johnson of the FBI, and the newscaster, Thornhill. The worlds of *Tootsie, Thelma & Louise*, and *The Shawshank Redemption* also call for fairly large casts. *Sideways* is much smaller in scope, a deftly balanced chamber piece that stays focused mostly on four major characters— Miles, Jack, Maya, and Stephanie. A few others appear, but they never stay for more than a single scene.

Also, the cast members should mix with each other in intriguing ways. This usually means creating characters with distinct personality differences. Strong contrasts between characters create strong conflicts, which of course lead to explosive drama or sharp-edged comedy. Part of the fun of *Tootsie*, for example, is watching how these diverse people bounce off of each other. Jeff, the laconic roommate. Sandy, the hysterical friend. George, the exasperated agent. Julie, the lovely star. Ron, the egomaniacal director. Les, the sweet widower. Van Horn, the foppish old pro. Rita, the brusque producer. And let's not forget the delightful contrast between selfish Michael and his alter ego, openhearted Dorothy.

You might also consider how your characters reflect off of the protagonist, how they help to reveal the protagonist through their similarities or differences. In *Tootsie*, for example, the male characters echo aspects of Michael: Jeff, the pure artist; George, the driven professional; Van Horn, the hambone; and Ron, the sexist pig. This isn't something an audience will notice but they absorb it in a subconscious way.

You are manipulating an ensemble the way a composer orchestrates a piece of music, choosing which instruments are used and when they play. The way you orchestrate should not be random. Everyone should have a good reason for being there. If not, you should cut them, regardless of how much you may like a character. When a character pops into your mind, make that character audition for you and justify his or her reason for being included in the story.

Dimension

Remember Enid in *Ghost World?* How real I thought she seemed? So real that I wondered what became of her, even though she was only a character in a movie? How does a writer do that, create a character out of thin air that seems to resemble a living, breathing human being? The key is to make characters dimensional—round, full, in the way real people are.

Granted, some movies are more character-driven than others, and so they should have the most dimensional characters. In

movies that are more plot-driven, the characters are more efficiently engineered. But in all good movies, the characters should
have some semblance of dimension. Two key things will help you
achieve this—desire and contrasts.

Desire

It's been discussed that most protagonists have an immediate goal,
something clear and tangible, and it's this goal that drives the
story. In *The Wizard of Oz*, for example, Dorothy wants to get back
to Kansas. That's her goal. And it's been discussed that often underlying the surface goal is a deeper desire, something more internal and abstract, which signifies what is really at stake for the
protagonist. Because Dorothy is a powerless little girl whom no
one listens to, she yearns to take more control over her life, to stop
being blown around by the wind, and it's this deeper desire that
makes her want to travel over the rainbow and it's the same desire
that makes her want to return home.

But not only protagonists are driven by desire. All significant
characters should have strong desires. For the Wicked Witch of the
West, it's all about getting the ruby slippers. That's her movie. The
Scarecrow desires a brain; the Tin Man, a heart; the Lion, courage.
Even those menacing apple trees have desires: They want to stop
people from picking their apples. These other characters might
well have deeper desires, too. For the Wicked Witch, the ruby slippers are the immediate goal, and the deeper desire is to control
Oz (which the slippers will help with in some unexplained way).

There are times, as with *Sideways*, when the protagonist's goal is
not all that clear and tangible, when the goal looks more like a
deeper desire. This phenomenon is even more common with secondary characters. Their goals are not driving the movie, as is the
goal of the protagonist, so you have more leeway. Darryl in *Thelma
& Louise* is not driven by an immediate goal, just the deeper desire
to stay the biggest fish in his tiny little pond. In *Tootsie* Sandy's goal
of winning the part in the soap opera is quickly disposed of, after

which her actions are driven by the deeper desire to protect herself from rejection and pain.

Desire lies at the heart of every great character. Give each and every one of your characters some kind of a desire. It will give them purpose and drive, which will help bring them to life. And their desire will help you know what they will do in any given situation, and why. What better way to know someone than to know what they want most in life?

Contrasts

People in real life are not simple. A stereotype is a character that is predictable and one-note—the unbending minister, the sensitive poet, the peppy cheerleader. But you seldom see this kind of simplicity in life. Virtually every person on the planet has contrasts within their personality. The minister with a gambling addiction, the poet who plays rugby, the cheerleader who contemplates suicide. People in real life, in fact, are a mass of contradictory impulses, needs, and habits. We want to go out and conquer the world, and at the same time want to curl up by the fire and take a nap. The more we get to know people, the more unforeseen personal wrinkles we notice, and the more they come to defy our expectations. Characters in movies should reflect this complexity.

One-dimensional stereotypes will rarely hold our interest for very long. It is the multifaceted characters that capture our attention, linger in our imagination, and feel like real people to us. If you think of memorable movie characters, you will invariably find characters with fascinating contrasts. Is Scarlett O'Hara in *Gone with the Wind* nothing more than a scheming southern belle? Is Vito Corleone in *The Godfather* nothing more than a crime boss? Is J. J. Gittes in *Chinatown* nothing more than a sharp-eyed detective?

For starters, you have to be careful about allowing any character to be all good or all bad. People aren't like this in real life, and most of the characters in your movie shouldn't be like this, either.

Characters that are completely faultless may be admirable, but they can also be boring, perhaps even irritating. If you're writing a character who seems "too good," look for ways to give the character a rough edge or two. Not all characters require huge faults but they need *some* flaws or weaknesses. John McClane is a hero in every way: courageous, resourceful, quick-witted, a righteous champion of the common man. The guy would be just a little too wonderful to bear, except that he's pigheaded when it comes to his wife's success. It's also a nice little touch that he's nervous about flying. These traits make him human, which makes him more believable and appealing.

A character who is totally evil, though perhaps not dull (villainy does have its undeniable pleasures), will be made even more compelling when given some mitigating qualities. Hans Gruber in *Die Hard* is a ruthless villain who thinks nothing of committing mass murder in the name of profit, but at least he's remarkably clever and even kind of charming. He would be less intriguing if were dim-witted and dull. The ultimate evil guy, Hannibal Lector, has a whole slew of appealing traits: He's brilliant, cultured, witty, polite, intolerant of rudeness (just ask Miggs, in the neighboring cell), intellectually curious, and sincerely fond of Clarice. These fellows are bad, way bad, but they, too, have some hints of humanity and, interestingly, it's their good qualities that make them all the more dangerous.

Of course, contrasts within a character go far beyond questions of good and evil. Most dimensional characters, like most people, lie somewhere in the middle on the continuum of good and evil— far from saintly, far from demonic. They contain a very human mixture of appealing traits and those that are less than appealing.

Jack in *Sideways* is a pretty dubious character. With his compulsive lying and obsessive womanizing, he's probably not someone we would want to marry our sister. But his buoyancy and humor make him hard to hate, and there's something touching about his devotion to Miles, whom he sincerely wishes the best for. I imagine that we all know someone like this, someone whose behavior appalls us at times but whose friendship we can't quite do without.

Julie in *Tootsie* seems to have it all. She is beautiful, intelligent, and successful, with a child she adores and legions of worshiping fans. But all is not so perfect in her private life. She seems to have a problem with self-esteem, which leads her to questionable taste in men and a propensity to drink too much. Probably we all know someone like this, someone blessed with brains and beauty but who can't reconcile his or her inner demons.

The very richest characters are a genuine kaleidoscope of contrasting traits, as is Michael Dorsey in *Tootsie*. On the good side, he's a true artist—talented, passionate, dedicated, in it for the art, not the money. He is loyal and supportive to his friends. His determination and cleverness are beyond question. On the not-so-good side, he's impossible to deal with, stubborn to a fault, and a total jerk with women. Both his good and bad sides come to the fore when he escorts Sandy to her audition. He spent time coaching Sandy, and he comes along with her because he's a good friend who cares that she does well. When Sandy is refused the audition and on the verge of despair, Michael tries to provide assurance. But the moment he learns that Terry Bishop has stolen his role in a play, he drops Sandy like a burning coal and rushes off to badger his agent. Michael shifts between good and bad qualities as quickly as he slips in and out of heels, and this makes him a truly unforgettable character.

If you want to reader a character instantly more dimensional, give the character one or two contrasting traits. With a major character, feel free to add more. Not only does this make the character more real and appealing, but it allows them to do things that will surprise us. We're a little startled when we see that Julie allows herself to be manhandled by Ron and a bit taken aback as we notice her drinking too much. These surprises make her all the more interesting to us.

The contrasts you give characters have to be believable, though. You can't just toss them in as a way to dimensionalize. Don't give the serial killer a pet that he loves without providing a reason to understand this affection. There needs to be an underlying consistency that unites all of the character's traits. Why, for example, is it believable that someone as lovely and successful as Julie would allow herself to be neglected and humiliated? This is never explained, but we can infer that her beauty and pliability with men were the very things that helped propel her to soap stardom, and now she is suffering the consequences. Julie's contrasting traits are consistent with her personality.

Do all characters need contrasting traits? No, not all. Often, it's perfectly acceptable to have a one-note character in a small role, especially if it's an effective note. There is not much variation to hammy John Van Horn in *Tootsie* or the menacing terrorist Karl in *Die Hard*, but these characters hit their notes just right. For them, that's enough.

If you look closely, you'll see that *The Shawshank Redemption* doesn't pay too much attention to the contrast rule. The characters are well rendered, but most of them tend to be really good or really bad people. Except at the start, Andy is pretty much a saint, and Warden Norton is never anything but a hypocritical and cruel prig. We would all want Red for a friend and none of us are sorry to see Boggs beaten to a pulp. This isn't due to sloppy writing but because *Shawshank* is a sort of parable or tall tale. It's a deliberate choice and it works. This kind of simplicity will also work in any movie that is more comic book than real, including such movies as the X-Men and Spider-man films. Even here, though, you'll find that most superheroes and supervillains have some kind of weakness.

Profiles

The more of your screenplay you write, the more you will learn about your characters. They'll become more organic, more dimensional, and perhaps even start to surprise you by saying and doing unexpected things. Like Frankenstein's monster, sometimes our creations take on unruly lives of their own, and that's a very good thing. But the more you know about your characters at the *beginning* of the writing process, the more quickly and easily you can put them into action, and start their process of coming alive. You may choose to base a character on someone you know, or know of, and that will give you a headstart. So will envisioning a particular actor.

You can also use profiles. Some writers find it helpful to come up with a profile for their major characters—a detailed life history, or perhaps a list of interesting biographical facts. Here are the types of questions you might choose to answer about your characters:

Name

Physicality

    Looks

    Style of dress

    Gestures

    Other physical distinctions

Background

    Basic facts: sex, age, ethnicity, religion, etc.

    Family

    Childhood

    Friends

    Romantic partners

    Locations lived in

    Occupation

Personality

Best qualities

Worst faults

Deepest secret

Biggest fear

Habits

Favorite foods, sports, books, movies, TV shows, vacation destinations, etc.

What does the character love?

What does the character hate?

You might also explore some less conventional things about your characters. Sometimes the oddball details are the most illuminating of all. For example:

What does your character keep in the refrigerator? The medicine cabinet?

What kind of footwear does your character favor?

What's your character's idea of a perfect day off?

Who is your character's favorite celebrity? Historical figure?

What kind of animal is your character most like, and why?

Most of the things you come up with for this list won't actually surface in the movie. The audience will never learn that the protagonist's first kiss was in the planetarium during a seventh-grade class field trip, or that their biggest fear is being eaten alive by wild boars. Though undisclosed, however, these bits of history will inform the visible actions of the character. Think of your character as an iceberg: a little bit showing, a whole lot hidden in the waters below.

It's not essential to work with profiles. Some writers just intuit as they go. You should always find the way that works best for you. The advantage of the profile is that it helps you understand your characters more fully at the outset and it gives you a wealth of material to draw upon as you write. If you're stumped on how a character might react to a situation, you can consult your profile. And, of course, you have complete liberty to alter the profile at any time.

To illustrate the usefulness of profiles, let's see how a profile of Louise from *Thelma & Louise* may have informed the story. What about her education? Louise probably didn't go to college and perhaps she never allowed herself to have any big career ambitions, and therefore she has ended up as a career waitress. This fact makes her all the more eager to get out of town and, eventually, to leave her old life behind. If she had been a high-powered career woman, like Holly in *Die Hard*, she wouldn't be as likely to find herself in a situation like that in the parking lot with Harlan. And if she did, she wouldn't be as likely to shoot him. And, if she did, she wouldn't be as likely to flee the scene without contacting a lawyer. Her background helps make the story plausible.

What about Louise's personal habits? Louise is neat, even meticulous. We see this in the care she takes with her appearance, her packing, her car. This doesn't have any major impact on the course of the story, but it adds something. It makes her journey into messiness more interesting. When she tosses her lipstick away, it's not just a flip gesture, but a dramatic break from her past.

Obviously, this is a two-way street. Very often the needs of the story will inform the biographical facts, not the other way around. The whole story, for example, probably wouldn't have happened if Louise had not been raped in Texas. But there is much to be gained from knowing your characters intimately as you go to work on a script. When *Thelma & Louise* was being filmed, Geena Davis (the actress playing Thelma) knew that if she needed any little detail about her character, even down to what sort of toothpaste she used, the answer would be known by the writer, Callie Khouri.

Even the names are important, very much so. Choosing the right name helps establish the right tone for a character. Names are perhaps even more helpful for the reading experience than the viewing experience because we see the name on the page repeatedly. So take the time to select the best names. You don't want to be too literal about this. Shakespeare may have been able to name characters Andrew Aguecheek and Toby Belch, but, unless you are writing something wildly satirical or stylized, it's usually best to take a more understated approach. Just find a name for the character that feels like it fits, and perhaps resonates in some small way.

Look at some of the names in *Die Hard*. *John McClane* is a good, strong regular-guy name. *Hans Gruber* reeks of greed (money-grubbing?) *Holly* sounds nice, but not too soft. *Powell* sounds a bit like a gunshot (something he's haunted by). *Argyle* is lively and comic. *Ellis* is a little oily. There is something vaudevillian about the FBI guys being named *Johnson* and *Johnson*. We don't think about these names when we watch the movie, and we shouldn't, but each name feels right.

All the Actions

It's one thing to dream up fully dimensional characters in your head. But you then have to figure out how to bring those characters to life on the page and, eventually, on the screen. If you don't do that effectively, your characters won't ever emerge out of your head. So how do you go about this job of showing the audience who your wonderful creations really are?

In prose, the writer can tell us all about the characters and even let us enter their thoughts but, for the most part, these options don't exist in film. We may learn a little about characters by what other characters tell us about them, which can be helpful, but even that technique is limited. In movies, characters are best revealed to us through what we see them *do*.

We've seen how a protagonist follows a path of action to pursue his or her goal, but let's expand the concept of *action* to include everything a character *does*. As the art of screenwriting is about showing, not telling, show us the actions of your characters. These actions may be supported by the dialogue. Or the dialogue may be in opposition to the doing. Think of your old friend who says, "Trust me, I won't let you down," and then borrows your car, gets drunk, and drives it into the harbor. In this case, what the character does is in direct opposition to what he says. The actual action here is the colossal failure to deliver on the spoken promise of "trust me." As important as dialogue is, what a character says is never quite as important was what the character actually *does*.

As you get to know your characters, you will find a general through-line for their actions—they way they handle situations— but then you'll need to figure out how you will show us their actions bit by bit, scene by scene. And from that collection of actions we pull together a sense of who these people are.

Let's look at a few examples of character actions. As we go through the following, notice how some of the actions are shown verbally, some nonverbally, some with a combination thereof. Any of these methods will work.

Our understanding of characters starts with the smallest actions, the minutia of their behavior. These small actions can speak volumes.

Near the beginning of *Die Hard*, shortly after he has landed in L.A., McClane is met at the airport by a chauffeur, Argyle, who escorts him out to a waiting limo. When next we see them they are in the car:

```
Both Argyle and McClane are in the front seat.
```

Notice, McClane sits in the front seat, beside the driver. Most of us would take the backseat in a limo, even if, like McClane, we were riding in one for the first time. Indeed, the passenger is *supposed* to take the backseat. But McClane is not a backseat guy. He's a regular Joe, a man of the people, someone uncomfortable with pretense and formality. He wouldn't feel right in the backseat. This tiny action, revealed in one sentence, says a lot about McClane, and it even clues us in to how he will stand up against the arrogant terrorists, and why he is so uncomfortable with his wife's sudden change in social status.

Similarly, in *Sideways*, a simple action manages to show us a great deal about both Miles and Jack. After some delay, Miles has picked Jack up at his fiancé's house, and the two have finally gotten on the road. Settling in for the trip up to wine country, Jack takes a bottle of Champagne from Miles's stash and starts to undo the foil:

```
                    MILES
          Don't open that now. It's
          warm.

                    JACK
          Come on, we're celebrating.
          I say we pop it.

                    MILES
          That's a 1992 Vintage Byron.
          It's sacrilegious.

Jack untwists the wire. Instantly the cork pops
off, and a fountain of champagne erupts.

                    MILES (CONT'D)
          See what I mean? It's pissed
          off.

Jack is pouring two glasses.
```

```
                          JACK
              Shut up.
                  (handing Miles a glass)

              Here's to a great week.
```

The action and reaction surrounding the opening of the bottle gives us the characters in a nutshell, foreshadowing everything they will do. Miles is all about putting things on hold, waiting for the perfect occasion that will never come. Jack is not one to deny himself any gratification, no matter the circumstance.

In *Tootsie*, when Michael gets caught with his pants down (quite literally) while trying on Sandy's dress, he chooses to cover the situation by having sex with her. Deeply flattered, having admired Michael for many years, Sandy is all too happy to comply. But when Michael gets out of bed, immediately afterward, what does Sandy do? Assure Michael it was a wonderful experience? Demand Michael stay the night? No, not Sandy. As always, she assumes the absolute worst.

```
                        MICHAEL
              How 'bout I call you tomorrow.

                         SANDY
              I know there's pain in every
              relationship and I'd like to
              have mine now. Otherwise,
              I'll wait by the phone and
              if you don't call, then I'll
              have to have pain and wait
              by the phone. You could save
              me a lot of time.
```

Characters will take dozens of small actions in the course of a movie, and they all matter. Things register so strongly when we see them on screen that we assign meaning to every little nuance. So choose these small actions carefully, making them say what you want them to say.

As important as small actions are, however, movies are not about everyday events. They are about the most dramatic times in the lives of the characters, occasions when they are tested, pressured, forced to make momentous choices. It is the large actions that people take at such times that reveal most profoundly what they are made of. Will they fold or rise to the occasion? Will they act rashly or wisely?

In *Thelma & Louise,* Louise is temporarily separated from Thelma at the roadhouse. When she finally finds her, Thelma is on the verge of being raped by Harlan in the parking lot. Louise aims the gun (the one Thelma gave her) at Harlan and forces him to back off. Thelma is saved, but the situation is not quite resolved.

```
Louise lowers the gun and stares at him for a
second. Then she turns and walks away. Thelma
does, too.

                    HARLAN
            (pulling up his pants)
        Ditch. I should have gone
        ahead and fucked her.

Louise stops in her tracks.

                    LOUISE
        What did you say?

                    HARLAN
        I said suck my cock.

Louise takes two long strides back towards him,
raises the gun and FIRES a bullet into his face.
```

Killing a guy to stop him raping her friend is one thing, but Louise doesn't shoot him in the middle of the attack. She kills him *after* the direct threat is over, which is a whole other matter. Until this point, Louise has been seen as a bit of a tough cookie, and it's been hinted that she's had some bad experiences with men, but, until she fires the gun, we've had no idea how damaged she actually is. When she blows away Harlan, it reveals the sheer rage brewing inside her, the utter determination to never be a victim again.

In *Shawshank*, Andy takes a large action that is altogether more joyous in its effect than Louise's. Momentarily left alone in the guard station with a load of newly delivered supplies for the prison library, he discovers, to his wonder, a pile of record albums. As he digs reverently through them he finds something almost too good to be true, a Mozart opera, a thing of shining beauty brought into the prison. Andy is not one to let the moment slip by:

```
Andy wrestles the phonograph player onto the
guards' desk, sweeping things onto the floor in
his haste. He plugs the machine in. A red light
warms up. The platter starts spinning.

He slides the Mozart album from its sleeve, lays
it on the platter, and lowers the tone arm to his
favorite cut. The needle HISSES in the
groove . . . and the MUSIC begins, lilting and
gorgeous. Andy sinks into Wiley's chair, overcome
by its beauty. It is "Deuttino: Che soave ze-
firetto," a duet sung by Susanna and the Con-
tessa.
```

But then the guard, off in the bathroom, hears the music, and calls out. What does Andy do?

```
Andy shoots a look at the bathroom . . . and
smiles. Go for broke. He lunges to his feet and
```

barricades the front door, then the bathroom. He
returns to the desk and positions the P.A. microphone. He works up his courage, then flicks all
the toggles to "on." A SQUEAL OF FEEDBACK echoes
briefly . . .

. . . and the Mozart is suddenly broadcast all
over the prison.

This is an immense action. Andy is well aware of what the consequences may be—a beating, a long stretch in the "hole," becoming the object of great mistrust among the prison staff. And
yet he still chooses to broadcast the Mozart prisonwide. Everything stops. All the numbing routine of prison life grinds to a
halt. Everyone listens, transported. At tremendous risk, Andy has
brought a few brief moments of freedom and rapture to every
prisoner in Shawshank Prison. It is actions such as this that bring
characters to life, and it is actions such as this that make movies
live in our mind.

Take a Shot

Pick five real-life people, using a mix of those you know well and know
only slightly. For each person, identify one action that strongly defines
who that person is—i.e., scrubbing the kitchen sink, arriving late for an
appointment, picking an unnecessary quarrel, etc. Then go back through
your list of people, this time identifying one action for each that shows a
contrasting side to this person. For example, perhaps you know a person
who has no trouble speaking eloquently in front of a crowd but who gets
tongue-tied in a meaningful one-on-one conversation.

Stepping-Stone: Protagonist and Cast

Create a profile for your protagonist by answering all of the questions listed in the Profile section of this chapter. You will find a downloadable version of this questionnaire at www.WritingMovies.info.

Chart your protagonist's arc by listing at least three to five stages of his or her development, summing up each stage in a few words or sentences.

List the other major characters that you plan on using in your movie, and for each one state his or her purpose in the story. Every major character needs a strong reason to be there.

CHAPTER 4

The Page: Words That Move

BY JOHN GLENN

```
EXT. OCEAN - NIGHT

Darkness. The sound of wind and spray.

The darkness is actually water. A searchlight
arcs across heavy ocean swells. Half a dozen
flashlights — weaker beams — racing along what we
can see is the deck of an aging fishing trawler.

Fishermen struggling with a gaff — something in
the water —

A human corpse.
```

So begins Tony Gilroy's screenplay for *The Bourne Identity*. When I first read the script of this spy thriller, I was spellbound, riveted every minute, totally inside the movie, even though I hadn't yet seen it on the screen. Floating with Jason Bourne in that cold ocean, maneuvering through the streets of Zurich with the cops on my tail, seduced by the intoxicating scent of Marie's skin. That's what a screenplay should do—suck you inside the movie, making it seem as real as a dream in the deepest part of the night.

Screenplays are an alien species in the world of literature, far different from any other kind of prose. They look different, follow a different code of conduct. This is why outsiders often feel as if they're trying to decipher the Rosetta stone when they first pick up

103

a screenplay. Screenplays also serve a different purpose from, say, fiction. They're not an end unto themselves, but a plan, a blue-print for a movie, something that is chiefly read by people in the business or those who aspire to be in the business.

Even so, the best screenplays read like gangbusters. You see, be-fore a screenplay even gets around to serving as a movie's blue-print, it has to serve another purpose. It has to be a genesis point, a flash of light that galvanizes people into the monumental task of making a movie. Or not. Tony Gilroy had to make the *Bourne Iden-tity* script so dazzling that executives would take an insanely expen-sive leap of faith with it. He succeeded. (The actual film was directed by Doug Liman, with additional script credit to W. Blake Herron.)

The best screenwriters make you see a movie on the page. This aspect of screenwriting isn't discussed nearly as much as the other elements—plot, character, and so forth—but it's no less impor-tant. When you read a beautifully written screenplay, you fly through it, flipping pages, experiencing the story. That script isn't just a bunch of words lying there on the white paper. Those words *move.* They are alive with all the motion and emotion of the movie inside the writer's imagination.

It took me a while to figure this out. I spent seven years bar-tending by night in Santa Monica, writing screenplays by day. Peo-ple in the business read my scripts, liked the characters, dialogue, blah blah blah, but invariably their verdict went something like: "We're just not sure that it's a movie." Finally, I realized that they weren't sure it was a movie because I hadn't made them *see* the movie, see it right there *on the frickin' page.* The very next script I wrote sold in one day.

Making them see the movie you've written is probably even more important if you're not a pro, if you're an unknown shop-ping a spec, like all the other bartenders in Santa Monica. Nobody knows your work or your story or anything about you. If your script's lucky enough to get inside the door, it's probably lying in a high stack to be skimmed through by some overworked/underpaid reader who's already weary of the job. If that script wants a shot at being made—or making a sale, or even getting somebody to jot down your phone number—you better not just write a screenplay. You better write a *movie.*

That's the subject of this chapter—how to capture a movie on the page.

Format

First off, you've got to get the format right.

There are standard screenplay format guidelines in the movie industry. If you're a hotshot screenwriter like William Goldman or the Coen brothers, you can gloss over these guidelines. I suppose even I have earned the right to let the guidelines slide a bit. It's different when they already know you. But if a non-established screenwriter ignores the basics of format, it's likely to tell people in the biz that an amateur wrote the script and within two seconds it will be headed toward the nearest wastebasket. So, learn the basics.

There is a format guide in the back of this book that goes into technical things like margins, spacing, and what gets capitalized, so we're not going to micromanage those ideas here. Additionally, you can buy screenwriting software that handles these elements for you automatically. And the truth is, you don't have to get every minuscule detail perfect; there is always a little license for error or creative interpretation. So, please don't break out in a cold sweat over format or you won't get much writing done.

(Also, let me point out that if you read shooting scripts—versions of scripts right before the production stage—they're liable to look a bit different from specs. They might have scene numbers and camera angles, and corners may be cut on description details, so what we're discussing here specifically is the spec script.)

The number-one format guideline is this: Use 12-point Courier font.

All professional screenwriters use 12-point Courier font. It's a tradition, a remnant from the days when contract writers clattered away at their typewriters in hidden bungalows on studio lots. But it's a tradition that everyone honors. Beyond this, there is a practical reason for using Courier. Each page of a screenplay equals approximately one minute of screen time. Everyone in the business tabulates screen time this way. Courier makes the equation work relatively well. Other fonts mess it up. So save Apple Chancery for your book of poetry inspired by astrological formations. Stick to Courier.

After that, the basics of screenplay format can be broken down into five simple components:

- scene headings

- scene description

- character name

- dialogue

- parentheticals

This is how those components look:

INT. DINER — NIGHT [*scene heading*]

Julie and Ben sit in a back booth at a greasy-spoon joint. Ben fiddles with the salt shaker, uneasy. [*scene description*]

                    JULIE [*character name*]
          You still smoke? [*dialogue*]
              (off Ben's odd look)
              [*parenthetical*]
          Cigarette burn on your
          finger. [*dialogue*]

Let's examine these five components more closely.

Scene headings (also called sluglines)

These give the time and place, in a very general sense. For place, simply tell us where the scene is located. DINER. ALLEY. OFFICE. For time, just use DAY or NIGHT. If it's really important, you can get a tad more specific with time, such as DUSK or EARLY MORNING.

Scene headings also indicate INT. or EXT. telling us if the scene is an interior (indoors) or exterior (outdoors). This is important info for those planning and shooting a movie, but it's also included in spec scripts, even though they're a long way from going into production. Again, it's tradition. Honor it.

Scene headings are meant to be skimmed, if read at all. So don't bother adding anything too important or descriptive to them, like A GREASY-SPOON DINER or BOOTH IN BACK OF A DINER. You'll save that for the scene description.

But know this: You must use a new scene heading every time there is a new scene. And there is a new scene *whenever the time or place shifts, even just a bit.* In other words, if you show a woman driving her car, getting out and walking through a parking lot, then entering the pharmacy and moving down an aisle—that's three separate scenes with three separate scene headings.

```
INT. CAR — DAY
EXT. PARKING LOT — DAY
INT. PHARMACY — DAY
```

If that woman was sitting in her car on a stakeout and we saw her at noon, then again, still in her car, an hour later, that would be two separate scenes with two separate scene headings, even though the headings would be the same.

```
INT. CAR — DAY
INT. CAR — DAY
```

Scene description (also known as action)

Scene description is often referred to by us screenwriters as "action" but since we've already used the term action to mean several things in this book, it'll be simpler to call it "scene description" here. It's pretty much everything in a scene that isn't dialogue—descriptions of people, places, things, sounds, physical actions. As we'll discuss very soon, scene descriptions should mostly stay confined to what is seen and heard.

Scene descriptions should always be written in the present tense, as if whatever you're describing is happening right now, in the moment. So you would never do something like this:

```
She SLAMMED the door of her car and stalked toward
the store.
```

You would do it like so:

```
She SLAMS the door of her car and stalks toward
the store.
```

Character name

This merely means the name of the character that is speaking. But you'll need to decide whether you want to call a character by the first name, last name, nickname, or title. And make sure you use the same name throughout a script. For example, don't switch from GEORGE to GENERAL WASHINGTON halfway through. The only exception is when a character actually turns out to be someone different, as when an amnesiac MAN discovers his name is BOURNE.

Dialogue

This refers to what the characters say, the exact words that they say. You never do something like:

```
Jake tells Lisa that he can no longer bear living
with her.
```

You have to write the actual words that Jake says as dialogue. Jake will feel better and so will whoever is reading your script.

Parentheticals (also known as line actions)

These are used to indicate how a line of dialogue is delivered or to describe an action that is directly tied to the dialogue. They are placed in parentheses, hence the name. Be sparing with them, and we'll discuss this a bit later in the chapter.

Okay, that's it for the basics of screenplay format. Not so bad, huh?

Camera Directions

Should you put camera directions in a screenplay? Mostly, the answer is no. If you read a shooting script, you're likely to see camera directions, maybe a whole slew of them. But it's best to avoid them in spec scripts. A spec is a long way from going into production; its main purpose is to reveal your story. Camera directions will get in the way of your storytelling, resulting in something like this:

```
Hope scans the room.

DOLLY IN ON a roll-top desk.

Hope hurries over, pulls open the top drawer. Her
eyes dart over the contents.

ZOOM ON a letter with a seal of purple wax.

ANGLE ON HOPE

Her face falls slack.
```

It's cumbersome. We're paying more attention to the camera directions than the action. Also, when you write camera directions, you're liable to get things wrong, which will expose you as an amateur, something you want to avoid. (Don't forget about that wastebasket reserved for amateurs.) So my advice is to steer clear of camera directions altogether.

You can, however, convey a sense of what the camera is doing without using camera directions. This is actually a good thing to do because it makes your script cinematic (even if they don't end up shooting it your way). Take the example I just used. You can very easily get across all of those visual ideas, like so:

```
Hope scans the room, sees a roll-top desk.

She hurries over to it — pulls open the top drawer.
Her eyes dart over the contents. She sees . . .

A letter with a seal of purple wax.

Hope's face falls.
```

Putting an image on a line by itself, as in the above example, makes it jump out at us, just as it would with a DOLLY or ZOOM or ANGLE ON. And it's a helluva lot easier to read. You can also indicate where the focus is by doing something like this:

```
HOPE — her face falls.
```

Still with me? Great. Let's keep moving.

Only Sight and Sound

Show, don't tell. That's the byword for movies. And screenplays. When we experience a movie, the only kind of information we absorb is what we see and what we hear. That's it. Everything springs from those two sensations—sight and sound. Since your screenplay is supposed to replicate the experience of a movie, it follows that your script should convey only what is seen and heard.

Look at this scene description from *The Shawshank Redemption*:

```
The BUZZER SOUNDS, the cells SLAM OPEN. Cons step
from their cells. Andy catches Red's eye, nods his
thanks. As the men shuffle down to breakfast, Red
glances into Andy's cell —

— and sees Rita in her new place of honor on Andy's
wall. Sunlight casts a harsh barred shadow across
her lovely face.
```

Read over those lines carefully and you'll notice that nothing is there that is not visual or aural. Nothing. We get a very strong sense of the prison—the mood, the routine, the relationship between Andy and Red, the magic of the Rita Hayworth poster. But we get it all from what is seen and heard.

What about the other senses? Smell, taste, touch? You don't include those in a screenplay because you can't *see* smell. Or taste. Or touch. You can't *hear* them either. However, you can see and hear a character's *reaction* to these stimuli. So if you want to convey these senses, you could do it like so:

```
Bacon sizzles in a frying pan. Tim leans toward
the pan and inhales, eagerly. He reaches in to
seize a piece of bacon. Shoots back his hand.

                    TIM
          Damn!!!

He sticks his finger in his mouth to ease the
burning.

Then he picks up a fork, stabs a slab of bacon,
lifts it up, takes a bite. He chews, closing his
eyes with pleasure.
```

There, we managed to convey smell, touch, and taste through sight and sound, and without too much trouble at that.

What about thought? When you're writing prose, you're free to include the thoughts of the characters. Indeed, that's one of the charms of reading fiction, the ability to dive into the minds of the characters and see what's going on there. With screenwriting, sorry, thoughts don't work. You can't see thoughts, can't hear them. So you can't do something like this:

```
Bacon sizzles in a frying pan.

Tim reacts in horror, remembering how his father
was  tragically  killed  in  a  horrible  fire  at  a
bacon factory.
```

That's a memory, a thought. It won't show up on film so you shouldn't include it in a screenplay. If that tragic fire is important information, you'll have to find another way to convey it. You could show Tim's horrified reaction then dissolve into a flashback of the fire at the bacon factory, but, as you'll learn later in this book, flashbacks usually aren't a good idea. So you'll probably have to do something like this:

```
Bacon sizzles in a frying pan.

Tim rushes to the stove and turns off the flame.

                    TIM
                 (furious)
        Mom, how could you? After
        what happened to Dad?
```

And then the conversation turns to that fateful day at the bacon factory. Okay, it's still not great screenwriting but at least it's not violating the sight-and-sound rule.

Let's look at some better examples of how screenwriters manage to convey thoughts while staying within screenplay boundaries.

This bit from *Die Hard* comes right after McClane narrowly escapes a barrage of machine-gun fire:

```
McClane remains motionless in the air duct. Three
quarter-size holes inches from his face. Sweat
covers his face, drips silently onto the aluminum.
```

It's real clear what McClane is thinking here: "Holy shit! That was close!" Or maybe he's thinking, "Holy shit! A bullet almost went through my brain!" Regardless, whatever he's thinking most likely starts with "Holy shit!" and has something to do with not being dead. We know what McClane is thinking because we see *three quarter size holes inches from his face* and we see that *sweat covers his face*.

Truth is, you can cheat a little with thoughts. Just a little, though. Look at this bit from *Sideways*, right after Miles bungles a romantic moment:

```
After a few seconds, Maya breaks away and steps
past him, heading back into the living room. Miles
realizes he's blown it and silently berates
himself.
```

Here the script is actually giving us a thought: *Miles realizes he's blown it*. But the thought isn't coming out of nowhere. It's directly related to physical action—Maya breaking away and Miles silently berating himself. If the actor plays the moment right, we'll be able to sense exactly what he is thinking.

In another bit from *Sideways*, the script cheats even more:

```
She takes a seat opposite Miles on the couch. They
look at each other without speaking. Just what is
the vibe here?
```

Here the script is actually quoting Miles's thought: *Just what is the vibe here?* And the thought isn't as directly tied to physical action as in the previous bit. The two characters are just sitting there in silence. Still, the thought is closely related to what is happening in the moment and it's possible for an actor to convey it through the performance. Now and then, you can get away with something like this as long as it's possible to convey the thought on screen. If Miles were remembering the fire at the bacon factory, that wouldn't work.

Finally, three minor points in the see/hear department:

Don't use the words *we see* or *we hear* to indicate what is being seen or heard, unless it is unavoidable. For example, it's better to write *Darkness* than *We see darkness*. It's more direct.

Don't describe the style or placement of the opening credits in your script. Credits are figured out in the production stage, and sometimes movies don't even have opening credits. Sure, credits are cool, but forget about 'em.

Don't describe the musical soundtrack at all. At the production stage, a composer will figure out how to capture the mood of the moment in music. It's okay, though, to refer to source music, that is, music that the characters hear in a scene (for example, when a character plays a recording or attends an opera). But with source music, refrain from citing a specific contemporary song—rights can be a problem and do you know how expensive a tune like "Satisfaction" would be? Instead, put it this way: *He plays something with an irresistible old-time rock beat.*

Take a Shot

Pick a two-minute slice of your life from this week, a slice that includes you having a conversation with someone. Write it up in screenplay format, including both physical action and dialogue. This should run about two pages. Don't worry about creating great drama, and don't worry about how to manage the margins, spacing, and capitalization. Just focus on getting comfortable with basic screenplay format. But do confine your writing to only what is seen and heard.

Effective Description

Dialogue and description. That's pretty much what a screenplay is. We'll make you masters of dialogue in a later chapter. Right now let's make you masters of description.

The first goal with your description is to be clear. You don't want your readers needing to read a line twice to get the gist of it. Once that happens, you've pulled the reader out of the cinematic dream state you're trying to create. Polish your descriptions until they're clear as crystal. Leave no chance for confusion or ambiguity. Beyond that . . . here are some tips and techniques for creating effective screenplay descriptions.

Economy

Novels are meant to be savored like a leisurely stroll in the park. Screenplays are meant to fly like the wind. You get no more than 120 pages to cover what is probably a great amount of story. You gotta make it move. Actually the goal is to make the descriptions read at roughly the same pace that you would be absorbing the sights and sounds of the moment described.

So don't overwrite. Economize. Keep it simple, clean, spare. At the same time, your descriptions need to be vivid and evocative. That's the big challenge with screenplay description, finding that balance between economy and detail, achieving resonance with an absolute minimum of words. It's not easy, a task requiring laserlike precision.

This description of a honky-tonk bar from *Thelma & Louise* is about as long as you should ever get:

```
This place is jumpin'. There are ten pool tables
with crowds all around. The long bar is filled
with customers. There are tables and booths. The
room is dense with smoke. There is a dance floor,
but no one is dancing yet because the band is
```

```
still setting up. There are a lot of single men.
Many heads turn and follow Thelma and Louise to an
empty table.
```

The description is given this much space because the setting is important, the locale where the whole movie will turn around. We need a real sense of the joint's atmosphere—crowded, loose, a bit sinful, filled with lusty men. Even so, if this were a novel this description might go on for the better part of a page. Here it's perfectly captured in just a handful of lines.

Whenever your story moves to a new locale, it's good to give a sense of that place, but often you can do it as briefly as this description from *Thelma & Louise*:

```
As the sun sets, the T-bird drives deeper into the
vast desert.
```

That one line paints a perfect picture for us.

You need to keep your descriptions of physical action brief, too. Look at how economically this description from *Thelma & Louise* captures both setting and the actions of numerous people.

```
The TV is ON and the place is a mess. Darryl, Hal,
Max, and other cops spring into action as the
phone RINGS, putting on headsets, turning on tape
recorders. Darryl picks up the phone.
```

You can read that in about the same amount of time it takes to watch the moment unfold, and that's the way it should work.

The key is to craft your descriptions in such a way that a few carefully chosen words are loaded with power. Let's take another look at that passage from *The Shawshank Redemption*:

```
The BUZZER SOUNDS, the cells SLAM OPEN. Cons step
from their cells. Andy catches Red's eye, nods his
```

```
thanks. As the men shuffle down to breakfast, Red
glances into Andy's cell —

— and sees Rita in her new place of honor on Andy's
wall. Sunlight casts a harsh barred shadow across
her lovely face.
```

That's only fifty-three words of description. But those fifty-three words evoke far more than what is actually on the page. You know the old saying: A picture is worth a thousand words. In screenplays, the reverse is true. Each of your words should conjure a multitude of pictures. If those words are carefully selected and arranged, they can trigger all kinds of information in our mind—movement, expression, memory, mood, thought, feeling, relationships, sensory stimuli. Here, let me illustrate.

The buzzer sounds, the cells slam open. That buzzer is loud, assaulting, a rude thing to hear in the morning, worse than your alarm clock. When those cells slam open, that's not a gentle sound either. This is a noisy, rough, hostile place. Those cells are part of a large cellblock, a world of iron bars and industrial design. And there are guards around, hovering, waiting for someone to step out of line.

Cons step from their cells. A small army of men stepping forward, all at once, misfits and thugs forced into conformity, breeding silent anger. Each emerging from a night spent on a flea-bitten mattress and pillow, a few magazines, pencils in an old soup can, a commode with no lid, not much else.

Andy catches Red's eye, nods his thanks. Amid this hell of despair and danger, Andy and Red know how to find each other in the crowd. They have managed to form a real connection, a bond that may last for life. Though no talking is allowed, Andy's nod is enough to show his deep gratitude to Red for obtaining a desired item for him.

As the men shuffle down to breakfast, Red glances into Andy's cell— It's noisy when all those cons head to breakfast, in unison, like a herd of cattle. They shuffle, no spring in their step, no excitement over a day that will be like every other day. The guards are right there, lest anyone decide he wants to do something other than head to breakfast right now. Red has to keep moving, but even so he wants to check out the thing he obtained for Andy.

—and sees Rita in her new place of honor on Andy's wall. Sunlight casts a harsh barred shadow across her lovely face. The poster of Rita Hayworth occupies a place of honor, like a goddess on a pedestal. There's something magical about her. We sense the sunlight that plays over her is actually battling the prison bars, a struggle between light and dark, despair and hope. Rita lingers in our mind. We know she will lead to something important, life changing, but we're not sure what. We'll have to wait to find out.

Those fifty-three words conjure a whole world.

Syntax

Syntax refers to sentence structure. In screenplays, you want to lean toward sentences that are clear and simple and not too long. Sentences that wind on forever, with all kinds of twists and turns, so many you're not quite sure where you are, as in this sentence, are to be avoided.

But screenplay sentences don't have to follow the normal rules. You may have noticed some questionable grammar in a few of our screenplay passages. Okay, look, even screenwriters should have a good grasp of the grammar basics. Sloppy grammar will look like the work of a sloppy writer. That said, screenplays aren't prose; they're a different form altogether. And screenwriters are free to bend the rules of grammar a bit in their effort to create a script that zips along at the pace at which a movie plays.

Though it would drive your seventh-grade English teacher bonkers, you can get away with something like this in a screenplay:

```
Norma stares at the phone, fingers tapping — ring
damn you, ring! — eternity passes — not a sound.
```

Yes, several rules of grammar are blatantly ignored there, but it nicely conveys the action and emotion of the moment, with great economy. And that's what you want.

You are also free to use sentence fragments, sentences that don't have the requisite subject and verb. Check out this bit from *Die Hard*:

```
McClane raises his machine gun, aims at Hans. Hans
pulls the trigger.

Click. Astonishment. Click-click-click. McClane
steps in carefully, reclaims his pistol.
```

Those fragments—*Click. Astonishment. Click-click-click.*—perfectly capture the staccato rhythm of this moment, not to mention the sound and sensation. (Your seventh grade English teacher would also want some conjunctions in those sentences but she's not here right now, is she?)

Check out this bit from *Shawshank Redemption*:

```
High white clouds in a blazing blue sky. The trees
fiery with autumn color. Red walks the fields and
back roads, cheap compass in hand. Looking for a
certain hayfield.
```

This isn't a fast moment, as in *Die Hard*. Red is strolling through the woods. Here we actually do have a walk in the park, so to speak, and the fragments here are longer. But they give us a quick sense of the scenery unfolding around Red as he moves through it, a sense of pastoral meandering.

Screenwriting is a bit like poetry in its license to bend the rules of grammar. And, luckily, screenwriters have a slightly better chance at making a few bucks off their trade than do the poor poets of the world.

Vertical Flow

Here's a big way that screenplays differ from most prose. Prose is written horizontally. We read big blocks of text, our eyes continually moving from left to right. We also read screenplays from left to right (unless they're written in Hebrew, which tends to annoy studio executives), but we don't have big blocks of text.

We have short bursts of text. Surrounded by lots of white space.

As a result, screenplays have a vertical, rather than a horizontal, flow. Our eyes spend more time moving down the page rather than across the page. Again, it's a bit like poetry.

It's best if someone can read one page of a screenplay in roughly one minute. Don't write with a stopwatch in hand, but do keep yourself from putting too much material on any one page. As a general rule, it's best never to have a paragraph that runs more than four, maybe five, lines across the page without a space break. Older screenplays tend to have bigger blocks of text, but nowadays screenplays are leaner and meaner than ever. Personally, I never use a paragraph of more than three lines.

Take a look at this passage from *The Shawshank Redemption*:

```
Norton scoops a handful of rocks off the sill. He
hurls them at the wall one at a time, shattering
them, punctuating his words:

                    NORTON
          It's a conspiracy! (SMASH)
          That's what this is! (SMASH)
          It's one big damn conspiracy!
          (SMASH) And everyone's in on
          it! (SMASH) Including her!

He sends the last rock whizzing right at Raquel.

No smash.

It takes a moment for this to sink in. All eyes go
```

```
to her. The rock went through her. There's a small
hole in the poster where her navel used to be.

You could hear a pin drop. Norton reaches up,
sinks his finger into the hole. He keeps pushing
. . . and his entire hand disappears into the
wall.
```

The writing is vertical. It moves fluidly down the page.

Also notice how the vertical movement captures the pace and rhythm of the action. The space breaks and white space help to isolate individual moments. These moments are given room to take hold in our minds. That *No smash,* for example, is a heart-stopping moment in the film so it's appropriate for it to have a line all to itself.

You might even want to combine your vertical writing with sentence fragments to create something like this:

```
Jessica unlocks the door of her house, opens it.

An empty room.

Furniture, lamps, rugs, paintings.

All gone.

Stolen.
```

Here the vertical flow captures Jessica's dawning realization that her entire home has been wiped out. You wouldn't want to write your whole screenplay like this, but this technique can work well for especially dramatic moments.

Word Choice

You will make your descriptions more economical and more dynamic if you choose the best possible words. And that usually means choosing the best possible nouns and verbs. People often

think that using adjectives and adverbs is a great way to spice up
their description, but usually the reverse is true. Adjectives and
adverbs can water down description.

Let's say you write:

```
A tiny dilapidated house stands by the road.
```

Yeah, we get the idea, but it doesn't really pack as much
punch as:

```
A shack stands by the side of the road.
```

Here it's just a matter of replacing the noun *house* with a more
specific noun *shack,* which alleviates the need for the adjectives *tiny*
and *dilapidated.* The second version is briefer and better.

Let's say you write:

```
Sally looks sexy.
```

That adjective *sexy* doesn't tell us much. It's general, bland, just
lies there on the page. Not sexy at all. So let's trade in that adjective for some strong nouns and verbs.

```
Sally sashays by, shimmering in satin.
```

This is better partly because we're showing rather than telling.
We're giving Sally a sexy action rather than just saying she's sexy.
But also the words are better. We've replaced the adjective *sexy*
with two strong verbs—*sashays, shimmering*—and a strong noun—
satin. It's more vivid, more evocative. (If my seventh-grade English
teacher is reading this, yes, I'm aware that *shimmering* is actually
acting as a modifier here, but it's still pretty close to a verb.)

Verbs are the words of motion. And movies are all about motion. Characters streak through space or flee serial killers or dash
to pick up their children from daycare on time or . . . whatever

else you have them doing. Thus, verbs are the most important words in your screenplay. Select them well.

Get specific with your verbs. Let's say you write:

```
Martin walks down the street.
```

That doesn't tell us much and it's not very interesting. You can try to spice it up a bit with an adverb, like so:

```
Martin walks slowly down the street.
```

Maybe a little better but that adverb *slowly* adds letters without adding much punch. The description becomes much better if you replace the ho-hum verb/adverb with a single specific verb. Like so:

```
Martin saunters down the street.

Martin trudges down the street.

Martin lumbers down the street.
```

All of those are better. They tell us how Martin moves down the street, creating a picture in our minds and even telling us something about Martin's emotional state. Strong verbs are more than just words. They give us images. They give us characters in action.

Look at this bit from *Sideways*, where Jack and Miles arrive for a double date:

```
Jack plops down next to Stephanie while Miles
politely eases in on Maya's side.
```

Both Jack and Miles are simply sitting here, but we wouldn't get nearly as much out of the moment if the script gave us:

```
Jack sits next to Stephanie while Miles sits next
to Maya.
```

Jack is eager, ready for action, not terribly concerned that he's cheating on his fiancée, and the *plops* conveys that. Miles, on the other hand, is tentative and nervous and we get that from the way he *politely eases in.* Here the adverb *politely* actually is adding something so it's okay to use it.

Look at this bit from *The Shawshank Redemption,* when Andy is breaking out of prison:

```
Fingers appear, thrusting through the heavy-gauge
wire mesh covering the mouth of the pipe. Andy's
face looms from the darkness, peering out at free-
dom. He wrenches the mesh loose, pushes himself
out, and plunges headfirst into the creek. He
comes up sputtering for breath.
```

There are plenty of verbs in there, and most of them are strong ones. *Appear, thrusting, covering, looms, peering, wrenches, pushes, plunges, sputtering.* This is a dramatic moment, perhaps the most dramatic moment in the movie. We feel the struggle, the desperation, the overwhelming suspense through all those wonderful verbs. The writing is truly alive.

Character Introductions

When a character of any importance first appears, it's good to give the character a little introduction, to convey a sense of that character straight out of the gate. Sometimes shooting scripts skip that step because the people involved already know the characters, but for specs, you want the character introduction. Again, you're not writing a novel so don't get carried away. Give it to us quick, but also make it effective.

Major characters usually get two to four lines of description. Here's how Andy is introduced in *Shawshank Redemption*:

ANDY DUFRESNE, mid-20s, wire rim glasses, three-
piece suit. Under normal circumstances a respectable, solid citizen, hardly dangerous,
perhaps even meek. But these circumstances are far
from normal. He is disheveled, unshaven, and very
drunk.

And here's how Red is introduced in *Shawshank*:

RED emerges into the fading daylight, slouches
low-key through the activity, worn cap on his
head, exchanging hellos and doing minor business.
He's an important man here.

Both introductions give a hint of the character's physicality, and
that's not a bad thing. A sense of the physical (including age)
helps us to picture the person. But don't go overboard with the
physical, describing such things as hair color, eye color, height, or
every article of clothing. For one thing, you have no idea who will
end up playing the role and what kind of wardrobe will be chosen.
More important, though, physical details alone don't convey the
essence of the character.

And that's the crucial thing with character introductions. They
should help us intuit something greater about the characters—
their essence, their inside, their soul.

Character introductions are the one place where you have some
license to violate the sight-and-sound rule with a brief authorial
comment. You can add in little things that give us a sense of the
character, things we might not immediately see. For example, with
Andy we're told that he is a *respectable, solid citizen, hardly dangerous,
perhaps even meek*. We may not glean this by seeing him at this
point, disheveled and drunk, but it's a good thing for us to know.
Same with the way we're told Red is *an important man here*. These
insights are giving us the essence of the character, in a nutshell.

It's also nice that both these introductions merge with what's happening in the moment: Andy sitting in his car, drunk, with a gun, contemplating revenge on his cheating wife (which we learn in the subsequent lines). Red is moving through the prison court-yard, going about his daily routine. Though we're taking a few words to introduce the characters, the forward motion of the script continues without much pause.

By the way, you want to avoid casting the role, with something like "a Morgan Freeman type." For one thing, you don't know that Morgan will play the role, but you also don't want to close the role off to other possibilities, maybe even a very different type of actor who would work beautifully. (Case in point: in the original novella, Red is an Irishman; Morgan Freeman is decidedly not Irish.) It's fine for you to envision a particular actor when you write, but keep it to yourself.

With supporting characters, usually you need just one, maybe two lines. Here's how Karl is introduced in *Die Hard*:

```
His name is KARL, big, with blond hair like a rock
drummer.
```

Here's how Powell is introduced in *Die Hard*:

```
The customer is POWELL, young for a police vet-
eran, old for the rest of the world.
```

Both descriptions are quick, but effective. With Karl, we stick with the physical, but that manages to give us the essence because he doesn't just have blond hair, it's *like a rock drummer*. We sense that he's cool, hip, arrogant. The description of Powell is com-pletely abstract but also good at conveying his essence. We're told he's young in years but old in experience and that conveys the sense that this man has been weighted down by some hard times.

With very small parts, characters who appear for only one scene or so, you don't need a character intro or even a name. You can just call them State Trooper or Hysterical Nun or Big-eyed Orphan, or whatever tag conveys the gist of the character. The reader gets who they are from the moniker alone.

At the start of the chapter, I told you how great Tony Gilroy's screenplay of *The Bourne Identity* was. Now, let me show you. Here's a character introduction for Conklin, the government man tracking down the protagonist, Jason Bourne:

```
TED CONKLIN. Ivy League Ollie North. Buttoned down.
Square  jaw.  Everything  tucked  away.  But  there's
tension  in  the  air.  Work  on  the  desk.  Cot  in  the
corner.
```

Only twenty-seven words. But look at how much potency those words contain.

Ivy League Ollie North—military background, clean-cut, good schools, intelligent, bound by duty, follows his own code of honor regardless of the law.

Buttoned down—conservative, disciplined, old-fashioned, not a man who spends hours gossiping over coffee.

Square jaw—powerful (inside and out), determined, masculine, no one calls him a wimp.

Everything tucked away—neat, logical, precise, protective, dwells in a world of secrets.

But there's tension in the air—some of those secrets are dangerous, deadly, explosive, this is not a place for relaxation, or yoga, or feng shui.

Work on the desk—a computer, papers, files, documents, to-do lists, probably a paperweight.

Cot in the corner—works long hours, not concerned about comfort, probably not much of a home life, a monkish existence.

Not only is this an excellent character introduction, which also encompasses setting, but this passage embodies all of the principles of effective description we've discussed. This is screenwriting at its very best.

Parentheticals

Though it's not the sexiest subject, let's briefly return to paren-theticals. They can be confusing and are often misused. In particu-lar, they are frequently mixed up with scene description. The real purpose of a parenthetical is to describe how a line of dialogue is delivered or to indicate a brief action that goes directly with a line of dialogue. In other words, parentheticals are linked to dialogue; they are not just another place to include scene description.

So you don't want to put a major action in a parenthetical, like so:

```
                    SETH
          Don't crowd me!
               (He pulls out a pistol
               and gestures for
               everyone to stand
               back, causing the
               crowd to roll back in
               a wave)
          That's better.
```

That's too big of an action to go in the parenthetical, actually something more important than the words spoken. It will work much better like this:

```
                    SETH
               Don't crowd me!

He pulls out a pistol and gestures for everyone to
stand back, causing the crowd to roll back in a
wave.
```

                              SETH
                        That's better.

If you were to use a parenthetical, it should be related to the dialogue, like so:

                              SETH
                          (desperation)
                        Don't crowd me!

But here's the key thing about parentheticals: Use them sparingly. Directors and actors dislike having their dialogue overdirected in a script and, besides, if your dialogue is good it will convey the right tone without the need for explanation. In the bit above, for example, we don't really need the parenthetical about desperation because it's obvious enough in the dialogue and action that this guy is desperate. It's overkill.

Parentheticals are best reserved for those times when it's not immediately clear how the line is to be delivered, as in this example:

                             MARIA
                        (sarcastically)
                        What a lovely day this has
                        turned out to be.

Here's a good use of a parenthetical from *Tootsie*:

                            MICHAEL
                        You're worried about the
                        audition, aren't you?

                             SANDY
                        No, I'm not. Because I know I
                        won't get it, I'm completely
                        wrong for it.

```
                    MICHAEL
           What's the part?

                     SANDY
                (crying)
           A woman!
```

Only Sandy would cry on that line because she's so insecure about her womanhood. The parenthetical is helpful.

Now and then you can include a very minor physical action in a parenthetical, if it's closely related to the dialogue, like so:

```
                      HOSS
                 (a tip of the hat)
           See ya, missy.
```

And sometimes you'll use a parenthetical to indicate if a character switches talking from one character to another, as in this example from *Tootsie*:

```
                      JOHN
           Yes, I see. Will that be on
           the Teleprompter? "Loudly?"

                       RON
           Yes.
                (to Dorothy)
           Now, toots, you enter here,
           you cross to here, and your
           corridor scene is here.
```

Without the parenthetical, we might think Ron is calling John "toots" and that would put a whole new slant on the moment.

Voice

In addition to everything else you've learned about putting a movie on the page, there's something else. Voice. You hear the term *voice* bandied about by literary types a lot more than by screenwriters, "I prefer Faulkner's voice to that of Hemingway because of its hypersensitivity to consciousness and . . ." Screenwriters don't discuss voice so much, but the very best screenplays have it. Voice is like the aura emanating from the script.

To put it more concretely, voice is the style of the writing. It comes from the sum total of the choices the screenwriter makes about all those things we've discussed—economy, syntax, vertical flow, word choice, the way thoughts are handled, and, yes, dialogue, too. All of these elements add up to an attitude, a personality, a *voice* that colors the reading experience.

With screenplays, usually the best route is to use a voice that is fairly subtle, present but not so "loud" that it will interfere with clarity or overpower the story itself.

Look at this passage from *Thelma & Louise*:

```
Next to the cash register on the counter on dis-
play are those little tiny bottles of liquor.
Thelma picks up a little bottle of Wild Turkey and
puts it on the counter. The Old Man rings it up.
She takes another one and puts it on the counter.
The Old Man is still ringing stuff up.
```

And this passage from *Sideways*:

```
A furtive search of Jack's pockets reveals noth-
ing. Then Miles notices a HIGH-PITCHED SOUND waft-
ing from an open door down a short hallway.

Miles feverishly begins foraging through debris on
the floor. Again nothing. Meanwhile the noise from
```

```
the bedroom grows louder — female MOANING in odd
rhythmic unison with a man's voice.
```

Neither of these screenplays scream "voice" at us, but if you look closely you will notice a difference in the voices. *Thelma & Louise* is down to earth, kinda homespun. Short sentences, no fancy words, quaint phrasing like *those little tiny bottles. Sideways* is more erudite, longer sentences, and more elevated words, like *furtive, wafting,* and *foraging.* Both scripts are entertaining to read, but in a slightly different way. (For what it's worth, both of these scripts were deemed Best Screenplay by the Academy of Motion Picture Arts and Sciences and the Writers Guild of America.)

How do you find voice? First, it comes from you, the writer. We all have a distinctive way of expressing ourselves when we speak and interact with other people. Do you come off as laid back, scholarly, plainspoken, poetic, square, hip, tough, warm, ironic? Your voice will emerge from your personality. That's a good thing. We don't want all people to be the same and we don't want all screenplays to read the same.

The voice can also be influenced by the nature of the story. A fast-and-furious action/adventure screenplay will probably have a voice different from a quietly modulated drama. Voice can be influenced, as well, by the personalities of the main characters. Miles in *Sideways* is well educated, probably has a master's degree. Thelma and Louise probably never graduated from college. Their background fits with the way those screenplays are written. There is a good chance that the stories and characters you choose to write about will bear some relationship to your own personality, and that's bound to help the voice come together.

But, look, voice is not something you should sweat over too much. It's best when it comes naturally, and it comes naturally with practice. In my case, as I churned out script after script, my voice started growing stronger and more distinctive, especially when I caught on to that little notion that I'm not just writing words, but capturing a movie on the page.

Now, full disclosure. Some writers run wild with voice. This includes some of the best (and most highly paid) screenwriters, Shane Black of *Lethal Weapon* fame being the most notorious example. But let me offer a word of warning. Don't try this at home until you're very comfortable with your voice, not to mention the basic mechanics of screenwriting. If you push your voice too far too soon, it may backfire, resulting in a script that's trying too hard to copy someone else's style, or worse, turning your script into a perplexing mess.

Still, it's helpful to see how some great writers push the limits of voice in a screenplay. So here goes.

The Matrix, by Larry and Andy Wachowski, plunges us into its futuristic weirdness by morphing high-tech jargon into poetry:

```
A blinking cursor pulses in the electronic dark-
ness like a heart coursing with phosphorous light,
burning beneath the derma of a black-neon glass.

A PHONE begins to RING, we hear it as though we
were making the call. The cursor continues to
throb, relentlessly patient.
```

My Best Friend's Wedding, by Ronald Bass, serves up a romantic comedy peppered with its heroine's frazzled neurosis:

```
She snatches up the hated phone, and wanders aim-
lessly into . . .

. . . her bedroom. West Village view. Defiantly
jumbled, aggressively eclectic. Traces of wonder-
ful taste mixed with I-like-it-you-got-a-problem-
with-that? She stumbles around, rehearsing . . .

                    JULIANNE
          This is awkward timing,
          Michael, I just joined this
```

>   convent, and they never give
>   your deposit ba . . .

Stops. Full-length mirror. She straightens her
hair, to look her best.

>   JULIANNE
>   Michael, I'm married.

Not enough.

>   JULIANNE
>   . . . and I have two weeks
>   to live.

Lastly, let's go back to *The Bourne Identity*, where Tony Gilroy
captures the story's frantic pace and paranoia with a relentless attack of machine gun–like imagery:

BOURNE exits the bank. The red bag full to its
limit. He's walking briskly now. Looking for a
taxi. Nothing in sight.

BOURNE crossing the street. Shit, there's A COP
on the corner — turn — change pace — make it look
natural —

BOURNE around a corner. And it's looking good for
a moment — but only a moment — TWO MORE COPS walking a beat — walking this way — turn — cut — cross
the street —

BOURNE heading down a boulevard. Trying to look
small. Pulse starting to race. Fighting the paranoia. Where the hell is a cab? Turning back
fast as A SIREN starts bleeding in from behind
him —

It's just an ambulance.

BOURNE turning back. Forcing himself to focus. And fuck — there's A METER MAID, and she's stopped writing up a ticket — she's staring at him and —

BOURNE trying not to panic — don't run — smile — stay small — get to the corner — scan the options — but —

THE METER MAID — she's watching him go and she's pulling her radio and —

BOURNE hitting this next corner — banging a right — forcing himself not to run — glancing back and —

THERE'S ANOTHER COP — but this one is jogging — searching — he's got his radio out and — FINALLY TO —

BOURNE bailing on the street — disappearing.

Words that move. A movie on the page.

Stepping-Stone: Key Descriptions

Choose one of the key settings in your movie and write a detailed description of it, running as long as you like. Include the way it looks and also the general feel of the place. Then whittle the description down to no more than three sentences, focusing on only what can be seen or heard.

Choose one of the major characters in your movie and write a detailed description of him or her, running as long as you like. You may include physical appearance but also give a sense of the character's essence. Then whittle the description down to no more than three sentences. With character description, you have permission to move beyond what is seen and heard, including some authorial comment.

CHAPTER 5

Scenes: Exploring and Exploding Moments

BY TAL MCTHENIA

There's a scene that tears me apart in Peter Bogdanovich's *The Last Picture Show* (written by Bogdanovich and Larry McMurtry). Sonny is a teenager in a bleak Texas town in the 1950s. He's had an affair with Ruth Popper, the forlorn middle-aged wife of the high school coach. Eventually Sonny abandons Ruth to chase after a pretty blonde his own age, but after life batters him around, he returns to pay Ruth a visit.

Ruth answers the door, a ghost in a bathrobe. Manic laughter roars from a comedy show on TV. Sonny asks if he can come in for coffee, and Ruth apologizes for not being dressed in the middle of the day. Her hand shakes crazily as she tries to pour the coffee, and at last, she just can't keep it together. She hurls the cup and then the coffee pot against the wall. Coffee streaks down the wall and the wet grounds clump atop the refrigerator.

Then Ruth tears into Sonny—his sudden absence, his pursuit of the blonde girl—finally speaking her mind for what might be the first time in her life: "I guess you thought I was so old and ugly you didn't owe me any explanations."

And then Ruth goes silent. Sonny, because he's ashamed of himself and relieved at her anger, offers her his hand. Ruth, because she's fond of the feeling of his young skin, takes it. She uses his hand to caress her face, then wipe away her tears.

136

Sonny remains mute. But by coming to see her, he's asked without asking if they can resume their affair. And now he waits for her answer.

Ruth tries to speak and fails, but we know what she's thinking. Yes, Sonny has ruined their love and yes, of course, he'll leave her again. There's no good choice here. Would she rather open up to fleeting warmth and inevitable abandonment or just wither up and die? This is the film's final scene, and Ruth's answer is ambiguous. Her face now lifeless, she straightens Sonny's collar, and says gently: "Never you mind, honey. Never you mind . . ."

In mere minutes, this scene paints a breathtaking view of the human heart. The scene explores the complex silence between these two people and then explodes with the emotion it finds inside. And that's what scenes are all about: the exploration and explosion of moments. At the level of scene, we writers explore our characters most intimately—who they are, what they want, how they behave in every situation. And during that exploration, very often, the event explodes: rage, passion, anguish burst out of the characters, unexpected by writer or audience, like a coffee pot hurled against a wall.

Through this process emerge vivid moments that sear themselves into the audience's heads and hearts. A forgotten silent film star visits the set of a modern "talkie," shoos away the microphone that destroyed her career, and basks in the fleeting spotlight of an old electrician who still remembers her (*Sunset Boulevard*). A neurotic environmentalist and a hothead firefighter slam each other in the face with a rubber ball, over and over again, to achieve a delirious state of existential bliss (*I ♥ Huckabees*). A young woman plays horror-movie trivia with a killer on the phone, driven to such unbearable heights of terror that her death comes as a relief (*Scream*). A bruised-up Brooklyn boy rides the subway all night in his white disco suit, realizing it's time to grow up (*Saturday Night Fever*). These are moments in film that we'll never forget.

When we join scenes together, moment to moment, we create a larger, unified story. And that's what a movie is: a continuous flow of moments. A progression of scenes.

What a Scene Is

A scene is a unit of story that takes place in a single location during a continuous period of time. Movies usually have forty to sixty scenes. That might sound like a lot, but remember that, technically, a scene shifts any time the place or time shifts, even just a bit. So, many scenes are quite brief. The multitude of scenes lets movies have motion, fluidity, visual variation, and a broad sweep of time and place.

Scenes are often part of a *sequence*—two or more scenes connected to tell a mini-story. For example: In one scene, a slovenly bachelor shops for exotic produce in the grocery store; in the next, he struggles to cook the produce in his kitchen; in the next, he shaves his overgrown soul-patch in the bathroom; and in the final scene, the doorbell rings, and he kicks a pair of dirty socks under the couch on his way to the door. This four-scene sequence tells a mini-story: Slovenly bachelor prepares for a date.

Scenes come in varying lengths, anywhere from an eighth of a page to three, four, or more pages. In contemporary film scripts, scenes almost never run more than three pages, and while every scene should justify it's length, that's particularly true of longer ones. Some movies, like *Tootsie*, which unfolds almost like a play at times, lend themselves more to longer scenes. And some movies lend themselves more to shorter scenes; an action movie like *Die Hard* never stays still for very long. In general, though, a movie should consist of a fluid blend of short, medium, and (perhaps) a few long scenes.

No matter the length, every scene must have three essential elements in order to contribute effectively to the story.

- Relevance: The scene must be important, if not crucial.

- Conflict: The scene must contain a clash of objectives and obstacles: what someone wants and what's getting in the way.

- Structure: The scene must have a beginning, middle, and end.

Now, lets see how these concepts work in some actual scenes.

Here is a short scene from *Tootsie*. Michael's agent has just told him that no one in the business wants to work with him. Michael takes this as a personal challenge and then we see . . .

```
EXT. MADISON AVENUE - DAY

Teeming with people, coming and going. The focus
gradually forces us to notice one woman mov-
ing toward us unsteadily on high heels. She is
Michael.
```

That's it, the whole scene.

Next, a medium-length scene, running about a page, from *Thelma & Louise*. The night before, Thelma has had earth-shattering sex with the handsome hitchhiker, and she's eager to tell Louise all about it over breakfast at the coffee shop. But when Thelma reveals that she has just left the hitchhiker alone in the motel room—alone with the money—Louise bolts out, panicked, with Thelma right behind her.

```
EXT. MOTEL PARKING LOT - DAY

They run across the parking lot around to the back
of the room. The door is ajar and no one is inside
the room. Louise goes in and Thelma stays outside
the door.
```

                   THELMA
        Goddamnit! I've never been
        lucky. Not one time!

Louise comes back outside. She doesn't say anything. She is stoic, fighting back tears.

                THELMA (CONT'D)
        Shit. That little
        sonofabitch burgled me.
        I don't believe it.

Louise sits down on the sidewalk in front of the
room. Thelma comes and sits beside her. Neither
one says anything for a moment.

                THELMA (CONT'D)
        Louise? Are you okay?

Louise shakes her head no.

                THELMA (CONT'D)
        Louise . . . It's okay.
        Louise? I'm sorry.
        I mean it.

Louise has seen the end of the tunnel and there is
no light.

                  LOUISE
        It's not okay, Thelma. It's
        definitely not okay. None of
        this is okay. What are we
        going to do for money? What
        are we gonna buy gas with?
        Our good looks? I mean . . .
        Goddamn, Thelma!

Louise quietly falls apart. This causes Thelma to
leap into action.

                         THELMA
              Come on. Stand up! Don't you
              worry about it. I'll take
              care of it. Just don't you
              worry about it. Get your
              stuff.

Louise is still sitting on the sidewalk.

                         THELMA (CONT'D)
              Come on! Damnit, get your
              stuff and let's get out of
              here!

Louise slowly gets to her feet.

                         THELMA (CONT'D)
              Move!
                 (to herself)
              Jesus Christ, take your damn
              time.

Thelma is hauling stuff out of the car.

And, finally, here is a longish scene, running about three pages,
from *Sideways*. Miles and Jack have been hitting the California
wineries, and for Miles, winetasting is serious business. But what
Jack wants more than anything is to get laid before his wedding
the next week.

INT. FOXEN WINERY — DAY

The pourer, a brunette in her early thirties,
breaks away from a BORING COUPLE down the bar.
This is STEPHANIE.

                         STEPHANIE
              Hey, guys. How's it going?

                    JACK

Excellent. My friend and
I are up here doing the wine
tour, and he tells me that
you folks make one hell of
a Pinot.

                    STEPHANIE

That's what people say.

                    MILES

You gotta excuse him.
Yeserday he didn't know
Pinot Noir from film noir.

                    JACK

But I'm learning fast.

Stephanie laughs. It's clear she likes big good-
natured lunks like Jack.

                    MILES

I'm trying to teach my
friend here some basics
about wine over the next
few days before he goes
off and –

WHOMP! Under the bar Jack stomps on Miles's foot.
Miles winces. Stephanie slides two glasses in front
of them.

                    JACK

That's right — I'm here to
learn. I never had that much
interest in wine before, but
this trip has been very

                    enlightening. Always liked
                    wine, of course, but I don't
                    know. Always more of a beer
                    man. Microbreweries and such.

She THUMPS the cork off a bottle of Chardonnay.

                            STEPHANIE
                    Well, no better way to learn
                    than tasting.

She pours almost flirtatious amounts.

                            JACK
                    Now there's a girl who knows
                    how to pour. What's your
                    name?

                            STEPHANIE
                    Stephanie.

Jack swirls the wine as though he were by now a
sommelier. They look, they smell, they taste.

                            STEPHANIE (CONT'D)
                    So what do you think?

                            MILES
                    I like it. Tastes great.
                    Oaky.

Stephanie reaches for another bottle and pours.
Jack's eyes never leave her.

                            STEPHANIE
                    Cabernet Franc.
                        (as they taste)
                    This is only the fifth year
                    we've made this varietal.
                    It's from our Tinaquaic

Vineyard. And it was also
Silver Medal Winner at the
Paso Robles wine festival
last year.

                    MILES
Well, I've come to never
expect greatness from a Cab
Franc, and this one's no
exception. Sort of a flabby,
overripe, thin —

                    JACK
        (ignoring him)
Tastes pretty damn good to
me. You live around here,
Stephanie?

                    STEPHANIE
Just outside Santa Ynex.
        (low, to Miles)
And I agree with you about
Cab Franc.

                    JACK
Oh, yeah? That's where we're
staying. Windmill Inn.

                    STEPHANIE
Oh, yeah.

                    JACK
You know a gal named Maya?
Works at the Hitching Post?

                    STEPHANIE
Sure I know Maya. Real well.

                    JACK
No shit. We just had a drink

with her last night. Miles
knows her.

> MILES
> Could we move on to the
> Pinot, please?

> STEPHANIE
> Chomping at the bit, huh?
> Sure.

As she turns to reach for the right bottle, Jack
winks at Miles. Miles shakes his head. Stephanie
pours each of them a full HALF GLASS.

> JACK
> You're a bad, bad girl,
> Stephanie.

> STEPHANIE
> I know. I need to be
> spanked.

She notices the boring couple, visibly annoyed
that she has been monopolized.

> STEPHANIE (CONT'D)
> Excuse me.

As she wanders down the bar, Jack turns to Miles,
his mouth wide open.

> JACK
> Yeeeah. I'm going to get
> this whole thing lined up.

> MILES
> What whole thing?

> JACK
> You. Me. Stephanie. Maya.

```
                    MILES
          Do you know how often
          these pourers get hit on?
          Especially the cute ones?

                    JACK
          Please.

     They glance down the bar at Stephanie. She smiles
     back.
```

Relevance

Every scene should be relevant enough to a story so that without it, we'd feel like something was missing.

Many scenes give us an essential "beat" of the plot—a key event or moment that moves the story forward, escalates conflict, shifts the balance in the film's overall struggle. A change, either positive or negative. If these scenes weren't included, the story simply wouldn't make sense. Thelma and Louise getting robbed escalates conflict: If it didn't happen, then they wouldn't need to resort to theft, which makes them look much more like outlaws. It's one in a cascade of mounting misfortunes that push them closer to the edge. In *Sideways*, Jack and Miles's encounter with Stephanie represents a key shift in Jack's hook-up scheme—from all talk to direct action—and it puts in motion the date and romance with Maya to follow.

Some scenes are important, but not as crucial to the plot. In *Tootsie*, Michael's first drag scene isn't strictly essential to the plot— after all, we see him in drag in the audition to follow—but it provides dramatic punch. It allows us a moment to absorb his makeover before seeing where he's going with it. Sometimes we need short scenes like this to hammer home a story or character change in a single moment.

Sometimes scenes don't feel essential to the plot as they're happening, but later they pay off. In the opening of *Die Hard*, McClane's nervousness on the plane might seem like an expendable character detail, but it leads to the advice about taking off his shoes, which is what causes him to be caught barefoot when the building comes under siege. And his barefootedness is one of the most pernicious obstacles of the film.

Some scenes aren't necessary for the plot, but they enhance our understanding of character and character change in a significant way, like the early scenes of Thelma and Louise packing. What and how they pack tells us a lot about who they are, which helps to highlight the changes they will soon undergo. The scene is our way of keeping track of overall character growth.

But note that even in those packing scenes, Thelma and Louise aren't simply "being." They are "doing." They are packing to go somewhere; they are pushing the story forward. And that's the thing. The best scenes move both plot *and* character ahead at the same time.

Screenplays need to be so compressed that you should seize any chance to let a scene multitask. The *Thelma & Louise* motel scene is crucial to the plot, but it also shows a profound shift for Thelma. She goes from being careless to responsible, and right here, for the first time, she takes care of Louise, instead of the other way around. And in the *Tootsie* scene, the plot advances (Michael is walking to his audition) and the character changes (his desperation for work reaches new heights) all in the very same screen moment.

How do we know if a scene belongs or not? Most writers write a whole bunch of scenes that don't make the final draft of their script. And often the final draft includes scenes that don't make the final cut of the film. Early in the script of *Tootsie*, there are scenes of Michael's failed auditions, a scene of him as a waiter taking the order of his ex-girlfriend, and a painful birthday party scene, all of which effectively communicate that he's not gotten so far in his acting career. In the final film, the ex-girlfriend scene is cut. Why? Likely because, when taken with these other scenes, it felt like one too many character moments, leaving the plot to idle.

But lest you think this example gives you license to be lazy ("just throw in all of my choices and let the director or editor sort them out later"), watch out. Too many of these "maybe/maybe not" scenes and the whole script starts to feel "maybe/maybe not." You can write lots of extra scenes in early drafts (exploring character, taking plot detours, covering the same beat in different scenes) but by the final draft, compress and refine your scenes so that most, if not all, advance plot and character together, in ways that are unique from the other scenes around them.

Conflict

Virtually every scene needs to have conflict, tension, struggle, the clash of opposing forces. And that conflict always relates to some aspect of the overall plot. In early scenes, conflict builds toward the film's major dramatic question, as in those first audition failures in *Tootsie*: a series of small *life* struggles (to succeed as an actor) that carry us to the central *film* struggle (to succeed as an actor, in drag). Once the protagonist's goal is defined, then each and every scene should be a chapter in that struggle, a step toward that goal. The movie is the war, and the scenes are the battles.

Scene conflict usually comes down to a struggle between two things—objective and obstacle.

Most of the major players in a scene should have something they want in the moment, an immediate objective. The scene objective is clean, clear, and concrete. It's what the characters work toward, via every line of action and dialogue, throughout the scene. It's their total purpose. When actors prepare a scene, they scour the text to locate their character's scene objective—the thing they're after, the specific reason for what they do and say.

And it is our job as screenwriters to make that objective apparent on the page.

The opposite of the objective is the obstacle: what is standing in the way of the character getting what he or she wants. The obstacle can be purely a physical thing, like bare feet on broken glass, or a fireball roaring up an elevator shaft. More commonly, the obstacle comes from another character in the scene. In fact, the obstacle for one character is usually linked to the objective of another character in the scene. Then you get opposing objectives. A character can also struggle with an internal obstacle. But internal conflict all by itself is difficult to show on film for more than a moment or so, and it usually needs to be externalized in some way—through conflict with something physical or another person.

In the *Tootsie* scene, the conflict is entirely physical. Michael simply wants to get down the street. He's on his way to audition for a part that he wants to win, but in this particular scene his objective is to just get down the street. His obstacle, believe it or not, is those damn heels. Yes, it sounds silly, but if you're a man who's never worn high heels, try walking down a busy city street in them.

In the *Thelma & Louise* scene, there's some early conflict over the stolen money. But the real conflict in the scene is between the two women. Thelma's objective is to overcome Louise's paralysis, and Louise wants to fold up and die. Opposing objectives.

Usually, one character "leads" the scene, with the action slanted toward his or her side of the struggle. And often, that character is the one whose objective is more concrete and active. Thelma drives the motel scene. At first, she tries to get Louise to be Louise again, the one in charge, by apologizing and showing concern. But her effort falls flat. Seeing Louise isn't going to snap back, Thelma takes charge and tries to get Louise up and back on the road.

Within this struggle between Thelma and Louise there is also intense internal conflict for both characters—Louise is sinking into despair, and Thelma is racked with panic and a sense of "bad luck." The internal conflict works here because it is externalized by the interaction between the women. An image of Louise weeping on the floor wouldn't be interesting by itself; it's a more interesting scene with Thelma trying to pull her up, out of the despair.

In the scene from *Sideways*, we have a three-way conflict, with Jack in the "lead." His objective is to pick up the flirtatious Stephanie, and he pursues this with his usual gusto. His main conflict comes from Miles, who wants Jack to shut up and Stephanie to pour, so they can all stick to the agenda of wine-tasting. Finding Miles immovable, Jack shifts tactics midstream by including Maya in the pick-up deal, hoping that this will get Miles on board (which it doesn't). Stephanie's objective (she is at work, after all) is to make sure both her customers, Jack and Miles, are satisfied. She's having fun flirting back with Jack, but she also reaches out to Miles with generous pours and some wine chat. When you have three or more characters in a scene, it's important to keep the objectives and obstacles of each character active and focused.

Notice that in each of our three scenes, the scene objectives relate directly to the overall goals or desires for the characters. The goal for Thelma and Louise, for example, is to get to the border of Mexico. In the scene, that goal feels remote and impossible. But by getting Louise back on her feet, Thelma takes a key step toward making the goal of Mexico possible again. This scene is a battle in their war.

Structure

Like the film as a whole, most scenes and sequences have a beginning, middle, and end. They have a mini–three-act structure that tells a unified story.

In *Thelma & Louise*, the three acts might be described as: 1) discovery that the money has been stolen; 2) Thelma trying to deal with Louise's defeatism; 3) Thelma getting Louise going. Even the three-sentence *Tootsie* scene has a distinct three acts: 1) we see a vast anonymous crowd; 2) we see one particular woman in that crowd; 3) we realize that the woman is Michael.

In the *Sideways* scene, the first act is Jack putting on the charm, culminating with Stephanie's "almost flirtatious" pours—the signal that she's flirting back. The game is on. The second act is where the full conflict plays out. Jack steps up his advances, Miles fights back with his wine critique, and Stephanie plays it cool, but not really. The tension builds as Jack works up the double-date plan, which Miles doesn't seem to like at all. The turning point comes when Stephanie hints that she's into the idea. Her line "I might need to be spanked" is pretty much a clincher, right? This marks a change that will affect things beyond the scope of this scene. Then the third act deals with Miles trying to pour cold water on Jack's hot ambitions. It's too late, though. It's become a different kind of trip now.

Notice how these scenes grow, from line to line and action to action, beginning to end. Each moment is new and vital, with no repetition or backpedaling, and that's because the conflict isn't simply maintained. It is *escalated*. The three-act structure demands that tension and momentum constantly *build*.

How do we achieve that build? Keep the objectives out of reach by keeping the obstacles strong. Don't let the characters get what they want, and force them to shift tactics. Louise won't get up, so Thelma dons the "take-charge" attitude and gets physical. No matter how hard Jack and Stephanie try to loosen up Miles, he won't relent, so Stephanie has to "conspiratorially" agree with his snarky wine critique and Jack has to bring up Maya. They adjust their tactics and push harder.

You'll often find that the accumulation of smaller moments of conflict leads to a turning point at which the dynamic changes dramatically. Frequently, turning points come at the end, but a scene can certainly have more than one.

Often the best turning points surprise us and catch us off guard. There's a scene in *Die Hard*, when Hans and McClane finally meet face to face. Hans strives to convince McClane that he's actually a hostage, while McClane tries to tell if Hans is lying. The scene reaches a shocking turning point when McClane hands a gun to Hans. It seems that all is over. But the scene spins around again when Hans tries to shoot McClane only to discover the cartridge is empty. Turns out McClane was still suspicious. The unpredictability of this scene is what keeps us riveted.

Sequences

Most contemporary screenwriters construct their plots more through sequences than through stand-alone scenes. Once again, a sequence is a collection of scenes (with a shift in location and/or time) that tell a complete mini-story. In years past, films tended to have lengthier scenes in a single location, more like a play, because filmmakers were limited by budget and technology, and perhaps audiences were more patient. Not the case today, as films utilize sequences to create a brisk, lag-free pace and evoke a broader sense of time and place.

Here's a sequence from *Die Hard*. McClane has been up on the thirtieth floor of the Nakatomi building, joining the party and arguing with his wife. Then, downstairs . . . all hell breaks loose.

```
INT. BUILDING LOBBY — SAME TIME

The Guard at the front desk notices the Emory
truck on his monitor. The Guard continues to watch
the Emory truck and only half notices as a Mer-
cedes pulls up in front of the building and two
extremely well-dressed BUSINESSMEN (late twenties)
climb out and start up the stairs for the door. As
they cross the lobby to the Guard's table to sign
in, we hear their conversation.
```

                              MAN #1 (THEO)
                        (animatedly)
                    . . . So Kareem rebounds —
                    listen, this is a great play
                    — feeds Worthy on the break,
                    over to A.C., to Magic, back
                    to Worthy in the lane and —

Suddenly the other man pulls out a Walther pistol
with a silencer and aims it at the Guard's forehead. Before the Guard can react he pulls the
trigger.

                              THEO
                        (dryly)
                    Boom . . . two points.

The speed with which the murder takes place sets
the tone for the rest of the action. The killer
moves behind the desk, stepping over a small pool
of blood from the Guard.

His name is KARL, big, with long blond hair like a
rock drummer. Karl takes off the silencer and
looks at the video monitor of the Emory truck. The
first man, Theo, opens his briefcase, takes out a
portable CB radio and speaks into it.

                              THEO (CONT'D)
                    We're in.

ON THE SCREEN

The driver nods at the security camera as several
men climb out of the rear of the van and begin un-
loading wooden crates by the service elevator.

INT. ELLIS'S OFFICE — NIGHT

McClane looks at all the lavishness around him and picks up a phone by the toilet. He opens his wallet and takes out the phone number Argyle gave him. A photo of his children stops him.

It's of Holly, the two children, and himself in happier days: six months ago, before Nakatomi came calling to Holly's door. McClane flips it over. On the back in crude but painstaking hand of a five-year-old it says: WE MISS YOU, DADDY. LOVE LUCY (and in more primitive letters) JOHN.

McClane returns the photo to his wallet, dials the number.

INT. BUILDING OPERATIONS CONTROL ROOM

Theo enters the small control room and comfortably sits behind the maintenance keyboard. Whistling a vaguely familiar tune, he TYPES in some commands and locks down the passenger elevators up to the 30th floor. Then with several more computer commands, systematically causes:

THE HEAVY STEEL GATES TO THE PARKING GARAGE CLOSE

THE ESCALATORS TO THE GARAGE COME TO A STOP

CONTROL ROOM — SAME

Theo finishes typing and disconnects the keyboard and pulls out the wires from beneath the panel.

INT. LOBBY — SAME

The doors to a service elevator open to reveal HANS GRUBER, impeccably dressed, lean and handsome, he steps out into the lobby like he owns the building — and in a way he does.

Theo steps to the door of the control room and tosses Hans a computer card.

Hans goes to the front door, waves the card over a magnetic plate. An LED blinks and the door LOCKS with a THUD.

Hans looks out at the street. Appropriately enough, "not a creature is stirring." Century City is quiet.

An elevator door opens revealing TEN MORE MEN, all armed with Kalashnikov machine guns and carrying canvas kit bags. One of them, EDDIE, a rugged American in his twenties, goes to the dead guard and immediately begins changing into his clothes. Meanwhile:

A.) Karl takes a tool case from the elevator and joins his brother TONY, first playfully grabbing him. They head for the basement stairwell;

B.)Theo leaves the control room and nods to Hans;

C.)Eddie finishes adjusting buttons and snaps on his pilfered uniform, takes his position behind the front desk.

HANS

Looks at his watch and seems pleased. He steps into the service elevator with the others and presses the button for the 30ᵗʰ floor.

This sequence, comprised of four scenes, tells the story of the terrorists taking control of the building. Like a single scene, this—and all effective sequences—contain the three key elements of relevance, conflict, and structure.

The relevance is obvious. This first breach of security sets in motion the entire story and provides key information about these dastardly villains. Structurally, there is a very clear beginning, middle, and end: 1) the shooting of the guard; 2) the infiltration in full swing; 3) mission accomplished.

The sequence's conflict isn't as obvious. The struggle we *see* is between the terrorists and the building (the front desk guard, the security measures). But that's a lopsided battle, with the building offering little resistance; that poor guard gets blown away before he can blink. Sometimes, and this is one of those times, there is no overt conflict erupting in a scene, but a kind of simmering sense of conflict to come. In this particular sequence, we feel the tension between the quiet Christmas Eve in Century City, where "not a creature is stirring," and the very un-Christmasy sight of guys with machine guns stalking through the lobby. To amplify this tension, the writers spliced in a short scene of McClane thirty floors up, oblivious to the terror that's now rising in the elevator.

Sequences can cover a small span of time and space, or a larger one. Small-scale sequences take what could be a single, continuous scene and "blow it out." In *Sideways*, for example, there is a sequence where Miles lets it slip that Jack is getting married and Maya freaks. This could easily have played as a single scene. But it's been split into a sequence, carrying the conversation from their grassy picnic to a chase in the parking lot to a drive in the car and to a final parting outside Maya's apartment. The movement makes the encounter more visually dynamic and gives the sense that the argument builds for even longer than the "highlights" we're seeing.

Other sequences encompass a greater span of time and space. In *The Shawshank Redemption*, for instance, one sequence tells the story of Brooks's release from prison and attempted reentry into the outside world. We travel to various locales and cover what occurs probably over the course of several weeks. We see: Brooks leaving Shawshank; watching traffic and planes whiz by; struggling to keep up at his grocery store job; feeling lost and alone in his boardinghouse room; and then hanging himself. Each scene in this sequence is very brief, but together they deliver this man's heartrending struggle to find his way in the free world.

Another variation on the sequence is the *montage*—a series of brief images (rather than whole scenes) that tell a story. *Tootsie* has montages galore: Michael shopping for clothes, Michael becoming Dorothy, Dorothy becoming America's new cover girl. The montage is a quick, visual way to convey the essence of a cluster of related events, usually without dialogue.

How do you know if an event demands a single scene or a whole sequence? Let yourself experiment with this question, either on paper or in your head. Check back with your three core scene elements—conflict, relevance, and structure—and decide which choice, scene or sequence, most cleanly delivers all three of those elements. Suppose the slovenly bachelor from our earlier sequence example is the hero of a fast-paced spy caper, and the date ringing the doorbell is actually an assassin. As much fun *conflict* as there might be in seeing him clean up and cook, and as much as the prep sequence tells a *structured* three-act story, is it really *relevant* to the plot? Or might it be more efficient simply to have him kick the socks under the couch (for a dash of character) and answer the door, leading into the essential "date-turns-deadly" moment to come? Alternately, in the *Shawshank* example, a single scene of Brooks in his room preparing to hang himself would certainly deliver the *relevant* beat of his post-release demise. But in terms of *conflict* and *structure*, it would feel rushed, abrupt, unmotivated, and significantly less dramatic. Instead, the writer lets the event expand out into a sequence, with each mini-scene working almost like a distinct "act" in Brook's growing despair.

I'm guessing that the writers of *Tootsie* played around with a whole sequence of Michael getting dressed and made-up as Dorothy before settling on the single scene of him, already as Dorothy, on the street. That single scene surprises us more than a sequence would and it gives us the pleasure of imagining a whole earlier sequence in our minds. Also, later in the script, we do get to see Michael agonizing over Dorothy's outfits, so if we'd seen it already, it wouldn't be as funny later on.

In *Die Hard*, the writers could have hacked out the whole siege sequence and zeroed in on the initial "we're in" moment, leaving the details of the infiltration to our imagination. But without a full sequence, we wouldn't really know our enemy. We wouldn't see how utterly terrifying and skilled they are, and we wouldn't feel that all-important dread.

And that's, ultimately, one of the best ways of deciding between scene and sequence: How will the audience feel as they're watching it? Do we want a dawning realization (sequence of Michael becoming Dorothy) or a quick-punch surprise (scene of Michael already as Dorothy)? Do we want a glimpse of intrigue (scene of Hans and team arriving) or a no-holds-barred "shock and awe" campaign (complete siege sequence)?

Take a Shot

Imagine a character who plans a dinner party with high hopes, only to have it turn into an utter disaster. Map out how you would tell this mini-story in a sequence of four scenes. Give some thought as to which four scenes related to the dinner party will best tell the story. Then write the sequence in screenplay format, conveying only what is seen and heard.

Other Key Elements

Once you're pretty sure your scene or sequence has the three core elements—relevance, conflict, and structure—it's time to push further. From rough sketch to vivid painting, let's explore several other storytelling techniques that can help make your scenes become fully lived-in moments.

Visuals

Some movies may slant more toward pure visual storytelling and some movies may include lots of dialogue, but virtually all movies utilize both the visual and the verbal. The art of writing a good scene involves knowing when and how to use these two elements.

That short scene from *Tootsie* has no dialogue whatsoever, but for many people, that's the very scene they remember most out of the whole film.

Single-character scenes like this are a great place to mine for images and behavior—story we can "see" rather than hear. This can be particularly true of *private* single-character scenes, like Thelma and Louise each packing alone in their rooms. Almost like studying animals in their natural habitat, these "observations" allow us to find hidden character shadings within physical behavior, and they do so far more efficiently and effectively than spoken dialogue.

But just because you have more than one person in a scene doesn't mean you need a lot, or any, dialogue. The *Die Hard* sequence has only a few words of dialogue and those don't have much to do with what is actually going on. What we see the characters doing is where the real drama lies.

In the scene from *Thelma & Louise*, there are plenty of spoken lines, but the visuals are still primary. Louise never says the money was stolen; her look says it all. Watch how she crumples. What words could ever say despair as well as that action? And Thelma's tugging makes her new "take-charge" persona concrete and physical. What the characters do tells the emotional story almost as clearly as what they say, and the scene might play just as effectively with the volume turned all the way down.

Sideways is definitely more of a dialogue-driven film, but even in the wine-tasting scene, look at how rich the visuals are. The actions of Stephanie's pours (bigger and bigger) are like unspoken lines of dialogue in her flirtation with Jack. And the wine gives Miles, who often remains silent, plenty of physical behavior that lets us in on what's happening for him emotionally: his anger, his fear, his need for control.

When you're drafting scenes, there's a temptation to write it all out in dialogue form first, or at least to allow dialogue to guide the process. To wait for later to fill in the visuals and the action, mostly just as "punctuation," or, as they say in theater, "business." But film is first and foremost a visual medium, so challenge yourself to let the visuals *lead*. Ask yourself: How can this moment of story be expressed through images and actions? Think of images and actions more than dialogue.

Visual storytelling is often a matter of finding the physical tasks and props to activate the scene. Michael trying to walk in high heels. Thelma needing to get Louise up and on her feet. Stephanie pouring the wine. "Live" in the scene in your imagination to find the props and tasks that emerge naturally from the environment and situation. But don't pick just any prop or task at random. If you think about it, each of these examples of visual elements cuts right to the heart of what the scene is about.

Visual thinking can also help you unlock innovative scene-writing techniques. In *Thelma & Louise*, for example, Thelma robs a convenience store. We see her go in the store, and then we see her come out of the store with a wad of money. But we don't see the robbery occur as it happens. Instead, we see Darryl and the police/FBI guys watching the robbery via playback of the black-and-white surveillance video. It's an arresting way to show this action and it also lets the scenes multitask—we learn about the robbery and we see that the authorities have *also* learned about the robbery, all in one fell swoop.

Stylistic trickery like this, however, isn't something you impose on a scene simply to "jazz it up." It's something that helps tell the story more dramatically or efficiently. But storytelling style must come from within the story itself. *Thelma & Louise* has lots of characters in lots of different locations; the scene with the surveillance video comes out of the story's essence. *Sideways*, on the other hand, is a simpler story, so it's told in a more straightforward, unadorned style.

Challenge yourself to find the most powerful moments of your film through images. Embrace those images that will burn into our minds, those images that cut right to the thematic and dramatic heart of the film. Thelma and Louise kissing, holding hands, the Thunderbird sailing over the Grand Canyon. The story of these images is exactly what the whole film is about. In *The Last Picture Show*, the wet, wasted coffee grounds atop the refrigerator—that's Ruth Popper's soul.

Setting

Don't underestimate the power of your scene's location. Where the scene takes place should have a profound effect on the action itself, so choose locations that maximize the scene's conflict or underscore the moment's emotion. In the *Tootsie* scene, we could have seen Michael walking down a quiet Greenwich Village lane. But that's nowhere near as challenging (or visually striking) as seeing him walk down a "teeming" Madison Avenue. Brooks's boardinghouse room in *Shawshank* is up a steep flight of stairs and is described as "small, old, dingy." A perfect room for suicide.

You may be envisioning scenes that take place in an intimate private space, such as a house or a car or a quiet table at a restaurant. These locations may make your characters feel safer, but is safer more dramatic? Move your scene from private to public. Relocate the characters to a church pew or a china shop; open up the windows on the car and put them in traffic; better yet, make them walk down a crowded street. And in that restaurant (or café or bar), pull them out of that quiet corner and exploit the latent dramatic power of the strangers all around them. These "extras" don't need lines; they can bring a scene alive by their mere presence. After all, crazy things happen to people in public; they feel anxious or watched or emboldened. All good things for maximizing conflict.

Even the choice of interior or exterior is important. Exteriors can add a sense of visual breadth. Interiors often feel claustrophobic and muted. Which vibe is more appropriate to a scene? As you move from inside to outside (and your script should definitely mix it up throughout), let the contrast work for your drama.

Sometimes it will be obvious where a scene must be set. In our *Sideways* scene, for example, it needs to be in a winery. But you can still make the most of the location, exploiting what would naturally be part of the environment. In that scene, pay attention to that "boring couple down the bar." They reinforce that we're in public, which adds a little spark to the flirtation, and their need to be attended to adds a nagging tension to Stephanie (and the scene). It's a little thing that adds a lot.

Subtext

In a good scene, there is more going on than what we actually see and hear. There's something happening underneath the events and action, something unspoken and unseen, something that we *feel*. Let's call this deeper layer the *subtext* of a scene, the meaning beneath the surface. Subtext is an important concept in dialogue, and one that will be covered in the following chapter, but let's examine how it applies to a scene as a whole.

In the *Tootsie* scene, the subtext is the new layer of Michael that emerges when we see him in drag: "This guy will stop at nothing!" In the *Die Hard* sequence, the subtext is the awe and dread the terrorists invoke: "These guys are really bad news." Simple enough.

You have to dig a little more to see the subtext of the *Thelma & Louise* scene, but it's very much there: Louise is shedding her caretaker role, and Thelma is finally taking charge. In the overall scope of their friendship, this is a momentous shift of power. In the *Sideways* scene, Jack's flirtation is so overt that it can't really be called "subtext," right? But watch Miles closely and you'll sense the scene's subtext: Miles treats Stephanie with unnecessary coldness; he's closing himself off to women altogether; he is scared.

Think of subtext as a scene's secret, the hidden story, and usually the clues to it are in the script. In fact, however muted its revelation, the subtext is often the most important thing we take away from the scene. And the subtext of a scene reverberates throughout the movie. From one scene to the next, these subtextual messages form a current of deeper meaning that we follow and process as the film progresses.

Take a look at that unforgettable scene near the end of *Sideways*, when Miles drinks a bottle of wine out of a Styrofoam cup along with his fast-food hamburger. The scene is brief, contains no dialogue, and yet it is brimming with subtext. On the surface, all we see is a guy pathetically sipping wine in a burger joint. But when he refills his cup we catch a glimpse of the label on the wine bottle— Cheval Blanc. (Yes, that glimpse is in the script.) We remember the scene much earlier when he told Maya about owning this incredibly valuable bottle, which he was saving for a special occasion. We remember Maya telling him, "The day you open a '61 Cheval Blanc, *that's* the special occasion." Suddenly the scene explodes with dramatic meaning. We, the viewer, put two and two together and realize the subtext; after anguishing over some mythic perfect future, Miles is finally accepting his life as it is, on its own terms. And because of the subtextual emotional journey we've taken with Miles in scenes leading up to this one, this moment is overwhelming in its potency.

Audiences relish subtext because it pulls us out of simple passivity, engaging us in a sense of discovery. We make a special connection with the scene's meaning because the film allows us to find it for ourselves. Cringe for a moment as you imagine the *Sideways* scene with a voice-over memory of Maya's "special occasion" line. That's speaking the subtext, saying it aloud, and as soon as a scene starts doing that, it loses much of its power; audiences sag back in their chairs and wait to be told how to feel. Subtext, then, is a story that we whisper into our scenes, not one that we yell.

Focus

In that short *Tootsie* scene, we don't see Michael get off the bus on Madison Avenue, start walking, then eventually round a corner and disappear. We see him walking only as long as it takes for us to fully register that its *him*. The scene gets to the point, and does it fast, which is a key quality of effective storytelling.

Always make your scenes get to the point, quickly.

Okay, well, how do you know what the "point" of your scene is? Sometimes it's obvious enough—Michael walking to the audition in drag, the terrorists killing the security guard. Sometimes, though, it's a trickier question. Sometimes there is a more intriguing point lying beneath or between the obvious actions of the plot. (And, yes, often this intriguing point is closely related to the scene's subtext.) For instance, in the *Thelma & Louise* scene, the most overt action is the discovery of stolen money. That's what "happens" in the plot, but it's not the focus of the scene. Concrete events such as this are our story guideposts, to be sure, and in the early stages of planning they might be what we think the scene will be about: "Thelma and Louise discover the money's missing and get on the road again, more desperate than ever."

But as we explore the scene, we begin to discover that the real dramatic "meat" comes more from the character development than the simple plot event. *Thelma & Louise* isn't a "wild girls on the lam" pulp-action picture; rather it's the story of two women growing together as they grow apart from the world. Hence, the true point of this scene is Thelma changing and taking charge, a key juncture in Thelma's evolution. And notice how efficiently the scene focuses on that aspect. We don't spend a long time watching the women search for the money. They discover it's gone right away and Louise promptly falls apart. The bulk of the scene is in seeing what Thelma will do. And as soon as Thelma pulls Louise to her feet, the scene is over. Thelma's handling of the situation is the scene's real focus.

"Getting to the point" requires you to focus the scene's true conflict very specifically. It's about zeroing in on the most significant physical and emotional struggle within the plot event. It's about asking and re-asking (from draft to draft to draft) why and how this scene is an important building block in the particular story you're trying to tell.

Sometimes we have to write what we *think* the scene is about to get to what the scene is *really* about. It is quite possible that the *Thelma & Louise* screenwriter had to first write a desperate search for the money in the motel room in order to figure out what the more important conflict was: the power shift *after* the money search. The writer had to live in that panic and hopelessness, to push and go deeper into the conflict between the two women; she had to explore the moment and let it explode.

Once you know the most important conflict of a scene, you can apply a key screenwriting technique: *Enter a scene late and leave it early.* Start the scene not when the conflict is brewing on the horizon, but—*bam!*—right when it's staring us in the face, maybe even when it has already reached fever pitch. End the scene as soon as that conflict has been resolved, and not a moment later.

For a beautiful example of how "enter late/get out early" can work, take a look back at the long wine-pouring scene from *Sideways*. The script shows the complete encounter between Stephanie and Jack/Miles. But watch that scene in the movie. The filmmakers cut the intro part of the conversation, entering the scene when Stephanie slides the glasses to Miles and Jack. And we leave the scene as soon as Stephanie wanders away from the guys. This puts the last turning point—Stephanie showing real interest in Jack—at the very end of the scene, the climax. The long version is perfectly good, but the scene is made even better by entering when Jack's advances are already under way and ending as soon as it's clear he's successful. As soon as Stephanie really flirts back, the battle is over. In the truncated version, the scene still retains a nice three-act structure, but it's been centered around a more focused vision of the scene's conflict. (Also note that in neither of these versions do we actually see Jack making the date with Stephanie, which is the concrete plot event.)

By focusing the conflict, you can propel one scene into the next with greater drive. The scenes build on top of each other and gain increasing momentum, and the script moves from battle to battle, without delay. Just as the scenes remain focused on a specific and significant conflict, so too does the story as a whole.

Transitions

As important as it is to build an effective scene, it's just as important to build clear and engaging links from one scene to the next. Frequently, this means paying attention to the unwritten space *between* your scenes.

In real life, there's nothing left out from one moment to the next. A person opens his eyes, gets out of bed, puts on clothes, goes downstairs, makes coffee, waits for the coffee to brew, guzzles the coffee, drives to the office, hurries to his desk, and gets to work.

But that's not what normally happens on film; its boring, too literal. The art of cinematic storytelling comes from the choices we make about what to leave out, offscreen. We create meaning by connecting scenes that don't happen in a continuous flow: A person opens his eyes in bed, then gets to work at his desk. The meaning created via those two linked scenes might be: "Every waking moment is about work." The flow of events still makes sense, and that's certainly a key function of transitions—maintaining logic as we leap through time and space. Equally important, though, is engaging the audience by allowing them to piece the story together on their own.

The *Tootsie* scene is a classic example. The agent tells Michael his career is doomed. He retorts, "Oh yeah?" And then we see him in drag. We piece together his whole process of coming up with the drag scheme, and imagining that in our head is great fun.

Sometimes scenes tease a question or pose a challenge like this ("Oh yeah?") that is literally answered in the next scene, like a call and response. The screenwriter can even have sly fun with this kind of cut, as in this example from *Die Hard*:

```
McClane slowly lets out breath, praying softly:

                    MCCLANE
            Argyle. Tell me you heard
            the shot. Tell me you heard
            the shot and you're calling
            the police right now . . .

INT. LIMO — PARKING GARAGE

Argyle is on the phone. The music is playing.

                    ARGYLE
            I'm working, honey. Working
            hard. 'Course I'll be by
            later to pick you up, have
            I ever lied to you? My boss?
            He thinks I'm cruising to
            Palm Springs . . .
```

Another technique of teasing out tension between separate scenes is cross-cutting—shifting back and forth between one scene and another. In the *Die Hard* sequence, we see McClane mooning over pictures of his wife and kids while the terrorists are wreaking havoc downstairs. The contrast between these two emotionally disparate moments tells a bigger story than each moment does on its own. When done carefully, cross-cutting can bring a sequence's conflict right off the page.

A precious few times in your script, transitions can be simply to start a new section of story afresh. A significant break in time. A new strand of plot. But don't think of these moments as giving your audience a "breather." The rule of sustained conflict still applies. In *Sideways,* Jack's objective to pick up Stephanie is accomplished, and so, immediately, in the very next scene, he's preparing for the date. When advancing warriors win a battle on one hill, they don't linger and gloat over the fallen enemies. Their eyes are already on the next battle on the next hill, one step closer to the castle. In this way, the resolution of one scene's conflict determines the beginning of the scene to come.

Perspective

As in fiction, a screenwriter chooses a perspective from which to tell the story. Usually, that's a choice between showing only scenes with the protagonist, which is like a first-person point of view, and including scenes where the protagonist is not present, like a third-person point of view.

Sticking with the protagonist makes sense for some movies, if you want a really intimate portrait of a character. We experience the entire story alongside the protagonist; we know only what he or she knows. In *Sideways,* it might be tempting to see Jack caught in bed with the waitress by her gigantic husband, but this story stays very close to Miles, dramatically and emotionally. So it's better to patch the story together with Miles as Jack recounts it, and then to live with Miles through the full hideous terror of the later encounter with the waitress and husband.

Other movies let us see things more broadly. In *Thelma & Louise* we cut freely between the two women and everyone chasing them down. In *Die Hard* we see McClane alone, the villains, and all the people affected by the events—a perspective I call "action movie omniscient." If we were exclusively with McClane, things wouldn't be nearly as exciting. In such cases, we know more than what the protagonist knows. And the contrast between the various characters' different experiences of the same events adds a crucial layer of dramatic tension.

By finding the right perspective for your film, you can decide which scenes to include and which to leave out. So you should consider this question early in the process. At the same time, don't be afraid to consider a change of perspective as you're writing, if you find that much of the good stuff is happening offscreen, between or beyond the scenes on paper. Perspective shapes story, and story, in turn, shapes perspective.

Assembling the Pipeline

From an aerial photo, an above-ground pipeline appears to be a single, unified apparatus that carries water, oil, or liquid chocolate from one place to another. But look closer. The pipeline is actually a lot of smaller pieces of tube. Lengths of pipe fitted together, one after another, from beginning to end. These are like a film's individual scenes. And as polished and memorable as individual scenes or sequences may be, they are not meant to stand alone. They need to work as chapters of the whole script. A piece of pipe only matters when it's joined together with all the other pieces, doing their job collectively. If one scene ruptures or veers, the dramatic flow is impaired. Water spills out onto the desert floor, and the city is miserably thirsty.

Therefore, it is a major part of the screenwriter's job to figure out which scenes are essential to the overall story. And that's no small feat. At a certain stage of writing, it feels like all kinds of scenes could fit, and there's no clear way of winnowing down those choices. Do we show the first time they meet or jump in after they already know each other? Do we need to see him get fired from his job or can we just refer to that? We shouldn't be writing elaborate scenes for every little beat of the story, but on the other hand, if we leave too many gaps, it will feel like something's missing.

We also have to figure out where these scenes fit, where they make the most sense. Each scene should feel like it belongs exactly where you've put it in the script. Placement, as much as content, is essential to the effective unfolding of the story. And that's a pretty daunting task, too.

Even experienced filmmakers futz around after the film is shot, in the editing process. Take *Sideways*, for example. The finished film is pretty close to the script (the director was one of the co-writers), but if you watch the movie with script in hand, you'll find that some scenes were cut. You'll even notice that the order of some scenes was rearranged. This is a perfectly natural part of filmmaking. Drama takes on a whole new life when the cameras start to roll, and we can't expect to create a "change-proof" script. But we can and should make the flow of drama, from beginning to end, as seamless on paper as possible.

It's tempting to just start writing, finessing nifty transitions from scene to scene, creating a reasonable enough *illusion* of dramatic flow. But what's needed first is a coherent sense of the scenes' place in the larger story. Lay the lengths of pipe where you *think* they should go before welding them together. This is where outlines come in handy: a picture of the overall pipeline path. If you're writing with a reasonably thorough sense of the story's flow from one major event to the next, you'll have clearer guideposts. And you'll have a better sense of what you have to accomplish in roughly what amount of time. So begin with a chart of the film's major events.

The next stage of your outlining will usually involve a *beat sheet*, a list of every event (beat) you envision. A beat doesn't necessarily have to correspond to a single scene or sequence; it often does, but a beat may include numerous scenes that are part of the same general situation. For example:

The next day, Thelma starts to tell Louise about sex with J. D., but Louise asks about the money: it's still in the room, with J. D. They race to room and the money's gone. Louise crumples, Thelma takes charge.

Police, FBI set up camp at Thelma's house, tapping phone.

Thelma robs convenience store. Police, FBI see it on video. Thelma, Louise feel thrill of being outlaws.

Like all outlining methods, the beat sheet is for your eyes only, so make the form work for you. It can definitely help to push your beat sheet beyond the "what" (the concrete events) and include notes to yourself about the "why" (the emotional motivations and significance). For example:

They race to room, discovering money gone. Louise crumples, Thelma takes charge. (Here dynamic shifts, with Thelma leading the way more and more.)

At some point, you might want to progress to a "step outline" where you actually break the beats into scenes (steps), like so:

INT. COFFEE SHOP – DAY

Thelma tells Louise about orgasm. Louise realizes J. D. left alone in motel room with money.

EXT. MOTEL ROOM – DAY

They race to room, discovering money gone. Louise crumples, Thelma takes charge.

If you're like me, you'll get tired of staring at the computer screen during the outlining process, and you'll want to see something more tangible and physical. This is where you can break out those old-fashioned index cards. You can map out the plot of your script—beat by beat, scene by scene—on index cards, which are tacked, glued, or taped to a wall, poster board, or bulletin board.

The beauty of index cards is that you can scribble in added details for a particular beat or scene, you can tape on new clusters of ideas around scenes, and, most important, you can arrange and re-arrange to your heart's content.

Let the process get messy before it gets clean. Early on, your out-lined script may resemble lots of little clusters of pipe sections scat-tered in the desert. At some magical point, though, they start coming together, looking like that seamless tube in the aerial photo.

But don't let yourself sit back and admire for too long. Rather, scan/scour the whole arrangement over again, paying critical at-tention to how you feel as you move through the story. Is each scene an important battle in the script's war? Is it an important step in the growth of an important character? Does it represent a positive or negative change? Does one scene flow into the next, in terms of action and subtext? Is that flow engaging, connecting the dots but not overconnecting or repeating them? Is momentum building?

Sometimes you won't have the best answer until you are actu-ally in there writing. You might write a perfectly beautiful scene, but then it doesn't seem to have a place. Or it seems to be hold-ing up the momentum. This might mean axing it altogether. Conversely, you might start writing a scene that was supposed to be very minor, or maybe wasn't even supposed to be there, and you find it taking on a life in a way that is absolutely central to the story. An essential gem that's turned up in the unlikeliest of places.

That surprise discovery, when you're in the middle of a scene, is one of the deepest joys of screenwriting. In the back of your mind, you've got that sense of overall character growth, that map of over-all story arc. Consider this your safety net. And with your safety net in place, you're free to do all kinds of stunts. You're free to ex-plode within the scenes, to explore between the scenes. You are free to live fully, with characters and story, in moment after moment.

Stepping-Stone: A Visual Scene

Pick a scene that will probably appear in your movie. It'll work best if this is not one of the movie's "big" moments. Write the scene with no dialogue whatsoever, telling the story solely through visuals (and perhaps some sound). Then write the scene again, this time adding dialogue where necessary, but using what you discovered the first time to keep your new scene visual.

Beat Sheet

A beat sheet is simply a list of all the events (beats) in a story, placed in the order in which they will appear. Events may unfold in a single scene or a sequence. Many writers create a beat sheet before writing a first draft to give them a specific sense of what goes where. Some writers find it helpful to put each beat on a separate index card. With the cards, it's easy enough to cut, add, or shuffle the order. Here is how a beat sheet might look for Act I of *Thelma & Louise*:

ACT I
Thelma and Louise talk on phone about trip.

Darryl acts like jerk to Thelma, and Thelma decides not to tell him about trip.

Louise packs carefully, Thelma packs recklessly.

Louise picks up Thelma. Thelma gives Louise a gun (brought in case they encounter psycho killers). They speed off.

They're having a good time on the road.

Thelma gets Louise to stop at a honky-tonk bar. Harlan flirts with them. Louise doesn't like it, but Thelma craves attention. Thelma drinks too much, dances with Harlan.

In the parking lot, Harlan tries to rape Thelma. Louise comes to her rescue with the gun. In a moment of fury, she shoots and kills Harlan. Thelma and Louise drive away.

Thelma wants to call the cops. Louise doesn't, fearing no one will believe Harlan was raping Thelma.

They stop at a diner. Thelma is a wreck; Louise is trying to keep it together. They blame each other.

Stepping-Stone: Beat Sheet

Create a beat sheet for the main plot of your movie. (You'll be learning about subplots a little later.) You can list the events very simply, or give a bit more detail. It's up to you. Don't worry about getting everything perfect; the choice and arrangement of scenes is bound to change in the writing process. But the beat sheet will help you get a sense of the flow of the entire movie.

CHAPTER 6

Dialogue: Making More of Less

BY MICHAEL ELDRIDGE

A film that just knocked me out is *Broadcast News* (written and directed by James L. Brooks). Especially the dialogue. The plot is basically a love triangle set in a major network television newsroom. Two men, an accomplished field reporter and a newly hired airhead anchor, vie for the affections of Jane Craig, the news producer. Jane is a whip-smart woman who excels at one of the most demanding jobs around, but she's not without her problems.

Practically every line of dialogue in this movie is a gem, but let me point out one moment in particular. The entire news staff is at a party when a U.S. fighter jet is shot down over Libya. It's big news, and the team goes into overdrive. The head of the division, Paul, decrees that Tom, the airhead, will take his first shot at anchor for this breaking story. Jane takes Paul outside and argues that the pretty boy is nowhere near ready. Paul disagrees, saying that's only her opinion. Adamant, Jane states that it's *not* opinion. And the rest of the dialogue goes:

```
                    PAUL
         It must be nice to always
         believe you know better.
         To think you're always the
         smartest person in the room.
```

```
                          JANE
                  (from her depths)
                No, it's awful.
```

In those three words—"No, it's awful"—Jane sums up the whole dilemma of her life. Yep, she *is* always the brightest bulb on the porch, and because she *knows* that, she can't just let things go when they don't seem right to her. But this attitude isolates her, drives people away, and leaves her lonely, neurotic, apt to close her office door, turn off her phone, and go on a good crying jag. (As one of Jane's colleagues say, "Except for socially, you're my role model.") All of Jane Craig, her faults and strengths, shoot through in those *three words*.

That's how you make dialogue effective in film. You whittle it down and ensure that every word counts. It's the art of making more of less. Every line should contain layers of information, emotion, characterization, meaning, so much so that the audience can't even get a piece of popcorn to their mouth without freezing in mid-nibble to concentrate on what the characters are saying.

Here's another reason you need to keep the dialogue whittled down. Film is a visual medium. Those visuals trump talk. You can—and should have—great scenes, where there is little dialogue or none at all. Less dialogue means more room for visual storytelling.

Yet most of what you see in an actual script is, in fact, dialogue. And many people reading scripts focus primarily on the dialogue. When those actors on the screen speak, we pay close attention to what they say. Dialogue is one of the most crucial elements of any screenplay. Great dialogue can help your screenplay, your entire story, take flight and soar like a big ol' jet liner, while bad dialogue, on the other hand, rips the wings off and sends that plane hurtling to the ground. Such fiery explosions are good for action movies. Bad for your career.

The Illusion of Reality

First off, you want your characters to sound like real people. Good
dialogue has a natural feel and flow. This seems simple enough; after all, most of us are pretty experienced at running our gums. But
the fact is, it's not always easy to pull off on the page.

Here's a good bit of natural-sounding dialogue from *The Shawshank Redemtion.* Red and Andy are "celebrating" Red's thirty-year
anniversary in Shawshank and yet another parole rejection.

```
EXT. PRISON YARD - DUSK

Red emerges into the fading daylight. Andy's wait-
ing for him.

                    RED
          Same old, same old. Thirty
          years. Jesus. When you say
          it like that . . .

                   ANDY
          You wonder where it went. I
          wonder where ten years went.

Red nods, solemn. They settle in on the bleachers.
Andy pulls a small box from his sweater, hands it
to Red.

               ANDY (CONT'D)
          Anniversary gift. Open it.

Red does. Inside the box, on a thin layer of cot-
ton, is a shiny new harmonica, bright aluminum and
circus-red.

               ANDY (CONT'D)
          Had to go through one of your
          competitors. Hope you don't
```

```
                mind. Wanted it to be a
                surprise.

                        RED
                It's very pretty, Andy.
                Thank you.

                        ANDY
                You gonna play something.

        Red considers it, shakes his head. Softly:

                        RED
                Not today.
```

Let me point out a few basic things that will help you achieve this kind of naturalness.

Don't worry about perfect grammar. People don't always speak grammatically; no reason they should in movies. Notice how Andy drops pronouns—"Wanted it to be a surprise"—and doesn't use complete sentences—"Anniversary gift." He also uses the very ungrammatical "gonna," as people often do in real life.

Use contractions. Red doesn't say, "It is very pretty." He says, "It's very pretty." In real life, people almost always use contractions when possible. Lack of contractions is a sure path to stilted speech.

Keep it moving. Don't let any character ramble on for too long before the other character speaks. Real-life conversation usually bounces back and forth like a Ping-Pong match. Note that you can also get that back-and-forth going between character "lines" and bits of physical action. Red is pensive in the *Shawshank* scene so Andy does most of the talking, but his lines are interrupted with bits of action with the harmonica. Rule of thumb: You shouldn't go more than three or four lines each time a character speaks unless there is very good reason.

A good way to ensure that your dialogue is natural is to read it aloud. It should fall trippingly off the tongue, feel real to you as you speak it. If your dialogue is phony, you'll know it as soon as you're forced to act it out yourself.

Aside from that, it's just a matter of developing your ear so you have a feel for the way people actually talk. Listen to how real people talk. Pay attention to what they say. What verbal tics do you notice? How is the way people really talk different from what you thought? You might even transcribe pieces of over-heard conversations to see what authentic talk looks like on the page.

But hold on a moment. Time to spin this around with a paradox. I've said that dialogue should sound real—but the fact is, dramatic dialogue is actually far removed from real-life speech. We falter all over the place when we speak, and often we take forever to get to the point. Mere transcriptions of conversations are duller than dishwater, and you'd be committing a felony against your audience if you made them sit in the dark and listen to it. Dialogue is not real-life speech, but it should give the *illusion* of being so. Dialogue is actually a highly compressed version of everyday speech. If drama is anything, it is the essence of life, the boiled-down version of the everyday that carries a punch and says something at all times. Any great story, from your whiz-bang actioner to your quietly pitch-perfect drama, keeps the audience on their toes at all times with new information. If you look back at that *Shawshank* passage, you'll see that every line has meaning, carries the drama forward in some way. Every word matters.

Now, take a look at the same scene from *Shawshank*, with the dialogue uncompressed.

```
EXT. PRISON YARD - DUSK

Red emerges into the fading daylight. Andy's wait-
ing for him.

                    RED
          Same old, same old. I was
          rejected by the parole board
```

again. Every time, same damn
thing. Thirty years. I've
been in this prison for
thirty years now. Jesus.
When you say it like that,
you gotta wonder where the
time went.

            ANDY
Yeah, you wonder where it
went. I wonder where ten
years went. But you . . .
thirty. I can't even begin
to imagine how you must
feel.

Red nods, solemn. They settle in on the bleachers.
Andy pulls a small box from his sweater, hands it
to Red.

         ANDY (CONT'D)
I bought you an anniversary
gift. You didn't think I'd
forget, did you? Go ahead,
open it.

Red does. Inside the box, on a thin layer of cot-
ton, is a shiny new harmonica, bright aluminum and
circus-red.

         ANDY (CONT'D)
I had to go through one of
your competitors. I hope you
don't mind my subterfuge. I
wanted it to be a surprise
and that was the only way I
could pull it off.

                          RED
              It's very pretty, Andy. Look
              at that, will ya? This
              baby's a beaut. Thank you.

                          ANDY
              You gonna just look at it or
              you gonna play something?

      Red considers it, shakes his head. Softly:

                          RED
              Sorry, I'm not in the mood.
              Besides, I don't even know
              if I remember how to play.
              Been so long. Not today.

This isn't exactly terrible dialogue. It sounds natural enough, might even be more realistic than the first version. But nothing is gained from beefing up the lines like this. In fact, you lose a lot. Read this passage aloud and see how long it takes. Dialogue takes much longer to say aloud than it does to read on the page, something you might not realize when you're madly typing away. The longer version of the scene would draaaaaag on screen. The first version of this passage moves much more quickly and yet says everything the longer version does. Compressed dialogue helps the actors, too, giving them more room to infuse every line with meaning rather than wasting their time yapping unnecessary words.

It's okay if your dialogue is long and windy in the first few drafts. You can trim, cut, reduce it to the perfect length later. You'll go through the same process. Here are a few techniques to help compress your dialogue.

The first is incredibly simple. Just cut out as many words as you can. If you have a speech with, say, four sentences, see if you can't lose two of them. Usually, you can.

It'll also help if you follow the principle of "enter late, get out early." That doesn't mean that every scene must fly by; it simply means that you want to start each scene at the moment when the drama is high. Then get out of the scene before the drama starts to flag.

Perhaps the most important thing is to know what your characters want every time they speak. Dialogue must be motivated by some kind of desire, be it conscious or unconscious. The question you have to ask, and you have to ask it for every line of dialogue, is this: *Why is this character speaking?* If you don't have a good answer, it's a cutable line. If you do have an answer, then you can focus the line better.

Another technique for compressing dialogue is to find the words that trigger another character to respond, preferably quickly and emphatically. The most basic trigger is the question mark. What's your name? We're triggered to respond. But triggers aren't just questions, they're words or ideas that compel a character to respond. Take a look at this passage from *Sideways*.

```
Jack and Miles are served breakfast by a young,
innocently sexy WAITRESS. Jack leers after her.

                    JACK
          Fuck man. Too early in the
          morning for that, you know
          what I mean?

                    MILES
          She's a kid, Jack, I don't
          look at that stuff anymore.

                    JACK
          That's your problem, Miles.

                    MILES
          As if she'd be attracted to
          guys like us in the first
          place.
```

```
                         JACK
              Speak for yourself. I get
              chicks looking at me all the
              time. All ages.
```

Each idea that comes up, Jack or Miles jump right on it with their response, contradicting and pushing each other—and thus accelerating the pace of the dialogue. Dialogue that is sharp and effective is a series of trigger-response-trigger-response, sharp volleys and returns. Not only does the dialogue keep clipping along, the conversation remains dramatic.

It's also interesting to consider which words or ideas a character personally considers a trigger. This can say a lot about the character responding, and the relationship between the characters. For example, you're in your study, working away on your brilliant screenplay. Your partner comes home, slams the door, and says:

```
                      PARTNER
            Will you take a look at
            yourself! You never have
            dinner ready when I get
            home! You just sit there
            and work on your little
            screenplay!
```

Now there are a lot of potential triggers there. If things are really on edge in this relationship, you might be triggered by that first shot: "Will you take a look at yourself?" Maybe you're most annoyed that your partner expects you to be the one who always provides dinner, and so you jump on the second line. Or let's say you're a relatively calm person and you don't mind that dinner is expected of you but that crack about your "little screenplay" is what makes you jump out of your seat and fight back. All of these are very specific character choices. (By the way, you should always stand up for yourself if someone is condescending about your screenplay. Write that movie and order some takeout.)

Take a Shot

Eavesdrop on a real-life conversation. Then try to write down the conversation verbatim, just as you heard it. It won't be possible unless you use a tape recorder, but try. Then write a much briefer version of the conversation in screenplay format, distilling the essence of the characters and the situation. It's fine if you fabricate dialogue to achieve this. Keep the new version under one page.

Stylization

Okay, so dialogue should sound real, but better than the conversational flotsam that we call real-life speech. Sometimes it's much better than real. Characters in movies often say things that are far sharper, smarter, wittier, more eloquent than what we poor mortals usually utter. While walking about in your day-to-day life, you may never have said something as good as, "Of all the gin joints in all the towns in all the world she walks into mine." But your characters can, and will, say stuff this good. You don't want to lose all semblance of naturalness, but it's often okay to let your characters phrase things incredibly well, creating lines that are truly memorable. This is all part of giving the illusion of reality.

Some movies take this concept even further and use dialogue that is somewhat stylized. This is a conscious choice made to suit the world of the movie. A good example is *Glengarry Glen Ross*, which David Mamet adapted from his own play. The movie is set in a capitalist hell, the dog-eat-dog world of real estate sales, a little shady and very rough. Here, two salesmen, Roma and Moss, are tearing into each other:

>   MOSS
> And what are you, Ricky,
> huh, what are you, Bishop
> Sheean? Who the fuck are
> you, Mr. Slick . . . ? What
> are you, friend to the
> workingman? Big deal. Fuck
> you, you got the memory of a
> fuckin' fly. I never liked
> you.
>
>   ROMA
> What is this, your farewell
> speech?
>
>   MOSS
> I'm going home.
>
>   ROMA
> Your farewell to the troops?
>
>   MOSS
> I'm not going home. I'm
> going to Wisconsin.
>
>   ROMA
> Have a good trip.

The dialogue brings you right into this viper's nest of salesmen. The characters are filled with so much rage and frustration that they pummel each other with words, in a roughshod, Gatling-gun style. The longer speeches burst out from the mouths of these characters as if they were expelling pieces of their souls, be they sad or violent, full of bile or brimming with guile. The dialogue is exactly *real* for that world, if not totally realistic.

Stylized dialogue is rare, more commonly heard in theater

than film nowadays, but it has been used to good effect in movies. Probably the most frequent use is in hard-boiled dramas like *Double Indemnity*, and futuristic stories like *The Matrix*. If you try it, you'll need to do it really well, but if you can pull it off, you'll plunge the audience into a whole new world.

How Characters Talk

One of dialogue's primary functions is to reveal character. How characters speak, what they choose to talk about, how they relate to the world verbally. These things speak volumes about people— their background, personality, sensitivity to certain situations.

For me, I know, truly know, a character inside and out when their dialogue starts to come easily. When it flows. Until then, I'll write some lines that clang like a wrench in an empty bathtub. I don't worry too much about it at the beginning. Usually I'll write my way into knowing the character, and, soon enough, all will feel right with the world. It's a gorgeous moment in the process. When you come to know these characters well enough to really make them *live*, suddenly your fingers are flying across the keyboard, and the dialogue starts to sing.

A common pitfall for many writers is making all the characters sound vaguely alike. Often, this will reflect the way *you* speak. It's natural; we go with what we know. Push yourself, however, to find the specific vocabulary, rhythms, verbal quirks, and attitudes of each of your characters. The more you can differentiate between each character's way of speaking, the more distinctive they will become.

See if that isn't true in this exchange from *Die Hard* between Hans Gruber and John McClane:

                          HANS
            Mr. Mystery Guest. Are you
            still there?

                          MCCLANE
          I wouldn't think of leaving,
          Hans. Unless you want to
          open the front door . . . ?

                          HANS
          I'm afraid not. But you have
          me at a loss — you know my
          name, but who are you?
              (scornfully)
          Just another American who
          saw too many movies as a
          child. Another orphan of a
          bankrupt culture who thinks
          he's John Wayne . . .
          Rambo . . . Marshal Dillon.

                          MCCLANE
          Actually, I was always partial
          to Roy Rogers. I really dug
          those sequined shirts.

                          HANS
              (harsh)
          Do you really think you
          have a chance against us,
          Mr. Cowboy?

      A LIGHT blinks on the elevator.

                          MCCLANE
              (long pause)
          Yipee-ki-yea . . .
          motherfucker.

     These two characters are worlds apart—Hans, the urbane Eu-
ropean criminal and McClane, the shoot-from-the-hip American

cop—and they sound it. There is a formal elegance to Hans's lines, apparent in phrases such as "You have me at a loss" and the perfect condescencion of "orphan of a bankrupt culture." McClane is a guy who says "dug," manages flippancy in almost every line, and has no problem with a little vulgarity. You could cover up the names and easily detect who was speaking, something you should be able to do in your own scripts.

Take a look at this exchange from *Thelma & Louise* between two very different characters who come from the exact same background, Thelma and her husband, Darryl:

```
                   THELMA
          Hon.

                   DARRYL
          What.

                   THELMA
               (she decides not to
               tell him)
          Have a good day at work
          today.

                   DARRYL
          Uh-huh.

                   THELMA
          Hon?

                   DARRYL
          What?!

                   THELMA
          You want anything special
          for dinner?

                   DARRYL
          No, Thelma, I don't give
          a shit what we have for
```

>   dinner. I may not even make
>   it home for dinner. You know
>   how Fridays are.
>
>   THELMA
>   Funny how so many people
>   wanna buy carpet on a Friday
>   night. You'd almost think
>   they'd want to forget about
>   it for the weekend.
>
>   DARRYL
>   Well then, it's a good thing
>   you're not regional manager
>   and I am.

We can hear that Thelma is sweet, or at least cowed, by the way she says "Hon" and the way she wishes Darryl a good day and asks his preference for dinner. We can immediately hear that Darryl isn't remotely interested in Thelma from his abrupt sequence of "What—Uh-huh—What?!" If there were any doubt about Darryl being a jerk, we'd get it from his vulgar, "I don't give a shit what we have for dinner."

There is often a power dynamic in scenes, with one character establishing more dominance than the other. Darryl is obviously the dominant one here, though Thelma makes a subtle comeback with her comment about people buying "carpet on a Friday night." We know she knows he's up to no good, even though she won't say it.

We also get a sense of the backgrounds of these characters, southern and probably not too highly educated. Their speech is very colloquial and neither would be able to match Hans's elegance nor McClane's flippancy.

This brings us to the question of dialects. Do not write them phonetically, à la *Huckleberry Finn*. It's too difficult to read, and you're almost guaranteed to offend someone. Simply say in your description that the character is from the South, or Irish, or whatever designation you need, then indicate the dialect with little touches. The southernness of the characters is easily apparent in this exchange between Thelma and Louise:

```
                    LOUISE
        How come he let you go?

                    THELMA
        'Cause I didn't ask him.

                    LOUISE
        Aw, shit, Thelma, he's gonna
        kill you.
```

The small details, such as "How come ..." and "Aw, shit" and "'Cause," give just enough regional flavor to get the point across.

Another way to reveal character through dialogue is to determine how a character would play to a certain audience. I'm not speaking of the audience watching the movie, but rather the audience the character is speaking to. We all change our way of speaking according to our audience—our friends, our boss, a check-out cashier, and so on and those modulations say a lot about us. If we see a man who's normally smooth and easy suddenly become tongue-tied in front of his mother, we know there's a problem in this relationship. The woman who can't say the right thing to save her life on a date, but is the picture of poise in the boardroom? We know her confidence socially needs to come up a level.

An example from my own experience. I was traveling in Connecticut with an old friend at the wheel of my car. He was speeding, and in Connecticut that's not good. I asked him, twice, to slow down. Then, the inevitable; we got pulled over. Two state troopers ambled up to either side of the car. And my dear friend rolled down the window and said to the mirror-shaded trooper, "Hey Deputy Dawg, trying to make your fucking quota?"

Oh, dear. Bang, we're both out of the car and getting patted down as cars whiz past on I-84. Good times.

But what does it tell you about my (former) pal? Rebel. Rude. Maybe not too bright. Problems with authority. Funny guy, certainly. Maybe a little selfish (*I* wasn't speeding, and yet I was facedown on the hood alongside him). Headed for jail eventually (indeed, he was). And all of that characterization comes from *one line of dialogue.*

Subtext

Again, we look to inspiration from real life to help us with dialogue. It's a little peculiarity of human nature that we very rarely say exactly what we mean. We avoid saying exactly what we mean because we're too polite or too afraid or perhaps we don't even know the truth ourselves. Conversations in real life are exercises in detective work. The same should be true of dialogue. Whenever you have characters say exactly what they mean, it's known as writing "on the nose." Very often when writers discuss each others' scripts, you'll hear someone say, "This is much too on the nose." It's not meant as a compliment.

So you want to bring subtext to your dialogue, at least a good part of the time. To break it down: *Text* is what a character says; *subtext* is what is truly meant.

Let's illustrate with a brief exchange from *Sideways*. Miles and Jack are at the bar of a winery. Jack begins flirting with Stephanie, the pourer. When Miles shows disapproval, Stephanie attempts to shut him up with a hefty pour of wine:

```
                    JACK
          You're a bad, bad girl,
          Stephanie.

                    STEPHANIE
          I know. I need to be
          spanked.
```

What's really going on here? Simple. Jack is coming on to Stephanie, she's letting him know that she'd be up for an evening with him (and she's up for more intriguing things than the standard missionary position). They don't come right out and say these things, but the subtext is pretty clear.

Subtext achieves three crucial things: It makes the dialogue more realistic; it adds a layer of dramatic tension, tension between the spoken and unspoken; and it makes the audience an active part of the drama—they have to really listen and piece things together for themselves, as you would do if you were eavesdropping from nearby. This last reason treats the audience as if they have a little intelligence while also giving them some voyeuristic fun. The above passage would fail miserably on all three counts if it were written too on the nose, like so:

> JACK
> I'd love to sleep with you,
> Stephanie.
>
> STEPHANIE
> Okay, tiger, that could
> probably be arranged.

Of course, subtext is not always as simple as it is here between Jack and Stephanie. Later in the film, after a double date (Jack with Stephanie and Miles with Maya), they all go back to Stephanie's place. While Jack and Stephanie disappear to make whoopee in another room, Miles and Maya are left alone. They are obviously attracted to each other, but both carry romantic baggage and their courtship is fraught with awkwardness. Instead, they discuss wine.

> MAYA
> Why are you so obsessed with
> Pinot? That's all you ever
> order.

Miles smiles wistfully at the question. He searches for the answer in his glass and begins slowly.

> MILES
> I don't know. It's a hard
> grape to grow. As you
> know. It's thin-skinned,
> temperamental. It's not a
> survivor like Cabernet that
> can grow and thrive
> anywhere . . . and withstand
> neglect. Pinot's only happy
> in specific little corners
> of the world, and it needs a
> lot of doting. Only the most
> patient and faithful and
> caring growers can do it,
> can access Pinot's fragile,
> achingly beautiful qualities.
> It doesn't come to you. You
> have to come to it, see? It
> takes the right combination
> of soil and sun . . . and
> love to coax it into its
> fullest expression. Then,
> and only then, its flowers
> are the most thrilling and
> brilliant and haunting on
> the planet.

In the context of the scene, we know they're not just talking about wine. This is a wooing scene, every bit as much as the previous exchange between Jack and Stephanie, but these are two very different pairs of people and they express themselves in very different ways. With Jack and Stephanie, the subtext was close to the surface. With Miles and Maya, two highly guarded people, it's submerged a few layers.

What's really going on here? Maya asks why Miles is obsessed with Pinot not only because she's interested in this particular grape (although she is) but because she wants to know Miles better. Then Miles launches into a long passage describing his penchant for Pinot. The speech is a mixture of various subtextual messages, no less complex than a bottle of superior wine. Really, Miles is telling Maya about himself, confessing that he is a difficult person. He's not happy-go-lucky like Jack, but under the right conditions he's a person very much worth knowing. He's actually making a case for those of us whose true potential isn't always easy to see. And by making such a painfully honest disclosure, he is showing Maya that he hopes she will understand and be that person who allows him to blossom.

Maya has invited intimacy, and Miles has reciprocated. And they have talked about nothing but wine. It's a breathtaking moment of drama.

As previously mentioned, generally it's best to keep your dialogue lines short and to the point. Every now and then, however, a long speech is right for the moment. Speeches should work like an aria in opera, a passionate expression that cannot be contained in a mere few words. Save your arias for those moments when your characters are bursting with emotion, and then make the dialogue worthy of those emotions. The Pinot speech is a wonderful aria, a high point of the movie.

In the two examples from *Sideways*, the characters are sort of saying what they mean, their words just dancing around the meaning a bit. For example, by simply changing a few words in Miles's speech, you could have him talking directly about himself. Other times, though, the text will have no direct relationship to the subtext.

That's how it happens in this passage from *Thelma & Louise*. When Louise and Jimmy go off to their motel room in Oklahoma City, Thelma is left alone in her room. There is a knock at the

door from J. D., the studly hitchhiker they dropped off a short
while ago.

Thelma opens the door and there stands J. D.,
soaking wet from the rain pouring down behind him.

> J. D.
> I just thought I . . . I
> know I'm supposed to be
> gone, but . . .

He's kind of looking over toward the road. He's
still slightly shy.

> J. D. (CONT'D)
> I'm not having much luck
> getting a ride.

He notices, looking past her into the room, that
Louise isn't there. Thelma just stands there looking at him.

> J. D. (CONT'D)
> Well, I guess I better . . .

> THELMA
> Wait . . . ! Um, where ya
> going?

> J. D.
> I don't know. Nothin'. What
> are you doin'?

The whole concern of his getting a ride, or where he may be going, isn't of any consequence at all. Those are just filler words because neither one of them wants to come right out and say what's
really on their minds. In truth, J. D. wants to be invited in but he's
playing polite, feeling out the situation. Thelma wants to invite

him in, only she's just a teeny bit reluctant, never having done anything like this before. All kinds of things are flittering around beneath the hemming and hawing.

And there are times when the text is completely the opposite
from the subtext. As the law starts closing in on Thelma and
Louise, the two women begin to sense there is no easy way out for
them. Since they are dead set against going to prison, they know
they will probably die. But instead of talking about their immi-
nent demise, they try to buck up each other's courage with a
pleasant pipe dream. Here's what they say while drivin' down that
road.

                    LOUISE
          We'll be drinkin' margaritas
          by the sea, Mamasita.

                    THELMA
          We can change our names.

                    LOUISE
          We can live in a hacienda.

                    THELMA
          I wanna get a job. I wanna
          work at Club Med.

                    LOUISE
          Yes! Yes! Now what kind of
          deal do you think that cop
          can come up with to beat
          that?

                    THELMA
          It'd have to be pretty good.

                    LOUISE
          It would have to be pretty
          damn good.

The scene is incredibly poignant because we know they know the truth but they can't bear to let their minds dwell on it. So they discuss something as far removed from death as possible, drinking margaritas by the sea. It becomes even more heartbreaking because when they talk of haciendas and changing their names we feel their intense desire to be free, acting independently for the first time in their lives, and now that they have begun to achieve this desire, they will not be given the chance to let it play out. And yet, neither one crumbles and cries. With these words, we see they are choosing to face their destiny with bravery and good cheer.

Most of the time, characters are aware of their own subtext. They may or may not be thinking to themselves that they're speaking with double meaning, but they have a general sense of what they're doing. There are exceptions, however, where a character is not aware of the double meaning. For example, a junkie who states, "I'm not an addict," may be in denial about his addiction. When Miles discusses the wonders of Pinot, he probably didn't set out to talk about himself; it was probably just a matter of his subconscious desires emerging through his words.

Subtext is one of the keys to great dialogue. Examine every line of dialogue you write to see if you can make it less on the nose. You'll find that in almost every case, the dialogue will improve with a little subtext. You're walking a tight line, of course. You have to make the subtext clear enough so the audience can understand what's going on, but you don't want to make it so obvious they feel insulted. Usually, the context alone will do it, but sometimes physical clues will help, as you're about to see. And don't worry about whether the actors will get it. Actors live for subtext, which allows them to act, rather than parrot overwritten dialogue.

Physical Accompaniment

Dialogue should not go unaccompanied. Characters do things before, during, and after they speak. You don't want to go overboard, directing every move the characters make, but you should pay attention to the physical action that goes with dialogue. Choose these actions as carefully as you choose the dialogue; they speak just as loudly, often more so. In fact, whenever you can convey something through action instead of words, do that, as it makes things more visual.

Look at this passage from *Tootsie*. Les, a regular guy with a farm, falls for Dorothy and proposes to her, with a ring and all. Then Les, poor man, discovers along with the rest of the world that Dorothy is really Michael Dorsey. At the end of the movie, Michael shows up at the bar that Les frequents, hoping to make amends. Here's what happens:

```
Les enters, takes his usual place at the bar.
CAMERA PANS to see Michael rise from a table
and move to a stool next to Les. Les turns back to
him. They stare at one another a beat, then Les
turns back to the TV. Michael reaches into his
pocket and puts the ring box on the bar; pushes
it toward Les, who does not take his eyes off
the TV.

                    LES
               (sotto)
          Get that off the bar, or
          I'll break your hand.

                    MICHAEL
          I thought you'd want it
          back.

                    LES
               (side of mouth)
          Outside. Give it to me
          outside.

Michael puts the box away.
```

The opening actions substitute for dialogue, brilliantly at that. We don't need Michael explaining who he is to Les; it's better to let these two men wordlessly stare at each other. And we don't need Michael explaining why he's returning the ring; it's obvious enough that marriage is out of the question, and it's funnier for Michael to simply set the ring on the bar. And then the ring becomes a great source of tension for Les because he's sitting in this very macho bar getting an engagement ring returned from a man, which launches us into the humorous exchange that follows. You could do this scene without the actions around the ring, but it wouldn't be nearly as visual, or as good.

Remember, also, that we all speak through body language and nonverbal clues. And here's the kicker, a lot of times, our physical language is far more revealing than what we say. It can even contradict what we are saying. Think of a charged situation; for example, asking someone out for a date when you have no idea if he or she is interested in you. What if it were to play something like this:

```
                    MAURICE
          Would you like to have
          dinner with me one evening?

                    SHEILA
               (not looking up from
               her book)
          Uh, sure, Maurice . . .
          Dinner might be nice.
```

Ouch. The truth here is pretty obvious. Look for those times when physical language can help bring subtext to the fore, and you will have a potent dramatic moment, rather than a limp line of dialogue.

Here's another situation. A woman has had a little too much to drink, gets sick in the parking lot of a bar. A man attends to her and makes a somewhat drunken compliment to her, even after she's puked. Nothing really bad, right? Now take a look at this moment from *Thelma & Louise:*

```
Thelma has been sick. She has Harlan's handker-
chief and is wiping her mouth. Harlan has backed
off for this part, but he's right back in there.

                    HARLAN
          How ya feelin' now, darlin'?

Harlan is leaning close to Thelma's head, and she
pulls her head away.

                    THELMA
          I guess I'm startin' to feel
          a little better.

                    HARLAN
          Yeah, you're starting to
          feel pretty good to me, too.

He pulls her to him and tries to put his arms
around her. Thelma pulls away.
```

When I read this script—forget seeing the film itself—I knew there was trouble on the way. My tension shot up, even though the dialogue, on the surface, is unthreatening. Here the physical accompaniment is perfectly played. First, Thelma's actions put her in a vulnerable position, throwing up in a honky-tonk parking lot. She is sick and practically helpless. Then check out Harlan's actions: "Harlan has backed off for this part, but he's right back in there" and "Harlan is leaning close." You immediately sense that this guy is invading her space, at the worst possible time. There's evil on his mind. We can see that Thelma senses the danger, too, because she "pulls away" twice, trying to get clear from Harlan. Also notice how the meaning of the action finally merges with Harlan's words, "Yeah, you're starting to feel pretty good to me, too." If Harlan had sneered, put his bad-guy voice on, and stated his intention flat out from the start, the moment wouldn't give us that same horrible sensation in the pit of the stomach.

We respond to physical actions and physical language in ways that we don't always feel through verbal communication. These feelings are often deeper, truer, more visceral. Keep this in mind. Seek out physical accompaniment that will support and expand on the meaning of your dialogue in every scene, and you'll go even further on your way to making every word count.

Exposition

Simply put, exposition is dialogue designed to give the audience information about plot, character, conflict, or backstory. But there's another kind of exposition: the moment when good movies can go bad. Here's the problem with exposition. It's necessary, because there's always information the audience must know. All too often though, it's handled badly.

My favorite example is when the archvillain explains his plan for world destruction to the hero, right before killing him. Silly as it is, you still see this in certain popcorn flicks. Of course, it's there for a reason. They need to set the stage, explain the situation, give the hero a chance to escape. We roll our eyes and forgive it, because it's a summer film and the air conditioning feels good. But all too often, even in films that should know better, exposition comes too on the nose. It's boring, stupid, and not believable.

So, how to keep exposition from killing your screenplay? The first and best advice: Use visuals. If it's possible to replace expositional dialogue with something visual, go for the visual. The visual will convey the information faster and more effectively. Let's say you've written a long dialogue passage in which a character explains that he hates his job as a traffic cop. Drop it. Simply show something like this:

> Frederico stands in the middle of the street,
> looking hot and miserable in his uniform. As he
> holds a line of cars at bay, he is answered with a
> symphony of dissatisfaction from the drivers, who
> honk and hurl verbal abuse. Frederico flips the
> finger at a driver.

We get it just fine, better than with the dialogue.

But visuals won't always work. You'll need dialogue at times. When you do, choose your situations well. Give only as much exposition as is necessary and select the right time for it. Remember *The Matrix*? For the entire first act, the movie teases us with mention of the Matrix without really explaining what it is, all the while making us very curious with unbelievably cool visuals. By the time we meet Morpheus, *we* are ready to take the red pill 'cause we're so damn eager to find out what the deal is with this Matrix.

How about a subtler example? An important aspect of Miles's struggle in *Sideways* is that he's clinging to memories of his ex-wife. We need to know about his marriage, but the exposition is carefully parceled out over the course of the film. First we get to know Miles a bit, growing curious about him, but we know nothing about his marital status. A little ways in, our first hint comes at his mom's house, when he looks at his wedding picture—visual exposition. We now know that Miles is, or was, married. In the next scene, his mom asks:

>   PHYLLIS
>   Miles, when are you going to
>   get married again?
>
>   MILES
>   Mom, I just got divorced.

We now know he was recently divorced. But we don't know how he feels about it until forty minutes into the film, when he and Jack are talking on a hillside in lovely wine country.

                        MILES
          Victoria and I used to like
          this view.
                (lost in nostalgia)
          Once we had a picnic here and
          drank a '95 Opus One. With
          smoked salmon and artichokes,
          but we didn't care.

                        JACK
          Miles.

                        MILES
          She has the best palate of
          any woman I've ever known.
          She could even differentiate
          Italian wines.

                        JACK
          Miles, I gotta tell you
          something. Victoria's coming
          to the wedding.

                        MILES
          I know. You told me. I'm
          okay with it.

                        JACK
          Yeah, but that's not the
          whole story. She got
          remarried.

                        MILES
          She what?
                (long pause)
          When?

Now we know everything—Miles is still stuck on her, she's re-married, and this is devastating news to him. The writers could have laid out all this exposition earlier in the film, but they wait until we care about Miles, until we're actually interested in his deepest pain. There is also the bonus of turning the revelation into an especially dramatic moment, soon followed the wonderful visual of Miles racing through a vineyard swigging desperately from a bottle.

Not only do you need to find the right amount of exposition and the right moment for it, but you need to find a way to sneak it into the dialogue, so we get what we need in the midst of what feels like a realistic conversation. Many a screenwriter has gone quietly mad trying to accomplish this feat. So let me give you a few strategies to help keep you out of the padded room.

Strategy #1: Often the quickest and clearest way is to have your character talk to someone with whom he or she isn't familiar. Your character will have to connect the dots simply because the stranger doesn't have any prior knowledge of the character's life. There's a pitfall here, though. If there's no plausible reason for the conversation, you'll get what I call the "bartender scene." You know, the scene where a character pours out his or her soul to a bartender or waiter or whatever. There's no real reason for the character to do this, and the bartender is of no importance to the story. It feels fake.

Early in *Die Hard*, there is a talk-to-a-stranger encounter that manages to avoid feeling like a "bartender" scene. McClane gets picked up at the airport by a limo driver named Argyle who starts asking questions.

ARGYLE
So, you divorced or what?

MCCLANE
She had a good job, it
turned into a great career.

> ARGYLE
> But meant her moving here.
>
> MCCLANE
> Closer to Japan. You're fast.
>
> ARGYLE
> So, why didn't you come?
>
> MCCLANE
> 'Cause I'm a New York cop
> who used to be a New York
> kid, and I got six months'
> backlog of New York scumbags
> I'm still trying to put
> behind bars. I don't just
> get up and move.
>
> ARGYLE
>   (to the point)
> You mean you thought she
> wouldn't make it out here
> and she'd come crawling on
> back, so why bother to pack?
>
> MCCLANE
> Like I said, Argyle . . .
> you're fast.

We get plenty of necessary backstory on McClane and his wife without feeling manipulated. Why? Argyle is set up as a bit of a Chatty Cathy, and McClane is so out of his element in this limo that he sits up front. So, they are practically forced to talk and the conversation leads naturally enough to the reason McClane has come to L.A. The whole scene feels perfectly natural.

Strategy #2: Place exposition in the midst of a heated exchange between characters. Exposition doesn't mean we need to take time

out from drama. Make it dramatic. People are more likely to over-
state things in heated encounters, giving us more information,
and the highly charged atmosphere will disguise the fact that
you're sneaking exposition into the mix.

Look at this scene from *Tootsie*, where Michael charges into the
office of his agent, George, demanding to know why he didn't get
an audition for a certain part. Michael is angry, pushing his agent
to exasperation.

>   MICHAEL
>   I bust my ass to get a part
>   right!
>
>   GEORGE
>   Yes, but you bust everyone's
>   else's ass too. A guy's got
>   four weeks to put on a play —
>   he doesn't want to argue
>   about whether Tolstoy can
>   walk if he's dying.
>
>   MICHAEL
>   The guy was an idiot. That
>   was 2 years ago.
>
>   GEORGE
>   They can't all be idiots.
>   That's the last time you
>   worked! You argue with
>   everyone. You've got one of
>   the worst reputations in
>   town. Nobody will touch
>   you.
>
>   MICHAEL
>   Wait a minute now . . . what
>   are you saying? That nobody

```
                    in New York will work
                    with me?

                         GEORGE
                    No. That's too limiting. How
                    about no one in Hollywood
                    will work with you either. I
                    can't even send you up for
                    a commercial. You played a
                    tomato for 30 seconds and
                    they went a half day over
                    because you wouldn't sit
                    down!

                         MICHAEL
                    It wasn't logical.

                         GEORGE
                    You were a tomato! A tomato
                    doesn't have logic! A tomato
                    can't move!

                         MICHAEL
                    That's what I said! So if a
                    tomato can't move, how can
                    it sit down? I was a great
                    tomato! I was a stand-up
                    tomato!
```

There is a busload of exposition in there and it's almost all on the nose. It works, though, because the situation is rife with conflict, not to mention devastatingly funny. You might also notice how effectively triggers are used to shoot the scene forward. Not everyone would get upset about being told to move as a tomato, but everyone isn't Michael Dorsey. (Also notice how this dialogue just jumps off the page at you. Great dialogue will do that. Readers will forget they are looking at a sheet of paper and will start seeing the scene, hearing the voices.)

I have to be honest, though. You can't always have characters exposing their lives to strangers and you can't always disguise exposition with a heated scene. Most of the time, you need to bite the bullet and get information across in a conversation between people who know each other and are acting rationally. This is toughest way to do it, but it must be done. Which brings us to . . .

Strategy #3: Crafty planning. We have our close companions with whom we talk about our lives, our histories, our jobs. But those conversations, rendered realistically, are next to useless for exposition. For example, earlier today, I had this very conversation with a good friend:

><pre>   FRIEND
   Done?

            ME
   Eh. No.

            FRIEND
   Man, you're slow.

            ME
   Alex called twice. I don't
   need you on me, too.
</pre>

Do you know what's going on? Of course not. That shorthand exchange is actually about this very chapter you're reading, which was a little . . . (ahem) late . . . to my editor, Alex. Now, for you to know that, I'd have to add more information. But I can't add too much, or we get something like this terrible exchange:

><pre>   FRIEND
   Are you done yet with that
   chapter you're writing for
</pre>

```
               the Gotham screenwriting
               book? You know, the one
               you're three weeks late
               turning in?

                         ME
               No. I'm not done, and I'm
               feeling very frustrated.

                         HIM
               You should be frustrated.
               It's terrible that it's
               taken you so long. You're a
               slow writer.

                         ME
               Don't insult me. I have
               enough problems. The editor
               of the book, Alex, has
               called twice asking for the
               chapter. I think he's
               getting annoyed with me.
```

What's the problem here (besides my missed deadline)? This is a conversation between two people who know each other, and all the extra information is completely out of place. We wouldn't have to explain it to each other. The dialogue feels false.

So, find a balance. Give just enough clues to let the audience in on things while still keeping the dialogue natural. When dialogue is done well, the audience will feel like they're flies on the wall but they'll also gain insight into the situation. Here's my third and best attempt at the scene:

```
Michael sits at his desk, looking at the empty
computer screen like it's his enemy. Next to him:
a typewritten sheaf of papers and a sheet with the
```

    heading GOTHAM SCREENWRITING BOOK: WRITER'S GUIDE-
    LINES.

    Michael's friend wanders into the room.

                    FRIEND
            Done?

                    MICHAEL
            Ehh. No, dammit.

                    FRIEND
            Come on, man, it's *one*
            chapter.

                    MICHAEL
            Don't start. Alex has
            already called twice.

                    FRIEND
            What are you late now, three
            weeks? If *I* were your
            editor, I'd kill you.

This version manages to reveal everything—what I'm working on, how late I am, my frustration, who Alex is and how he feels about me at the moment. And I daresay, it doesn't feel too forced. You'll also notice that I assisted my dialogue with some visual exposition—the papers on the desk. I never said you can't combine visuals and dialogue for exposition, did I?

Voice-Over

Lastly, we come to *voice-over*, known in the trade as V.O. Voice-over happens when a character speaks words of narration that are heard over the images shown on screen. Usually the character is speaking from another time and place than that being shown.

Most movies don't employ voice-over, and they shouldn't. Voice-over violates the rule of "show, don't tell," often turning a film experience into something more appropriate to the experience of a novel. Voice-over is a point of contention for many. There are knowledgeable people who say you should *never* use it. But I'm not much one for absolutes, save for the all-important "never use the toaster while in the shower." Voice-over can be an effective device if used for the right reasons.

But there are bad reasons. The worst is the one most commonly used by amateurs. Voice-over should never be used solely for the purpose of getting across exposition. It's tempting, I know. It's such an easy way to slip that exposition in quickly and cleanly. But this will slow the movie down for viewers, and it'll show readers you don't know the art of screenwriting. If there is any way for you to replace the V.O. with some other kind of exposition—verbal or visual—you should do it. V.O. should only be used if it enhances the movie in some other way, aside from exposition.

The simplest and most acceptable way to use V.O. is as a kind of prologue (narration only at the beginning) or as a framing device (narration used only at the beginning and end). You'll see V.O. used in these ways in such films as *Field of Dreams, American Beauty*, and *A River Runs Through It.* It can be a nice little touch that doesn't interfere with the bulk of the movie.

If you're going to sprinkle V.O. throughout the entire movie, as it was in such films as *Forrest Gump, Apocalypse Now*, and *Fight Club*, you need to have a compelling reason for doing so. What might these compelling reasons be? Here's a list:

- To bridge time
- To lend a literary or poetic touch
- To reveal interior thought
- Some other interesting reason

The Shawshank Redemption boldly breaks the V.O. rule, letting Red speak in voice-over abundantly throughout the entire movie. Whole pages are nothing but V.O. But there is a method to the V.O. madness; in fact, *Shawshank* has all of the reasons listed above. The film spans almost twenty years and often Red is simply helping us move through time. Also, there is certainly a poetic flavor to the V.O. And Red is revealing his inner thoughts, saying things he'd never voice to other guys in the prison. (It's not usually okay to do this, but it becomes more acceptable if coupled with some other reason.) Finally, Red is telling the story of Andy Dufresne, and the story is intended to have the flavor of a tall tale, even a myth. It's the latter reason that gives *The Shawshank Redemption* its own distinctive aura, and the V.O. is a big part of it.

Look at this voice-over passage from *Shawshank*—the scene where Andy arranges for the guys working on the roof to get some cold beer—and see if you can pick up how Red turns this tale of humdrum prison life into something mythic.

```
EXT. LICENSE PLATE FACTORY - DAY

As before, an object is hauled up the side of the
building by rope - only this time, it's a cooler
of beer and ice.

                    RED (V.O.)
              And that's how it came to
              pass,that on the second-to-
              last day of the job, the
              convict crew that tarred the
              plate factory roof in the
              spring of '49 . . .

EXT. ROOF - SHORTLY LATER

The   cons   are   taking   the   sun   and   drinking
beer.
```

                              RED (V.O.)
                    . . . wound up sitting in a
                    row at ten o'clock in the
                    morning, drinking icy cold
                    Black Label beer courtesy of
                    the hardest screw that ever
                    walked a turn at Shawshank
                    State Prison.

                              HADLEY
                    Drink up, boys. While it's
                    cold.

                              RED (V.O.)
                    The colossal prick even
                    managed to sound magnanimous.

Red knocks back another sip, enjoying the bitter
cold on his tongue and the warm sun on his face.

                              RED (V.O.) (CONT'D)
                    We sat and drank with the
                    sun on our shoulders, and
                    felt like free men. We
                    could'a been tarring the
                    roof of one of our own
                    houses. We were the Lords of
                    all Creation.

In addition to everything else it's doing, this is still good dialogue. Natural yet compressed, married perfectly to the visuals,
and every word counts.

Stepping-Stone: Subtext in Dialogue

Pick a scene that will appear in your movie, one with strong tension between two characters. Write the scene using dialogue that is on the nose. Then write the scene again, this time keeping the entire conversation in subtext; the characters should never touch on the real issue at hand. (If you're stumped on how to do this, keep the conversation on the subject of either pets or punctuation.) Then write the scene a third time, keeping the subtext but also letting the real issue rise to the surface where appropriate. Feel free to sprinkle in revealing physical actions.

CHAPTER 7

Subplots: A Side of Story

BY HELEN KAPLAN

Crimes and Misdemeanors (written and directed by Woody Allen) tells the story of Judah Rosenthal, a successful New York ophthalmologist and pillar of the community who is trying to end an affair with his mistress. When she threatens to expose him, Judah panics. Judah's rabbi advises him to confess to his wife, but there's an easier solution, and it's just a phone call away. After some soul searching, Judah calls his brother, a man with mob connections who arranges to make the mistress "disappear." Judah walks away a free and peaceful man. This is the crime of the film.

Running alongside the main storyline is a comic subplot about Cliff Stern, a filmmaker who makes "meaningful" documentaries no one wants to watch. Cliff's wife pressures him to make a film about her brother Lester, a wildly successful, womanizing TV producer. But when Cliff turns the documentary into a mockumentary, intercutting images of Lester with Mussolini and a talking horse, Cliff is promptly fired. Cliff also tries to woo Halley, a producer on the documentary, and this adulterous yearning is the misdemeanor of the film. But it's Lester who winds up marrying Halley, leaving Cliff tortured and miserable.

Crimes and Misdemeanors is an incredibly rich film largely because of its subplot, which brings comedy to an otherwise heavy story, and adds shades of gray to what could have been a black-and-white morality tale. The tragedy ends happily and the comedy concludes sadly, leaving us to ponder why these events resolve as they do. The juxtaposition between these two storylines gives this movie its resonance and is what haunts us long after we've left the theater.

Subplots are the side dishes, the seasonings and spice that perfectly complement the main dish. Imagine a burger without fries. Or eating sushi without wasabi, soy sauce, and ginger. And that's how it goes with subplots; they add dashes of dimension and diversity that give a film its ineffable kick.

With arms outstretched, Hampton Fancher, who wrote *Blade Runner*, told my graduate-level screenwriting class that the most commonly given note in Hollywood is "Open it up!" Hampton, being Hampton, added that the producers didn't know what they were talking about, or how a writer would possibly do that. When he pressed them, they would prattle, "Make my movie bigger, better, bolder, the themes more resonant, the characters more complex." "Here's what they were really trying to say," Hampton told us. "Work on the subplots."

Subplot Defined

So what is a subplot? A subplot is a storyline that is somewhat separated from the main action. If your main plot—the protagonist's quest to achieve his or her goal—is the superhighway, then subplots are the scenic byways, the side roads. They typically intersect the main plot at some point, but they can also wend their own way.

Here's how to tell if something is a true subplot: If you can remove most or all of it from the movie and still leave the basic story intact, it's a subplot. Here's how to tell if something is a *good* subplot: If you were to remove most or all of it from the movie, the movie wouldn't be nearly as memorable. Look, for example, at John McClane's friendship with the patrol cop, Powell, in *Die Hard*. Powell serves the plot, briefly, by calling in the police when the body falls on his car. But McClane's CB radio friendship with Powell is a subplot that you could cut and still be left with *Die Hard. Die Hard,* however, wouldn't be nearly as strong without it.

Though subplots are somewhat separate from the main plot, they shouldn't career off to a parallel universe. They are not there to tell a separate story, but to *enhance* the main story. They usually accomplish this in one or more of the following ways:

- Character: Develop a protagonist and/or a secondary character

- Plot: Intersect and influence the main storyline

- Theme: Underscore the movie's theme

The best subplots connect to the main plot in all three regards—character, plot, and theme. The more a subplot meshes with the story, the more the movie feels like Aristotle's "organic whole," (which we mentioned in chapter 2). By reinforcing character/plot/theme, subplots give films more dimension. And subplots offer diversity by providing a detour from the hero's journey, letting us experience some new scenery along the way.

There are no absolutes for plotting a movie, and the rules for subplots are even looser. But most films have one to three subplots, and that's not a bad number to aim for. Some films have more, as you'll see with *Tootsie* and *Die Hard,* and others have no true subplots. Subplots come in all shapes and sizes. A rare few are so big that they almost rival the main storyline, such as Cliff's subplot in *Crimes and Misdemeanors.* Others are so small that they function more as motifs, like the tongue-wagging truck driver in *Thelma & Louise.* Most fall somewhere in between. With subplots it all depends on the specific needs and whims of your story.

Since subplots are interwoven with the main plot, it can be difficult to tell what's a true subplot and what isn't. The lines can blur.

Like most things related to screenwriting, this is not a science. But it's helpful to identify subplots in order to understand how they work to enhance the story. In that spirit, let us look at the three most common types.

Romantic Subplots

Romantic subplots are by far the most prevalent and you'll find them in movies as diverse as *Blade Runner, Chinatown, Erin Brockovich, Fargo, North by Northwest, Rocky,* and *You Can Count on Me.* If your main story isn't a love story, a romantic subplot is one of the best ways to show another side of your protagonist. After all, stealing a peek at someone's romantic life can be quite revealing.

In *Die Hard*, we watch John McClane run barefoot through shattered glass, crawl through ventilation ducts, and jump from an exploding skyscraper while tethered to a fire hose. While the thrills are the main attraction, the subplots add layers of dimension, raising *Die Hard* to the top of its genre. The major subplot is McClane's strained marriage with Holly. Through this relationship, we see McClane's vulnerability and flaws, revealing that he's much more than a muscular man of action. He's a New York cop whose career has always come first, so much so that when his wife gets a high-paying corporate job promotion that takes her to the West Coast, he doesn't make the move with her. He even seems to resent her success. McClane's a bit of a chauvinist—but not completely. Six months after Holly's move, he flies to L.A. to make amends and see his kids for Christmas. Apparently, he regrets not fully supporting Holly's career, but he's not completely contrite, and he and Holly keep fighting about the same old things. This part of the subplot unfolds early and develops McClane so deftly that by the time Hans and his posse of international terrorists invade the building, we feel we know John McClane and we're invested in his hope for a reconciliation with Holly.

Relationships are an excellent way to chart characters' transformations, showing how they change, or refuse to change. At McClane's nadir, when he thinks his number is up, he's finally able to apologize to Holly. He participates in a type of last rites and asks Powell to pass on a message to his wife. "She's heard me say I love you thousand times. She never heard me say I'm sorry. I want you to tell her that, Al. I want you tell her, John said that he was sorry." This, of course, makes us care about him more than ever.

The Holly subplot also relates to the movie's theme, which deals with the triumph of the underdog. McClane is a regular Joe, a fact highlighted when he's thrust into the decadence, flash, and conspicuous consumption of Holly's new world, the Nakatomi Corporation. It all rubs McClane the wrong way—Holly reverting to her maiden name, the Rolex the company gave her, and Ellis, the coke-snorting hustler who seems eager to move in on Holly.

The Holly subplot intersects with the main plot at both the beginning and end of the film. It's Holly's job that brings McClane to the building in the first place. As soon as the terrorists strike, McClane and Holly are separated for a long time, but one of the strengths of this movie is that McClane is not just fighting the terrorists, he's fighting for a chance to reunite with Holly. Holly reenters the main plot when Hans Gruber realizes that she is McClane's wife and takes her as a personal hostage. Here the stakes for McClane are dramatically increased: he's literally fighting for Holly. What makes the climax especially hair-raising is that as Hans starts to fall forty stories to his death, he grabs Holly's watch band. Either he'll use Holly to save himself or drag her down with him. McClane releases the latch on Holly's Rolex, a symbol of the career move that threatened their marriage, Hans falls away, and Holly is saved.

One could argue that this is an antifeminist message. Don't worry, we'll counter that now with *Thelma & Louise*. Here, both characters have a romantic subplot. Louise has her relationship with Jimmy, and Thelma has her fling with J. D.

Jimmy intersects with the plot because he provides the money Thelma and Louise need for their escape. But mostly he's there to reveal another side of Louise, to give us a window into her closely guarded soul. Louise has a no-nonsense exterior and likes to have things lined up, just so. But with Jimmy, she drops her defenses, revealing a tenderness and vulnerability. We learn that she has longed for a more permanent relationship with Jimmy, and when she meets him in Oklahoma City, we see her let go of that dream, partly due to circumstances, but also because she realizes it could never work. We also see how deeply she loves Jimmy when she refuses to let him get involved in her crimes.

Similarly, J. D. helps to develop Thelma. Her instantaneous interest in J. D. signals that she's finally done worrying about her dud of a husband, Darryl. And after a night in bed with J. D. she finally learns "what all the fuss is about." She is opened up, sexually and otherwise. For the first time, she's ready to take the reins in her life.

The J. D. subplot intersects the main plot in two significant ways. First, J. D. steals their money, the loss of which prompts Thelma to hold up the convenience store, borrowing J. D.'s "gentlemanly" approach to armed robbery. Of course, this puts Thelma and Louise on everyone's radar, making it impossible for them to cross the border stealthily. But that's not the end of their troubles with J. D. because he tells the authorities that Thelma and Louise are headed to Mexico. As Louise says, "Right now we have only two things goin' for us. One, nobody knows where we are. And two, nobody knows where we're going. Now, one of our things that was going for us is gone!" So the J. D. subplot radically affects the main story, placing Thelma and Louise on an inevitable path to their end.

Thematically, *Thelma & Louise* deals with two women rebelling against a male-dominated world, where many of the men treat women poorly. Both Jimmy and J. D. do their share to support this view. Although Jimmy seems like a nice guy, he's not ready to step

up to the plate with Louise in a meaningful way. In fact, he wants
to be with her only when she's running away from him. Though
J. D. certainly has his charms, he's a liar and a thief.

   Tootsie masterfully incorporates four subplots, all of them
romantic: 1) Michael/Sandy, 2) Dorothy/Julie/Ron, 3) Dorothy/
Les, and 4) Dorothy/Van Horn. *Tootsie* is really a tale of juggling
two lives, and these romantic subplots give Michael plenty of balls
to keep up in the air. Because each subplot stems from Michael's
masquerade, you could argue that the subplots are a necessary
part of the main plot. But let's call them subplots anyway. You
could cut any one of them and still tell the story of Michael trying
to pull off this charade, but if you cut *all* of them, you would lose
the fun of juggling.

   Thematically, *Tootsie* deals with the relationship between the
sexes, and each of these subplots offers an insight into that theme.
There are the men who treat women badly (Michael, Ron, Van
Horn), the women who put up with them (Sandy, Julie), and two
people who have a wiser view of things (Les, Dorothy).

   The subplots also help to flesh out Michael's personality. We see
how denigrating he is to women by how he treats Sandy. As her
friend, he is caring and attentive, but once he sleeps with her, he
treats her badly; he lies to her, doesn't return her phone calls,
shows up hours late for their dates, and he even re-gifts a box of
chocolates to her (with a love note from someone else attached).
Michael gets a good look at himself when he's Dorothy, recogniz-
ing his own bad behavior in Ron and Van Horn. John Van Horn,
AKA "the tongue," spritzes his breath freshener a bit too enthusias-
tically as he gears up for his first screen kiss with Dorothy. Ron
whistles at Julie like a dog, cheats on her, and treats her with general condescension. These things are not lost on Dorothy, though
Michael might have been oblivious. Through Les, Michael learns
how to treat a woman well (even if that woman is really a man).
When Les confesses to Dorothy that being with someone is what
life is all about, Michael sees the point.

   Sandy and Julie both intersect the plot in significant ways. If

Sandy hadn't been turned down for the role of the hospital administrator on *Southwest General*, Michael would never have dressed in drag and auditioned for the role himself. When Julie and Dorothy almost kiss, showing Michael that he may have a chance with her as a man, Julie becomes *the* major obstacle to maintaining the masquerade because Michael wants her so badly.

The Julie subplot is an especially large one, so important that it walks the line between being considered a subplot and the main plot. However, it stands apart from the main plot in tone, adding a contrasting flavor to the mix. There's something wistful about Julie, and her presence lends a note of seriousness to the farce, giving the movie a deeper emotional range.

Through Julie, we chart Michael's progression. At first, Michael is just drawn to Julie sexually. As Dorothy, though, he becomes a true friend to her, and when Julie confides in him, he learns how men can really muck with women's self esteem. And if Michael is given a chance with Julie, we sense that he will treat her much better than Ron did, or how the old Michael would have done. He has literally walked in a woman's shoes and learned that it's not much fun being called Tootsie.

Friend and Foe Subplots

If a protagonist isn't a complete hermit or castaway on an island, he or she is likely to have a friend, or an enemy, who can be a source of a subplot. We learn a lot about people from how they interact with their friends and foes.

In *Die Hard* the Powell subplot intersects with the main plot when Powell checks out the building and a body drops onto his car. After he radios in what has happened, his work is done and he's no longer critical to the plot. Powell remains in the movie, however, because he has something unique to offer McClane— friendship, albeit via CB. Without Powell, we wouldn't feel nearly as close to McClane or understand his transformation. Powell also helps to underscore the underdog theme. He's a regular cop, like McClane, not one of the brass. So when he tells Mc-Clane how he and the other regular cops are emotionally supporting him, it means a lot to McClane. Notice also that Powell is more than just a buddy prop. He's a fully dimensional character with problems of his own; In particular, he's haunted by his having mistakenly shot a child. He, too, gets his moment of redemption in the end.

Argyle, another ally of McClane, is a smaller ally subplot, and he's there mostly for comic relief. It's a tense movie, and we need a few laughs along the way. But notice how he still connects on all three fronts. He helps with character by giving McClane someone to talk to on his ride into the city; he gets his plot moment when he crashes his limo into the terrrorists' escape vehicle; and he, too, nicely underscores the underdog theme.

In *The Shawshank Redemption*, Andy has three key friendships—Brooks, Red, and Tommy. Since Brooks and Red fall into our next category, we'll get to them later. But Tommy works purely as a friend subplot. He develops Andy by showing us Andy's fatherly side when he helps Tommy earn his high school equivalency. Tommy intersects with the plot in a major way, when it turns out he can prove Andy's innocence, and Andy is given real hope of being freed legally. When that hope is extinguished by Tommy's murder, Andy's despair spurs him to attempt his dangerous escape. This is a good example of how the outcome of a subplot can have a profound impact on the protagonist.

Adversaries can also be used in subplots when their storylines are distinct from the main plot. This is the case with Karl in *Die Hard*. Certainly, he's part of the terrorist posse, but Karl has his own issues with McClane. Specifically, he wants to avenge his brother's death, which is separate and apart from the terrorists' mission. So his "blood for blood" drama acts as a kind of subplot. Although Karl doesn't have much effect on the characters, plot, or theme of the film, his desire for revenge does increase the testosterone level of the fighting, making it especially brutal and elemental. In a movie like this, that's a good enough reason.

The tongue-wagging truck driver in *Thelma & Louise* also falls into the adversary camp. It's such a small subplot that it's almost more of a motif, like a recurring musical phrase. While the truck driver has no bearing on the plot as a whole, he helps chart Thelma and Louise's transformation. At first, they endure his taunts, such as when he offers to lick them all over. But later in the film, when they've grown bolder, they teach him a lesson. Thelma and Louise will never be able to exact their revenge on the whole world, but it's highly satisfying to see them give this one disgusting man his comeuppance. The truck driver underscores the theme because he represents what Thelma and Louise are rebelling against—men at their basest level. This subplot also provides a comic interlude before the film's very serious finale.

Non-Protagonist Subplots

Subplots typically involve the protagonist, but they can also center around secondary characters, letting us follow the secondary character on a journey that may not directly involve the protagonist. This kind of subplot is rare and it risks stealing focus from the protagonist, but it is sometimes the right choice. Secondary-character subplots are often used to illustrate theme. In *Crimes and Misdemeanors*, for example, Cliff's subplot highlights the movie's theme—the fickleness of life—by the way it contrasts with Judah's storyline. The killer gets away with murder, while a good man loses love and suffers. Usually the featured character in a non-protagonist subplot will be someone the protagonist knows, but not always. (Judah and Cliff meet only once, very briefly, at the end of the film.)

In *The Shawshank Redemption*, Brooks and Red both have friendships with Andy that could be considered part of the main plot.

But they also have subplots of their own, illustrating how each man adapts to life outside of Shawshank. Neither of these subplots significantly affects the main plot or show Andy's development. Instead, these subplots are there solely to augment the movie's theme of maintaining hope amidst hell.

When we first meet Brooks he seems resigned; he gave up long ago on the idea of being free. When Andy joins Brooks in the library, Brooks is thankful for the company, but Andy has arrived too late to change Brooks's psychological dependence on Shawshank. When Brooks eventually gets parole, he is emotionally lost, utterly unprepared to function in a world that's moved on without him. Everything goes by too fast—the bus that he grips in terror, the plane soaring overhead, the groceries that pile up before he can bag them. Brooks is so distraught that he fantasizes about robbing the Foodway so he'll be sent "home" to Shawshank. But he figures he's too old for that; instead he carves a message onto the ceiling beam of his room—"Brooks was here"—and hangs himself.

Red's subplot is tracked through his three parole hearings and culminates when Red, too, is released. We meet Red after he has served twenty years of his sentence and is ready for parole. At this first hearing, he removes his cap, tries not to slouch, and tells the parole board what he thinks they'd like to hear. He has few illusions that he will be released. A rubber stamp slams down: "Rejected." At his second hearing, he suspects that the proceeding is pro forma, and he's right. The only thing to have changed is that now Andy waits for him with a parole anniversary gift. For his third hearing, Red has no hope of things turning out differently and no longer pretends to be a model prisoner. He speaks honestly and, surprisingly, this time he is set free.

Red's life on the outside is eerily similar to Brooks's experience. He rides the same bus. He works at the Foodway. He even stays in the same dingy room as Brooks, lying awake at night, craving life in Shawshank where everything made sense. He glances at the beam where Brooks carved his final message, contemplating suicide himself. But he remembers his promise to Andy. He carves a new message into the ceiling beam—"So was Red"—and sets off on his journey to find Andy in Zihuatanejo.

Brooks tries to make it on the outside and fails; he's unable to make the transition. Red follows the same path, but is able to adapt. The movie's theme is well illustrated with Andy alone, but it gains even more power by the way it is developed through the parallel journeys of Brooks and Red.

Sideways is a very character-driven movie, which makes it difficult to separate subplots from the main story. Miles's novel, his ex-wife, and Maya could all be called subplots, but they're so integral to Miles's goal of improving his life, that they really act as part of the main story. Jack's friendship with Miles is also too much a part of the main story to be a subplot. Jack's sexcapades, on the other hand, are somewhat separate and function as a non-protagonist subplot, one that illuminates the character of Miles through contrast. For most of the film, Miles is the front-runner in an Olympics of loserdom. Jack might seem like an amoral lunk, but he's likable, semi-successful, and about to marry a beautiful and rich woman. Then we get to know Jack better. We see him get involved with Stephanie as a prenuptial last hurrah, lying to her and to himself when he briefly considers calling off his wedding to stay and manage a vineyard (despite his complete ignorance of wine). When Stephanie learns that Jack's getting married, she bashes him with her motorcycle helmet, but Jack still doesn't learn. He seduces the waitress, Cammi, and he leaves his wallet (with the wedding rings) behind when her husband catches them in bed together. When Jack pleads with Miles to help him and is no longer able to form words—emitting "low, primitive sounds" as "snot flows from beneath his bandaged nose"—we realize how deluded, immature, and pathetic Jack is. Now, relative to Jack, Miles no longer seems so bad.

The Jack sexcapade subplot also intersects the main story in some interesting ways. When Jack abandons Miles in order to be with Stephanie, Miles feels even more depressed; the carefully planned trip has failed, like everything else Miles touches. Later, Jack's shenanigans torpedo the one thing that is going right for Miles—his blossoming relationship with Maya.

Eventually, though, the subplot influences the main plot in a way that is actually helpful to Miles. Jack convinces Miles to sneak into Cammi's house to retrieve the lost rings, apparently irreplaceable because of their dolphin and Sanskrit engravings. Crawling on all fours, Miles ventures into Cammi's room where she's having sex with her husband while tied to the headboard. He grabs the wallet with the rings and sprints to the car with Cammi's naked husband chasing after, running barefoot on the asphalt, as Jack and Miles speed away. It's a moment of sheer triumph for Miles. As the script indicates, "for all his failures, this time he did something right." *Everything* has gone wrong for Miles, but this one heroic act gives him a genuine (and much-needed) boost in self-esteem. The subplot concludes at Jack's wedding where, over the wedding rings, Jack gives Miles a last mischievous glance.

The newscaster, Thornburg, in *Die Hard* is an example of a rather small non-protagonist subplot. He's used mostly to add scope, to show how the hostage situation in the building has become a big media event. Although that would be enough justification for his presence, he also connects with the plot by putting the McClane kids on the news, which helps Hans learn Holly's identity. In his brief appearances, Thornburg manages to do quite a bit of damage.

Take a Shot

Watch a movie, any movie. Identify all of the true subplots and describe the ways in which they enhance the story. Subplots are not always easy to spot, but almost all movies have at least one. (You can test yourself against our answers if you use one of the movies listed at www.Writing Movies.info.)

Subplot Structure

Think of a subplot as a story its own right, a mini-plot. Though subplots contain fewer events than a main plot, they still have a clear beginning, middle, and end.

In *Thelma & Louise* here's how the J. D. subplot breaks down:

Beginning: Thelma bumps into J. D. and he asks for a lift, but Louise makes Thelma refuse.

Middle: After convincing Louise to pick up J. D., Thelma gets to know him, has a fling with him, and then he steals all of their money.

End: J. D. spills to the authorities that Thelma and Louise are headed to Mexico.

And here's how it goes with the tongue-wagging truck driver:

Beginning: A truck driver in a semi-tanker with mud flaps of naked women, passes Thelma and Louise, flicking his tongue at them. (In the script, they see him one time before this.)

Middle: The semi passes them again, and the truck driver gestures obscenely at his lap.

End: The semi passes again, harassing them. Having had enough, Thelma and Louise signal him to pull over, berate him, and then blow his truck sky high.

A subplot should appear at least three times, even if some of those occasions are only fleeting (as with the truck driver's first two appearances). A passing action or reference in the middle of a scene devoted to something else is often enough to advance a subplot.

Subplots should also develop—evolve and change—just as a main plot does; they should lead somewhere. J. D. starts out as a lover, ends up as a thief. Thelma and Louise exact revenge on the truck driver's lewd behavior by destroying his semi. In both cases, there is a progression of events that leads to some kind of change in the situation. The J. D. subplot leads to a major problem—the women are broke and the authorities learn they're headed to Mexico. The truck driver subplot leads to a big moment of personal fulfillment for Thelma and Louise.

It's important to consider where you place your subplots. Look for a logical way to interweave the subplot and main plot. Often subplots are woven in throughout the entire movie, as with Jack's exploits. Sometimes they don't appear until the movie is well under way, as with Powell. Still others, like the one featuring Brooks, are finished well before the movie is over. Decide when it is a good time to take that trip down a side road and when it's time to get back on the interstate.

In *Die Hard*, Holly appears at the very beginning and the very end of the movie, and seen only periodically in between. It looks like this:

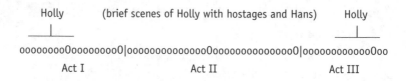

The positioning of the subplot is dictated by the needs of the story; in this case, the terrorists provide a barrier to any interaction between McClane and Holly throughout most of the movie. In an interesting footnote, one of the writers of the script explained that the terrorists were a metaphorical manifestation of McClane and Holly's troubled marriage. This isn't something viewers would or should notice, but a close look at the movie's structure shows how this works. Just after McClane and Holly have their big fight, the terrorists storm the building and the couple don't reunite until the terrorists are defeated. This is the kind of planning that really ties a plot and subplot together.

The Jimmy and J. D. subplots in *Thelma & Louise* occur mostly in one long interlude in the first half of Act II, though Jimmy first appears a bit earlier, and J. D. appears again later. It looks like this:

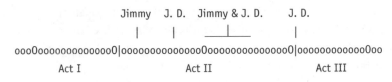

Sometimes it helps to devote a block of time to a subplot in the middle of the movie, especially when the audience needs to be spelled from unrelenting tension. After the trauma of the near-rape, murder, and flight from the law in *Thelma & Louise*, we welcome the romantic interlude. Notice the artfulness of J. D.'s introduction: Thelma first bumps into J. D. right after she finally tells her husband to "fuck off." It also makes thematic sense for the screenwriter to wrap up these subplots early in the story because the movie is really about two women liberating themselves from the world of men.

In *Sideways* Jack's sexcapades are sprinkled throughout the movie. It looks like this:

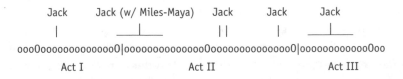

It takes the whole movie for our perception of Jack to change from aging Casanova to a helpless child. And the wedding ring retrieval sequence in Act III is perfectly placed. First, it gives us a hilarious interlude before we hit the movie's heaviest moments. Second, the heroic retrieval of the rings helps give Miles the courage to face his demons at the movie's climax.

Subplots are typically resolved before the main plot, but that's not a firm rule. In *Die Hard*, for example, all of the subplots are wrapped up after the main plot has finished. In fact, in an impressive bit of screenwriting, all of the subplots are resolved in one fell swoop lasting only three minutes. When the revenge-hungry terrorist Karl comes charging after McClane, Powell takes him down, and just when Thornburg swoops in with his microphone, prompting Holly to slug him—after which Argyle picks up her and McClane in his limo, and the couple drive off into the night, happily together.

Creating Subplots

How do you find subplots? A good place to start is with your protagonist. Ask yourself: How can the audience get to know this character better?

Because relationships work so well as subplots, think about your protagonist's crazy crushes, bitter exes, kooky roommates, country cousins, high school rivals, etc. Your protagonist might even meet a subplot character for the first time during the course of the movie. So let him go rollerblading and crash into the love of his life, or have her meet up with her husband's scheming aunt. Of course, any aspect of a protagonist's life is fair game. Work, hobbies, and religion are also rich territory to mine.

Keep asking yourself questions. How did the protagonist spend his time before he got embroiled in the events of the story? What does she do when no one is looking? What is this person like when lost in the woods or stuck on a ski slope? Get your protagonists out of their natural habitats and put them in strange, new places so you can see another side of them.

Once you've got some ideas for a subplot, how do you pick the best ones? Start with the ideas that best illuminate your protagonist. Contrasts within his or her personality are good things to consider. Show us a saint's temper and a villain's sense of humor. If your protagonist is a bully, what aspect of life makes him a pushover? If your protagonist is honest, what makes her lie? Then determine which of these ideas will intersect with your plot and theme most effectively.

While writing *Thelma & Louise*, Callie Khouri originally devised the J. D. subplot because she wanted to give Thelma a romantic experience. So Khouri started with a way to develop character. Khouri also knew that somehow Thelma and Louise would lose their money, and so she used J. D. to develop this plot detail, as well. J. D. became a charming sociopath, a true thief of hearts, who helps enlarge Thelma as a character, intersects with the main plot, and underscores the movie's theme. It's also possible to work the other way, to examine the needs of the plot and let a subplot emerge from them. Khouri could have created the J. D. subplot in reverse. She might have thought, "I'll have a hot hitchhiker steal their money," and only then realized that things could get more interesting if Thelma slept with him.

Sometimes a subplot springs from a direct requirement of the plot. For example, it's unlikely that the writer of *The Shawshank Redemption* thought, "Andy has made plenty of friends in prison but why don't we bring in one more, late in the story, just so everybody knows Andy is a great guy." Rather, the writer realized that something terrible had to befall Andy near the end so he would be forced to make his escape. The Tommy subplot is there to fulfill that need. The subplot is so well developed, however, it doesn't feel like a plot device.

It makes no difference which one you start with—plot, character, or theme. The important thing is that your subplots enhance the main story, ideally in more than one way. And regardless of how you get there, you want the subplots to feel like an organic part of the whole, rather than an afterthought, because some book recommended that the script should have them.

Let me now caution you about a few subplot traps.

It's easy to create too many subplots. This can lead to a confusing and overly busy screenplay. We need to know whose wedding we're dancing at. How many is the right amount? That depends on your movie. If your main plot is especially complex, one subplot is probably enough. If you have more than one subplot in mind, consider making one of them more dominant than the others. If you have many subplots, make sure that most of them are closely linked to the main plot. In *Die Hard*, all of the subplots are related to the terrorist takeover of the building. In *Tootsie*, the subplots all connect to Michael's masquerade. If you think about it, both of these movies have a strong need for multiple subplots. Take away the subplots from *Die Hard* and you're left mostly with a guy running around by himself in a deserted building. In *Tootsie*, Michael succeeds at playing Dorothy early and easily, but it's the subplots that put his disguise to the test.

It's also easy to be seduced by a subplot and wander off with it too often or too long. This is like going to the right wedding but dancing with someone other than your date a bit too much. If McClane spent half of *Die Hard* haggling with his wife on the phone about their marital problems, we'd be away from the main story for too long, and it would seem absurd. A subplot's size is best determined by how important it is to the main plot or protagonist. In *Tootsie*, Julie becomes very important to Michael and eventually becomes his primary obstacle. That's why she gets much more screen time than Van Horn; funny as he is, his presence isn't required for more than a quick dance or two.

Your subplots should be interesting, of course, but they shouldn't be so compelling that they overshadow the main plot. If Jack's libido led him into a building where he was taken hostage by international terrorists, we might stop worrying about poor Miles getting his life together. It's like the mother of the bride showing up in a white dress that is far more beautiful than her daughter's wedding gown. Upstaging the bride is always bad form.

Plot Strands

Some characters and relationships in a movie may look and act like subplots, but don't quite fit our definition of a storyline that is somewhat separated from the main plot.

In *Thelma & Louise*, for example, look at the characters of Hal and Darryl. They both have their own development with beginning, middle, and ends. Darryl certainly shows us something about Louise's character (and offers some great comic relief); Hal provides a necessary thematic contrast (showing us that not all men are Neanderthals). But Darryl and Hal are so integral to the main plot that you can't separate them from it. Darryl is the dead weight that's holding Thelma back, and Hal is the character who most wants to find Thelma and Louise, serving as something of an antagonist. Darryl and Hal are actually strands of the main plot. J. D., on the other hand, is a true subplot because you can remove the bulk of his storyline—his romance with Thelma—and the story remains intact. Someone else could have stolen their money. Someone else could have revealed they were going to Mexico.

Plot strands are storylines that may have their own development but are still essential to the main plot. In *Die Hard*, we would consider the Deputy Police Chief Robinson and the FBI's Johnson and Johnson plot strands because they directly relate to the activity in the building. The newscaster Thornberg or Karl's vendetta against McClane, however, could easily be excluded. We could even remove Holly without losing the main story (though we'd weaken the movie tremendously).

Let's say that you're in the midst of writing *Die Hard*. You've got the goofy police and FBI characters, but no Holly, Powell, Argyle, or Karl. You know you're supposed to have subplots in your story, but you think Robinson and Johnson and Johnson are your subplots. If, however, you understood the distinction between subplots and plot strands, you would see that you don't have any true subplots. Then you would go searching for some and you would discover the subplots that make this movie so strong.

On the other hand, you may be working on a script that has no true subplots. You try to include some but they merely distract attention from the main plot. You know that subplots are supposed to enhance the main story, so you feel you're doing something wrong. Well, you may be right. Your story may not allow for any true subplots. And yet you don't want to lose the dimension that subplots bring. Therefore, you make sure that one or two of your plot strands has enough substance to lend the kind of depth a subplot offers.

Yes, it is possible to have a good film without any true subplots. It's rare, but it's possible. Suspense and horror films may not require subplots because the tension of the main plot must be kept taut. *The Silence of the Lambs* is a good example. Clarice has well-developed relationships with two characters—her FBI superior, Jack Crawford, and Hannibal Lecter, the debonaire cannibal helping her solve the Buffalo Bill case. But both of these relationships are too connected to the main plot to fit our definition of a true subplot. These two relationships, however, are deep enough to give us a sense of dimension, and they both serve to develop Clarice. In the novel *Silence of the Lambs*, Clarice has a true subplot, a romance with an insect specialist, but, somewhere along the way, the screenwriter decided that a romantic subplot would dilute the tension, and rightly. So the film version of *Silence of the Lambs* works just fine the way it is.

If the distinction between subplots and plot strands helps, use it. If it's confusing, ignore it. But remember everything else about subplots because it may help add some new sides to your story.

Stepping-Stone: A Subplot

Brainstorm five potential subplot ideas for your movie. Pick the one that you think might work best (even though you may end up using more than one of these ideas).

List the ways that subplot might enhance your movie, in terms of character, plot, theme, comic relief, or anything else. Try to make it so that some element of the main plot would not be possible without the subplot.

Think about the subplot's structure, briefly describing the subplot's beginning, middle, and end.

CHAPTER 8

Plot II: Like a Roller Coaster

BY TOMMY JENKINS

Early on in John Ford's *The Searchers* (written by Frank S. Nugent), two girls, Debbie and her older sister Lucy, are kidnapped by Comanches after their parents are slaughtered. Their uncle, Ethan Edwards, sets out to find the girls, accompanied by the sisters' adopted brother, Marty. Ethan is played by John Wayne, and because it's John Wayne—the icon, the legend—we anticipate a heroic rescue. But Ethan is not a heroic man. He's driven more by his hatred of the Indians than his love for the girls.

The search takes years, turning into an obsessive quest. Ethan and Marty endure blistering nights of snow and scorching days with little water, hoping for just a hint of a clue as to where the girls are located. One day, Ethan finds Lucy's body and realizes she was raped before being murdered. His hatred and racism grow. Marty is pushed on by desire to save Debbie and bring her home. For Ethan, however, the mission changes to something more sinister. He's aware that as Debbie grows older, she too will be deflowered. She will become one of them. As Ethan says bitterly, "Living with Comanches ain't being alive." And he can't let her live that way. He'll kill her rather than let her become a Comanche.

After five years, the search leads to the Comanche camp where Debbie lives. Marty tries to save the girl, but Ethan throws Marty aside and chases Debbie down. She wears Comanche clothes, her hair is braided like a Comanche squaw. Ethan seizes her in his arms, lifts her high, as if he's going to smash her against the rocks and end it. But, in that moment, he sees the little girl he knew so many years before and the whole movie spins around with dizzying fury. Ethan brings her down gently, cradles her against his chest, and carries her off, saying, "Let's go home, Debbie."

Movies are like roller coasters. You climb that first hill—*clickety-clack, clickety-clack*—then *swoosh*, you are soaring downhill, then back up, then down, then twisting through a corkscrew, and so on. At times, you thrust your hands over your head, screaming with glee; other times you clench your eyes shut because you're scared to death. You're continually kept off balance, unsure of what's around the next bend. That's how you want your screenplay to work.

In this chapter, we'll examine three crucial aspects of plot—the lead-in, the second act, and the climax—that will help you create just such a ride.

The Lead-In

The first ten pages are considered the most important part of a screenplay. Now I'm sure you're asking, "The first ten pages? Really? Why are they is so important?" Think about it. Somebody in the business is reading your script. Probably this somebody has other scripts to read. Good chance this person has a whole stack of scripts to plow through in a weekend. And guess what? If they aren't grabbed by the throat in those first ten pages, they're moving on to the next script in the pile. There could be some great things to come, but they will never get to that dynamite moment on page 72 because you lost them on page 7. A great opening is equally critical to the finished film. So, even if you have millions of dollars and plan to produce your movie yourself, you better hook the audience during the first few minutes, because that's when they decide whether they like the movie or not.

Let's call the opening section of your script the lead-in. It runs from the first page to the "inciting incident," which usually happens around page 10—sometimes sooner, sometimes later. Instead of worrying about a certain page number, you can just think in terms of a great lead-in.

The lead-in should:

- Introduce the protagonist

- Establish the genre and setting

- Lead to the inciting incident

Not only do you have to accomplish those three things, you need to do it in a gripping way.

Let's start with the lead-in for *Tootsie*. Here's the first page and a half of the script. (I've made a few adjustments in the original script just to make it more closely resemble a spec.)

```
INT. ROOM — DAY

An actor's "character box." It contains: a mono-
cle, different pairs of eyeglasses, rubber appli-
ances, various makeups, a collection of dental
applications, an assortment of brushes. A hand re-
moves a small bottle. The other hand uncaps a bot-
tle of spirit gum.

One hand applies the spirit gum to a cheek. The
hands then apply spirit gum to a rubber scar, then
place the scar upon the actor's cheek.

The ritual continues as a moustache is applied.
The hands then search out the dental appliances
and pick one. The appliance is inserted into the
actor's mouth.

INT. THEATER — DAY

Blackness, or so it seems. Really a darkened the-
ater. We're looking out toward the auditorium.
```

                    A VOICE
          Next! Michael . . . Dorsey,
          is it?

MICHAEL DORSEY is looking out toward the darkened
auditorium. He is an actor, forty years old, intense, focused, a man on a mission. He holds a
script.

                    MICHAEL
          That's right.

Michael's face shows the scar, the moustache, and
perfect teeth.

                    VOICE
          Top of twenty-three.

                    MICHAEL
             (as a worldly man)
          "Do you know what it was
          like waking up in Paris that
          morning? Seeing the empty
          pillow where . . . wait a
          minute, cover your breasts!
          Kevin is downstairs! My God
          — what are you?"

A BURLY MALE STAGE MANAGER, cigar butt in
mouth, stands near Michael, also holding a
script.

                    BURLY STAGE MANAGER
          "I'm a woman. Not Felicia's
          mother. Not Kevin's
          wife . . ."

                    VOICE
          Thank you. That's fine.

```
                We're looking for someone a
                little older.

    INT. ANOTHER THEATER — DAY

    Michael stands on another bare stage, beside an-
    other stage manager. He slings a yo-yo, dressed in
    cutoffs, T-shirt and sneakers.

                        MICHAEL
                    (as a little boy)
                "Mom! Dad! Uncle Pete! Some
                thing's wrong with Biscuit!
                I think he's dead!

                        ANOTHER VOICE
                    (from the darkness)
                Thank you. Thank you. We're
                looking for someone a little
                younger.
```

Who do we see first? The agent? The roommate? Julie? Nope,
nope, and nope. We see Michael Dorsey. We have to know whose
story this is, who we are supposed to follow. And we need to know
it quickly. Don't dilly-dally when introducing your protagonist. Get
right to it.

And how do we see Michael Dorsey? In what setting? We see
him putting on makeup and auditioning for parts. We see him as
an actor. We see him in his world, the world of the movie. We also
see that he is adept at altering his appearance, something that
comes in handy later on. We sense that he is a perfectionist, that
he takes his craft very seriously. And we see how desperate he is for
a job, trudging from audition to audition, meeting only rejection.

It's also pretty funny. This is supposed to be a comedy, right?
One moment, he's playing a love scene with a burly stage manager, the next moment he's trying to get away with being a little
kid. You don't want people to be confused about the genre. You

don't want them to get to page 10 and say. "Oh wow, I didn't know this was a western." If you are writing a western, we should see horses and cowboys in the first few pages. If you are writing a hard-boiled detective drama, don't make us wait to see that tough detective getting hired. If you're writing a comedy, give us something funny right up front so we know we're supposed to laugh.

In *Tootsie*, we get a strong sense of the protagonist, his world, and the movie's genre in only a page and a half. Talk about being efficient! All this information is revealed in a compelling way, too. There's something mysterious about seeing those hands apply the makeup. We're not sure exactly who it is or what's going on but we're curious. Then we get the humorous auditions. The lead-in requires some expositional information, but you need to deliver it as entertainingly (and visually) as possible. Think about the roller coaster. Riding up that first hill gets the blood flowing, the heart primed for what's coming.

Very often the lead-in shows us the status quo of the protagonist's life, the norm that will be upset by the inciting incident. That's what happens in *Tootsie*. We're getting to know Michael in his everyday world. But it doesn't stop there. Remember, screenplays are very compressed. Scenes have multiple functions. So while we're learning about Michael, we're also setting up all kinds of things that will figure into the story to come. Nothing is random in a screenplay. Every moment is there for a purpose. The subsequent scenes in *Tootsie* show us more of Michael and his world, while also setting up plot elements. We see:

Michael teaching acting classes (showing us he really knows his craft)

Michael haggling with a director (showing us why no one will hire him)

Michael working as a waiter (showing us why he's so desperate to have an acting job)

Michael discussing his roommate's play (showing us that he
needs money because he wants to produce the play)

Michael attending his surprise birthday party (showing us
he's not getting younger and that he's something of a cad
with women)

Michael helping Sandy with an audition (for the role of the
female hospital administrator on a soap opera)

With all of this information woven in, deftly and quickly, we
are ready for the inciting incident. Remember, the inciting incident is a major event that sets the story in motion. Think of it
as the peak of that first hill on the roller coaster. Once you start
down that hill, the ride is on. If the lead-in has shown the status
quo of the protagonist's life, the inciting incident will upset that
status quo. That's what happens in *Tootsie*. Never forget that
movies are not about business as usual. Movies are about life-
changing events.

We could debate what the actual inciting incident for *Tootsie* is,
but I say it's when Michael escorts Sandy to an audition for a soap
opera and learns that Terry Bishop has been cast in a Broadway
production of *The Iceman Cometh*. (It happens 16 minutes into the
movie.) Michael flips out. How can that hack Terry Bishop get *The
Iceman Cometh*? Michael was planning on getting that part for himself! (In a scene deleted from the movie, it's revealed that Michael
and Terry used to be roommates, so there is a history of competition between them.) Michael is used to the humiliations of the acting business, but this isn't a typical rejection. This is the day he
breaks. Not only does the inciting incident in *Tootsie* upset the status quo, it is also a breaking point. Michael has to do something
drastic to change his life.

The news about Terry Bishop sets the whole story in motion.
Michael bolts from Sandy, even though she's in despair, and makes
a beeline to his agent's office to chew the guy out. His agent tells

him that no one wants to work with him because he's too difficult. Furious and wounded, Michael decides he'll show 'em all. He dresses up as Dorothy, does a brilliant audition, and gets the role Sandy wanted on the soap. Michael landing the job is plot point 1. Remember, plot point 1 is a major event at the end of Act I that launches the major dramatic question. (For *Tootsie*: Can Michael maintain the masquerade?) Here's where the roller coaster throws us into a whiplash turn, sending things in a new direction.

Now, look, this turn of events wouldn't be the least bit believable if it hadn't been set up properly by the lead-in. But it's been set up so well we *believe* Michael Dorsey is desperate and talented enough to pull this off. And you know what? We also *care* whether Michael can pull this off. We've seen his struggles and we've seen his commitment. Without that lead-in, we wouldn't give a damn. This is crucial: We absolutely *have* to care what happens to the protagonist.

Not all movies need their inciting incident to be a big breaking point like the one in *Tootsie*. Both *Thelma & Louise* and *Sideways* are movies about friends going on trips. They're road movies. So, in both, we spend a little time getting to know the friends, Thelma and Louise, Miles and Jack, in their everyday worlds. Then the inciting incidents occur when they set off on the trips. As a result, the inciting incidents come sooner (9 minutes in *Thelma*, 6 minutes in *Sideways*.) You have to determine what kicks off your story. In a road movie the story usually gets under way when the trip begins. In a detective movie it's usually when the detective gets the case. In *Chinatown*, for example, the inciting incident is when Jake Gittes gets hired by Mrs. Mulwray to follow her husband. These aren't moments of drastic change, but the status quo is interrupted all the same.

Die Hard works a little differently because the status quo is a bit out of balance right from the start. The movie opens with McClane flying to L.A., leaving the familiarity of New York and entering a new world. He's clearly uncomfortable and nervous about the trip.

We can tell from the start that he is not fully in control. *Die Hard* also waits longer than normal to hit the inciting incident (which happens 18 minutes in). But this extra time is necessary to establish firmly the relationship between McClane and Holly. This relationship anchors the movie, and they don't get to see each other again until the end. *Die Hard* actually has a very quiet lead-in for a fast-paced action movie. More often than not, action movies like to start with some kind of heart-stopping sequence to get you in that edge-of-your-seat mentality. Think of that rolling boulder in *Raiders of the Lost Ark* or the flashy opening of any James Bond movie. The leisurely lead-in of *Die Hard* is a risky move that ends up paying off very well. So, don't rely on convention. Find the lead-in that is right for your story.

The Shawshank Redemption shows us another variation, the lead-in providing a dramatic event that itself upsets the status quo. In the opening scene, Andy's wife is having an affair with another man and Andy is outside with a gun, drunk and ready to do something drastic. Then we jump to Andy's trial, where Andy is convicted of murder and sentenced to life in prison. The inciting incident occurs when Andy enters the prison (which happens 10 minutes in). Because the movie is about a man dealing with the horrors of prison, we need to see how he is thrown into that world. We don't really get to know Andy in the lead-in, but that's because he is an enigma who will gradually reveal himself over the course of the movie. Again, the lead-in fits this particular story.

A story can start at any point in time, but you want to carefully choose the best place to begin. Think about what your inciting incident should be, then consider what needs to come before so the groundwork is laid. And make sure you get there as quickly as possible. If you're going to take longer than ten pages, you better have a damn good reason. You know that feeling of watching a movie and waiting impatiently for the story to get going. You don't want that to happen with your script. Get that coaster rolling.

Take a Shot

Watch a movie, any movie. List everything you learn about the protagonist during the first ten minutes. Also take note of how these things are conveyed on screen. (You can test yourself against our answers if you use one of the movies listed at www.WritingMovies.info)

Act II

The big monster. Act II. Sixty long pages staring you in the face. It's daunting. Probably the most intimidating section of your script. The second act is the place where many promising scripts run out of momentum.

You've got a lot to do in the second act. Or, to be more accurate, you should *make sure* you have a lot to do in the second act. After all, you have to fill up those sixty pages with something. And you have to make it dramatic. Okay, don't start hyperventilating just yet.

Here are five big tips to help you maintain excitement and tension in the second act:

- Keep the conflict coming
- Raise the stakes
- Weave in subplots
- Divide the act into quadrants
- Give it highs and lows

Conflict

Conflict makes a story dramatic. As long as you have conflict, you will have drama. Your first act should have given your protagonist a goal, a big goal. Your second act should show the protagonist in pursuit of that goal. And it's your job to toss as many obstacles as possible in his or her way. Once you start putting up those obstacles, you'll start filling your pages with good scenes. Conflict sustains your second act. Whatever form it takes—external, internal, spiritual, emotional, physical—you need to have conflict. Remember the roller coaster? The roller coaster doesn't reach the middle and become a steady ride. No, as you race along there are twists and turns and climbs and plunges and lots of surprises.

Take *Tootsie.* We've got this guy who gets a job on a soap opera playing a woman, pretending that he himself *is* a woman. Now, in the second act, he must maintain that charade. He's good with makeup and he's a really good actor so he does pretty well with it at first. But this premise is going to have to sustain itself through the entire second act. How? Conflict. It just keeps coming. First, there's the conflict involved with maintaining his appearance. But you can spend only so much time showing a guy shaving his legs and plucking his eyebrows. So, you make it even tougher for him. He can't let his friend Sandy know because she'll die if she finds out Michael was the one who beat her out for the part and, to add more conflict, Michael sleeps with Sandy to cover the fact he was trying on one of her dresses. Then there's the lecherous ham on the soap who, wouldn't you know, takes a shine to Dorothy, Michael's feminine alter ego. And just so Michael can never catch his breath, Julie's father, Les, also takes a shine to Dorothy. All of these conflicts generate great scenes.

If you closely examine a character's goal, you should be able to create conflict in all kinds of places. Take the scene where the phone rings at Michael and Jeff's place. Simple thing, right? The phone rings. But Michael will not answer the phone because it could be the soap wanting Dorothy or it could be Sandy wanting Michael. If he answers as Dorothy and it's Sandy, that complicates things with Sandy. On the other hand, he doesn't want the soap thinking Dorothy has a man in her life. To top it off, he will not let Jeff answer the phone either. Jeff gets mad because people can't reach him at his own apartment. The conflict over being both Dorothy and Michael turns this situation into a great little moment about the struggle of maintaining these two identities.

That is what I mean by adding conflict. You don't miss opportunities to put your main character through the shit. It might be helpful to list every possible obstacle that your protagonist could encounter in pursuit of his or her goal. Nothing is too miniscule, not even answering the telephone. You probably won't use all of these obstacles, but you'll have them there whenever you feel that second act start to sag.

Raise the Stakes

Not only do you need lots of conflict, but you need it to escalate in the second act. Things must get progressively more perilous for your protagonist.

You accomplish this by raising the stakes. You hear this expression a lot. Somebody is always talking about raising the stakes, and how your script should raise the stakes in the second act. But what is it? Harvesting instruments of death for vampires? No, raising the stakes simply means that winning becomes more crucial, that the main character has more to lose, like when someone raises the stakes in a game of poker. Things get riskier for our hero, more treacherous. And your audience gets pulled more deeply into the story.

In *Tootsie*, the stakes get raised in two crucial ways. First, Dorothy's growing popularity increases the focus on her, which makes pulling off the charade more difficult. When Dorothy becomes a media star, she falls under greater scrutiny and there is greater chance she will be found out. If and when that happens, there will be hell to pay.

And then there's Julie. When Michael falls for Julie, it's no longer his career that's at stake. It's his heart. This opens him up to new obstacles, like spending time as Dorothy with Julie outside of work, even sharing a bed with her. At first the Dorothy disguise is a great way to get close to Julie but, after a while, it causes Michael unbelievable distress. He can draw nearer to Julie only as Dorothy, not as himself. As he falls in love, Michael's obstacles become more internal and decidedly more intense. Then there's the whole question of what will happen if and when Julie finds out about the masquerade. With Julie, the stakes are raised higher and higher for Michael. If he plays things right, he might get the girl of his dreams. If he screws things up, he may lose her forever.

In *Thelma & Louise*, the stakes are raised when Thelma robs a convenience store. They get the money they need, but now the girls are truly outlaws and the law is much less likely to view them with leniency. In *Sideways*, it's bad enough that Miles has to cover for Jack's infidelity to his fiancée, but the stakes are raised when he must lie about it to Maya, the first woman he's felt something for since his divorce.

Find ways to raise the stakes at least once or twice in your second act. Again, you might want to make a list. What could happen to make the rewards of the goal even greater? What could happen to make failure even more disastrous? You're bound to find answers that will lift your second act to new heights.

Subplots

You learned all about subplots in the previous chapter, so I won't say much about them here. But let me point out that subplots are a great device to help you get through the second act. Your main plot doesn't have to carry all sixty pages. You can sprinkle in subplot scenes here and there, like Jack's sexual hijinks in *Sideways*, or you can even take a subplot interlude, like the romances with Jimmy and J. D. in *Thelma & Louise*. Often Act II is where the subplots are dealt with most fully. In *Tootsie*, for example, the Julie subplot consumes a considerable portion of the second act. You've even got an 11-minute sequence in which Michael and Julie go upstate to visit Julie's dad, which is also where the Les subplot emerges.

Subplots offer a change of pace and allow for personal time

with your characters, all the while serving as your ally when it comes to tackling the second act.

Quadrants

Still, damn it all, you've got sixty pages to fill. Sixty pages!

Relax, we have a way to break the second act down to make it more manageable. Let's call this the quadrant method. Now, obviously all sixty pages have to fit into the story, each of them coalescing into a seamless whole. But instead of having to think about all sixty pages at once, you can break it down into four quadrants.

Let's use a visual. Visuals are nice, right? Helps us to learn. Look at this chart you saw in the first chapter on plot:

```
Inciting Incident    Plot Point 1    Midpoint    Plot Point 2    Climax
       |                  |              |             |            |
oooOooooooooooooU|ooooooooooooooooUuuuuuuooooooooO|oooooooooooooOoo
      Act I                        Act II                      Act III
```

Then, say, let's isolate Act II.

```
                    Midpoint       Plot Point 2
                       |                |
          |ooooooooooooooOoooooooooooooooooO|
                         Act II
```

You'll notice right there in the middle of the second act is the midpoint. Remember, the midpoint is a major event that happens in the middle of the story. Often it takes things to a new level, giving a slightly different vibe to the second half of the movie. The midpoint gives you something to build toward in the first half of Act II, and something to work off of in the latter half of the act.

The midpoint is usually a high point, a moment when things are going very well for the main character. In *Tootsie*, the midpoint is

the montage of photo shoots for Dorothy. Michael has achieved
great fame as Dorothy. Heck, he's succeeded at fooling the American public. In *The Shawshank Redemption,* the midpoint is when
Andy plays Mozart over the prison PA system. Here Andy finds a
new level of personal freedom.

There are exceptions, of course, where the midpoint is not a
high, but something calamitous. In *Thelma & Louise,* the midpoint is
when J. D. steals the money. Before this, Thelma and Louise had the
means to make it to Mexico, but losing the cash leads to Thelma robbing the convenience store and turning them into real criminals.

Okay, so the midpoint is a way to divide the second act into two
halves, approximately thirty pages each. But it doesn't stop there.
You can also divide the second act into four quadrants, approximately fifteen pages each. Fifteen pages is a lot easier to manage
than sixty. Trust me.

So how do you divide the second act into quadrants? Glad you
asked. You throw in markers 1 and 2.

Here's another chart:

```
        Marker 1   Midpoint   Marker 2   Plot Point 2
            |          |           |           |
        |ooooooo|oooooooOooooooo|ooooooo0|
                          Act II
```

In a screenplay these events usually fall approximately on the
following pages:

Marker 1: page 45

Midpoint: page 60

Marker 2: page 75

Plot point 2: page 90

The markers should be significant events that affect the action
in a negative or positive way. They're not as significant as the plot

points and climax, but they're not chopped liver either. (Keep in mind that these page numbers are not set in stone. Most likely you will have some variation, five or ten pages on either side. Just think of the page numbers as rough guidelines.)

In *Tootsie*, for example, it breaks down this way:

Marker 1: Julie invites Dorothy over for dinner to run lines (46 minutes in). It's significant because it's where Julie and Dorothy start to move from being colleagues to being friends. This friendship will lure Michael into falling for Julie.

Midpoint: The montage of Dorothy's fame (57 minutes in).

Marker 2: Dorothy's contract on the soap is extended (77 minutes in). It's significant because Michael had expected to be done playing Dorothy, but now he's being forced into sustaining the masquerade for a year.

Plot point 2: Dorothy and Julie almost kiss (86 minutes in). A bond has formed between Julie and Michael, so much so that they almost kiss, but Julie pulls away, not wanting to get involved with a woman. Michael realizes that he can't have Julie as long as he's trapped in the dress.

Here's how the quadrants really help. Each quadrant springboards off the big event that preceded it, and then, after about fifteen pages, you've got another big event to springboard you into a new quadrant. It's like your story gets a shot of adrenaline every fifteen pages or so.

In *Tootsie*, the first quadrant springs from plot point 1, when Michael gets the job. So the main focus in the first quadrant is Michael dealing with his new job on the soap. Then comes marker 1, when Julie invites him to dinner, and this springs into the second quadrant, where the friendship with Julie starts getting layered into Michael's new double life. Then comes the high of the midpoint montage. This is a springboard into the third quadrant, where Dorothy grows more confident, so much so that she starts changing lines on the soap and, agrees to go on a trip upstate with Julie. Then comes the bad news of marker 2, when the contract is extended for a year, which springs into the fourth quadrant, where Michael starts to feel trapped inside Dorothy, culminating with the most frustrating moment of all, plot point 2, when Julie wants to kiss Dorothy but resists because Dorothy is a woman. Remember, plot point 2 is a major event that sends the protagonist toward the story's conclusion, and usually it's a real low point.

The High/Low Flow

Another way to ensure that your second act stays interesting is to make sure you're giving your plot highs and lows. You don't ever want to stop throwing obstacles in the way of your protagonist, but if things go nothing but bad, it'll grow tiresome. That's why you need to give your protagonist some victories along the way. Michael gets some genuine satisfaction playing Dorothy and he sure doesn't mind the fast track to intimacy with Julie that being Dorothy allows him. For all his troubles in *Die Hard*, even John McClane gets to yell "yippe kay yay" a few times. Think of the most depressing movie you know. I'll bet that even there, a few little good things happen.

In a larger sense, this is why the midpoint tends to be a positive event and plot point 2 tends to be a negative event. This is especially true of any story that is going to have an upbeat ending, as *Tootsie* does. We get a big overall swing from high to low to high again.

It looks something like this:

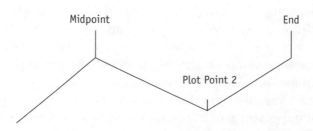

Midpoint   End

Plot Point 2

Now, if you have something of a downbeat ending, you very likely want a reverse effect so you still get the big swings from high to low. That's what happens in *Thelma & Louise*. At the midpoint, they hit their nadir when all their money is stolen. But then they start finding their groove as outlaws, finding liberation in their lives, which reaches a kind of high at plot point 2, when they look at each other as they drive through the desert, knowing they have found something they've long been searching for. And then, well, things go down at the end.

It looks something like this:

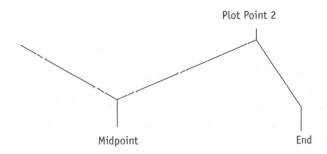

Plot Point 2

Midpoint   End

Damn, if those don't look like rollercoasters.

Take a Shot

Using the same movie from the previous assignment, list all the ways that the stakes are raised in Act II. (You can test yourself against our answers if you use one of the movies listed at www.WritingMovies.info).

The Climax

What is the most important part of your movie? The climax. "Now wait a minute, a while back you told us . . ." Nah, I said the first ten pages were the most important part of the screenplay. The most important part of the movie itself—the finished film we

actually watch in the theater—is the climax. If the ending disap-
points, everything that comes before is tainted. Hollywood ruins
lots of endings by pandering to what they think are the whims of
the mass audience, but that doesn't mean it's all right for your
script to disappoint at the end. Nope, your climax better deliver
the goods.

After all, this is it, baby. This is what the whole shooting match
has been leading to. And you have to do it in a deeply satisfying
way. Whatever is the most mind-blowing, stomach-plunging,
heart-stopping device on your roller coaster, this is the time to
use it.

The climax should do all of the following:

- Force the protagonist to take a final action against his or
  her biggest obstacle

- Bring about the answer to the major dramatic question

- Contain more dramatic punch than anything that has
  come before

The major dramatic question in *Tootsie* is: Can Michael maintain
the charade? Throughout the movie, Michael has been juggling
his two identities. But it's starting to drive him nuts. As Dorothy, he
has grown close to Julie but after they almost kiss at plot point 2,
he desperately wants to be close to her as Michael, which is impossible while Dorothy is still around. Things just get worse in Act III.
Michael has had to fight off the advances of Julie's father, who
wants to marry him, and Van Horn, who almost attacks him.
Michael begs his agent to get him out of his contract, but it can't
be done. Then, worst of all, Julie tells Dorothy that they can no
longer be friends. Michael has to do something drastic. That's
what you want to do, build momentum in this ramp-up to the big
finish.

So what happens at the climax? Michael Dorsey reveals that

Dorothy Michaels is really a man. To everyone. On national television. Live!

Michael takes this initiative himself; he is the one who rips off the mask. It wouldn't be right if someone had simply discovered his secret and reported it in the tabloids. Don't even think about using a *deus ex machina,* which is a fancy Latin term for a god coming out of the sky to save the day for the hero. And Michael is confronting his biggest obstacle here. What's the biggest obstacle? At this point it's his yearning for Julie, whom the disguise is keeping him away from. With Julie standing right there during the live broadcast Michael ends the charade.

That climax definitely gives us an answer to our major dramatic question. Nothing wishy-washy about it. We see that Michael can no longer maintain the masquerade. He can take it no more, not for another year, not really for another day. Not only does Michael out himself to his coworkers and Julie, he outs himself to the entire country. No doubt he'll be released from his contract after that. This is one of those cases where a protagonist willingly gives up the quest, and that's okay. But one way or another, the major dramatic question needs a definitive answer. Give us a yes or a no.

The *Tootsie* climax certainly packs a dramatic punch (Even literally so, when Julie hauls off and slugs Michael). What a great idea to have done it on a live show. Is it believable? Sure, within the context of this movie. It's been nicely set up. Earlier in the film, they had to retake a scene because a tech guy spilled celery tonic on the tape and we learn that this once caused them to do a show live. The tape guys screw up again and, boom, they have to do it live again. We buy it. And of course Michael makes the most of this moment, spinning an elaborate tale that seems straight out of Shakespeare.

Climaxes are usually very big moments. If you're writing an action movie, it better be the most intense bit of action yet. If you're writing a horror movie, it better be the scariest thing we've seen.

You get the idea. But it's possible for a climax to be a very quiet moment, if your script calls for it. As in *Sideways*, when Miles has his breakthrough by drinking a valuable bottle of wine in a burger joint. In its own subtle way, *Sideways* fulfills all our requirements for a climax.

Here's the thing about climaxes: They have to encapsulate everything. During the climax, the goal and the obstacles come together in their strongest and most concentrated form, answering the major dramatic question in one bold stroke, and here the protagonist reaches the farthest point yet of his or her evolution. And because everything comes together at the climax, the screenwriter has to know all the points that lead you there. That's why it's good to know the ending when you start mapping out your story. You're already thinking about how the plot will come to a head at the climax.

In fact, the beginning of a story links directly to the end, and vice versa. The more you can make your story a complete sequence of linked events, the better it will be. Think back to that opening page of *Tootsie*. What was Michael doing? Applying makeup, applying a mask. In the first half of the movie Michael perfects the mask, something that peaks at that photo-shoot midpoint. In the second half of the movie, Michael learns enough from the mask so he doesn't really need it or want it anymore. What does he do at the climax? He rips off the mask.

Which brings us to resolutions. A resolution is a winding down, a chance for the audience to catch its breath before being thrust back into the real world. But it also has another function. This is where you tie up any loose ends and give a hint of the protagonist's future. Shouldn't take more than a couple minutes. Once you hit the climax, things should be just about over.

Take the resolution of *Tootsie*. Michael and Sandy act in Jeff's play, and Michael returns the engagement ring to Les, making peace with him. Then we get a hint of what might become of Michael. Time has passed. He seeks out Julie. Julie is angry at first, understandably so, but she finally warms up, asking Michael if she can borrow his Halston. We don't know for sure that Michael and Julie will become a couple, but we have a suspicion they will. As long as the MDQ gets a definitive answer, there can be some ambiguity in the resolution. It's nice to leave us with a little something to wonder about, giving us a sense that the characters live on after the lights come on.

It's not always easy to find exactly the right ending for your story. It must have been pretty tough to find the right ending for *Thelma & Louise*. Think about it. We've got these two wonderful women running from the law because one of them has killed a man and the other has robbed a convenience store. So they're hoping to get to the border of Mexico.

Couldn't they just get away? With half the cops in America chasing them? This isn't a fantasy movie. But we sure as hell don't want to see these women caught, handcuffed, and hauled off to jail. That would go against their journey of liberation. And we definitely don't want to see them gunned down à la Butch and Sundance. What about somehow reuniting them with the dopey men in their life? Forget about it.

What's a writer to do?

Well, in this case, the writer found the perfect solution. Their green Thunderbird is forced to stop when they come to the gaping expanse of the Grand Canyon. An armada of squad cars barrel down from behind them. An FBI chopper soars overhead like a gigantic hawk. In a glorious burst of liberation they hold hands and floor that Thunderbird into the splendor of the canyon. They die, sure, but they choose the way to go. And what a way it is. (There's no resolution after this because there ain't nothing more to show.)

Someone wise (maybe it was Aristotle) said an ending should be inevitable but unexpected. Inevitable means it needs to feel like the right ending, the place where things have been heading all along. But if it happens as we expect it will, then it's predictable, perhaps even a cliché. So the inevitable needs to happen in a way that surprises us, catches us off guard. It's a tricky thing to pull off, but it'll give you the best ending.

The ending of *Thelma & Louise* follows this advice. At the end of Act II, the two women are driving through the desert. They don't say much, but we sense what they're thinking. They doubt they will get away and they even suspect they may die, and they make a kind of peace with whatever lies ahead. In Act III, they act with abandon, as if knowing that these are their last days on earth. But I bet if you were watching that movie for the first time and I leaned over the seat and said, "Hey, do you know how this movie is gonna end?" I doubt that one of you would have said, "It's obvious. They're going to drive into the Grand Canyon." You may have known they weren't going to get away, but driving into the Grand Canyon? I don't think so. Unexpected. Big time.

Thelma and Louise fail to achieve their goal and, of course, it's heartbreaking, but there's also something uplifting about it. They have found peace, excitement, freedom. This is a destiny they embrace. If your story requires a downbeat ending, it's usually best if you can find a way to make it somehow uplifting at the same time, as long as you can manage it without resorting to something phony or saccharine. That way, members of the audience won't feel like driving off a cliff after they leave the theater.

Can you have a real downer ending? Something with no silver lining at all? It's very rare, especially in mainstream movies, because, honestly, a movie with a truly downer ending seldom makes money. But if a rock-bottom ending is what your story calls for, that's what it should have. As an example, check out *Chinatown*. Jake's love interest is killed, leaving Jake a shattered man, and the bad guy gets away, absconding with a little girl who happens to be his own daughter *and* granddaughter due to incest. Although it's exactly the right finish for that movie, there ain't nothing uplifting about the end of *Chinatown*.

> ## Take a Shot
>
> This one deals with your own movie. In prose, describe a nightmare dreamt by your protagonist. The essence of the nightmare will be the absolute worst thing that could happen to your protagonist in the pursuit of his or her goal. The primary obstacle should appear in some way. This is a nightmare, so push things as far as they can go, without worrying about plausibility. When you're done, see if there's anything in your nightmare that could be incorporated into your actual movie.

Flashbacks and Secret Tracks

Hey, before I go, why don't we discuss two more roller coaster–like techniques.

A *flashback* is when the action loops backward in time for a spell, and allows the viewer to witness events that happened days, weeks, or years before. Now that I've told you what they are, don't use them. Let me rephrase that: Some movies use flashbacks to great effect, but you need to be extremely careful with them or you'll jump your story off its track. As with voice-overs, you should avoid flashbacks altogether unless you have a strong reason for using them.

The big problem with flashbacks is that beginning writers love to employ them as an easy way to convey information. For instance, you use a flashback to reveal a character's history, their backstory. Or you use a flashback to clarify a plot point. Wrong. Way wrong. You should never rely on a flashback solely for purposes of exposition. That is lazy storytelling. If used in this manner, flashbacks will only slow the story down, killing momentum, and, perhaps worst of all, brand you as an amateur. It's your job as a screenwriter to convey the necessary information in a manner that keeps the story moving forward, not backward.

So when can you use flashbacks?

The most acceptable way to use flashbacks, and really the best way, is as a framing device, a way to begin and end the movie. You start in the present with a character and then we flashback to show this character's story, then at the end we return to the present. We've all seen this done. Think of *Titanic.* Starts with Rose as an old lady, a guest on an archeological ship in the North Atlantic, flashes back to her story on the *Titanic,* then returns to Rose on the ship at the end. (Actually we return to old Rose a few times in the middle, but only briefly.) The use of flashback enhances the story because we see how the tragedy of the *Titanic* has continued to ripple into the present day, and we experience a kind of peace at the end when Rose drops the necklace in the sea and dies. The tragedy of the story is tempered by this resolution. (A variation on this technique is to use a prologue, a short opening section that shows the characters at an earlier period in time, as done with the three boys in *Mystic River.*) But even as a framing device, you should use flashback only if it truly enhances the story.

If memory is a crucial element of your plot, then flashbacks may be a natural facet of the storytelling technique. But the story better really hinge on memory to justify the flashbacks. For example, in *Ordinary People,* a character is unable to escape the memory of a tragic death, and in *Eternal Sunshine of the Spotless Mind* a character is having his memory scientifically erased.

Otherwise, you should use a flashback only if it's absolutely essential and/or the most interesting way to illuminate what's happening in the present. Flashbacks are not about the past; they have to enhance the present story and move it forward.

The Shawshank Redemption earns its flashback on both these counts. The movie even dares to place it at the climax. When Tommy is killed, it seems Andy has no hope of getting out of Shawshank. He's in utter despair. Red fears that Andy will commit suicide, especially when he learns that Andy has procured a length of rope. When Andy doesn't come out for the nightly roll call, Red fears the worst. But then we see that Andy isn't dead. He's gone!

Whoa!

The way the movie is structured, the escape must be a surprise. Therefore, we can't see it happening in the present. If we did, no surprise. However, it's also the most triumphant moment for the main character, so we sure as hell *need* to see it. And once we see Red peering through that hole in the wall, we are *dying* to know how the heck Andy managed to break out. In a sense, we've been waiting almost twenty years for this. Accordingly, we see the escape in a well-earned flashback—Andy cleverly stealing the warden's clothing and money from under his nose, crawling through the tunnel then through the sewer pipe, emerging beyond the prison walls, lifting his arms as he's cleansed by the rain. This is an immensely rewarding moment, made all the more so by the way it is revealed.

This brings us to our other technique, the secret track. What's that? Well, the secret track is a layer of the story kept hidden until the end, and when it's revealed we view the entire movie from a new perspective. You'll find brilliant secret tracks in such movies as *The Usual Suspects*, *The Sixth Sense*, and *Body Heat*. *Shawshank* has one, too: Andy's escape. We have no clue that Andy has been planning an escape until he has actually done it, and when we learn about the escape, Andy's journey takes on a new dimension for us.

Secret tracks are always a surprise, but they should be a satisfying surprise. It's difficult to pull off, requiring very careful plotting. The audience should be able to look back at the rest of the movie in the light of the secret track and see that everything makes sense, and yet you have to set it up without revealing too much, without giving away the surprise. It's like taking the "inevitable but unexpected" rule to the *n*th degree. In *Shawshank*, for example, we see Andy carve his name with the rock hammer into the wall. But we never suspect he's planning to tunnel with the hammer because we know he's a rock hound and he wants the hammer only for carving chess pieces, which he does. Besides, he even makes a joke about how it would be impossible to tunnel out with this tiny device. When it happens, however, we believe the escape, because by then we know that such a thing is not impossible for a man like Andy Dufresne.

You shouldn't attempt a secret track unless your plot calls for it, but if you can pull one off, you'll turn the story into a truly unforgettable ride.

Stepping-Stone: New Beat Sheet

Create a new beat sheet for your movie. This time include subplots, and factor in everything else you have learned since writing your first beat sheet.

CHAPTER 9

Tone and Theme: The Overlay and Underlay

BY JASON GREIFF

Tone

Let me tell you about one of my favorite movies.

It's about an ex-convict who marries a female ex-cop and, because the woman is infertile, they kidnap a baby to fulfill their parental urges. The desperate pair lives in a trailer in the middle of the desert, where they think no one will discover the abduction. Two jail mates of the ex-con break out of the state pen, take shelter with the newlyweds, and are soon plotting to lure the ex-con into a crime spree across the Southwest—that is, until they realize there's a reward out for the return of the baby. The ex-con's boss at the hellish sheet-metal plant not only wants to have sex with the ex-con's wife, but also becomes wise to the baby's identity. The FBI is on the hunt for the baby, too, as is a murderous bounty hunter, who plans to sell the baby to the highest bidder on the black market.

This movie is a hilarious comedy called *Raising Arizona* (written and directed by the Coen brothers). How could this story about a desperate couple kidnapping an infant possibly be a comedy? The answer: tone. Despite the bleakness of the events, *Raising Arizona* is painted in the bright colors of a Road Runner cartoon, and that makes all the difference.

The screenwriter Robert Towne (who counts *Chinatown* among his many credits), has said, "The most difficult thing to capture, and what finally makes a movie, is its tone."

265

I know you know the meaning of tone. But if I asked you to define it, I bet you'd have a hard time. It's a slippery term, no doubt about it. For now, let's say tone is the "feel" of the story, a feel that affects every element. Tone works like an overlay because it tints everything, giving a movie its distinct personality. It's not unlike the tints and hues chosen by a painter for a work of art.

Why Tone Matters

Movies are about getting people to feel, and the tone gives people an indication of *how* they should feel. Should they feel it's okay to laugh at a baby in peril? Should they feel sympathy for the giant ape climbing the building? Should they find the alien cuddly or terrifying?

If your tone isn't clear, you risk sending the wrong message. It's like e-mailing. Most of the e-mails I send are of a casual nature. I write as I'm thinking and click "send" when I'm done. When I don't get a timely reply from someone, it gives me a minor panic attack and I check what I wrote. I get particularly anxious as soon as I send off an e-mail to someone who can help or hurt my screenwriting career. I find myself rereading the message, checking (too late, though it may be) the tone of my message. Take the following e-mail I sent my agent:

> From: jasonigreiff@xmail.com
> To: [agent]@icmtalent.com
> Re: Disney's offer
>
> Hey—You tell that rat (Mickey Mouse) I won't accept anything less than a million for the script!
>
> Seriously,
> Jason

Thanks in no small part to this e-mail, I am no longer represented by this particular agent. My amiably sarcastic speaking tone was completely misinterpreted. While I meant it to come across as "Hey, we're buddies, we joke around about the business together," the agent interpreted my words as those of an insolent schmuck. The same thing applies to screenplays. If you don't present your intended tone clearly, you could get into all sorts of trouble. Script readers may misunderstand what type of screenplay they're reading. And wouldn't it be terrible if these script readers reject your screenplay simply because of a confusion of tone?

Audiences will have the same problem. A good example of this occurred with the first cut of Billy Wilder's *Sunset Boulevard*. It's about a screenwriter living in the mansion of a delusional silent screen star who believes she's going to make her return to the movies with his help. The feel of the movie is dark with comic undertones. *Sunset Boulevard* opens with the writer's voice-over as we see him facedown in a swimming pool, dead. But originally, the movie opened in the morgue and we heard other stiffs talking to each other in voice-over. It was meant to be macabre, but the preview audiences thought they were in store for a ridiculous comedy. It was not the tone Wilder had intended to set, and so he fixed it. *Sunset Boulevard* went on to win the Academy Award for Best Screenplay. The preview audiences for your screenplay will be your friends, colleagues, teachers, and others who read the script. If your personal readers aren't clear about your tone, fix it. Who knows, your Oscar just might be depending on it.

The Elements of Tone

Long before you prepare your Oscar acceptance speech, however, you'll need to figure out the proper tone of your story. It probably won't come to you instantly. This is something for you to ponder as you create your story and fine-tune it in subsequent drafts. We'll soon examine how to get your tone right on the page, but know that your tone will be the result of three core elements. Let's take a look at them.

Genre

The conventions of a genre greatly influence the overall feel of the movie. But you must also realize that not all movies within the same genre have the exact same tone. You will find tonal variations within each genre, and further variations caused by the practice of mixing genres.

For example, science-fiction movies tend to generate a sense of wonder and awe. But there are different types of "wonder and awe." Here are four sci-fi movies with variations on the genre's tone:

2001: A Space Odyssey: somber, intellectual, epic in scope

Star Wars: light, escapist, gee-whiz fantasy

E.T.: suburban, funny, heartwarming

The Terminator: dark, grim, relentlessly violent

Horror movies make us feel scared, on-edge, anxious. But notice the variation in tone among these four:

Dracula: mythic, seductive, tragic dimension

Rosemary's Baby: subtle, psychological, under-the-skin creepy

The Texas Chainsaw Massacre: gruesome, gritty, freeeaaky, full-throttle shockfest

Scream: titillating, fun-shocks, laced with self-referential wit, a slasher/mystery/comedy

Romantic comedies give us a sense that true love conquers all, and make us want to hold our partner's hand, or wish we had a hand to hold. But consider these variations:

Bringing Up Baby: screwball, wildly improbable, a gloss of sophistication

When Harry Met Sally . . . : urbane, neurotic, cute

There's Something About Mary: goofy, gross, pushes the limits of taste

Eternal Sunshine of the Spotless Mind: edgy, emotional, an odd mix of romantic comedy, drama, and science fiction

The variation in tone is even more diverse among dramas and comedies, genres that are pretty broad to start with. There are great differences in tone among such dramas as *Casablanca, The Godfather, Kramer vs. Kramer, Schindler's List,* and *Fight Club,* and among such comedies as *Some Like It Hot, Harold & Maude, Airplane!, Animal House,* and *Groundhog Day.*

So it's not enough just to know the genre. If you tell someone in the business you've written an action movie, they'll nod and think, Okay, what *kind of* action movie? You should know.

Light/Dark

The tone is also affected by how light or dark the movie is. Here we refer to light and dark in terms of "humorous/serious" or in terms of "levity/heaviness" in the actual script. The amount of light and dark in the visuals is mostly the business of the director and director of photography, but these decisions are usually influenced by the tone of the screenplay.

Picture a spectrum that looks like this:

Light_____Dark

On the far left side of the spectrum, you'll find movies like *There's Something About Mary,* in which the hero gets his "franks and beans" stuck in his zipper, a dog is shocked back to life with lamp wiring, and handsome NFL quarterback Brett Favre is rejected as a lover in favor of the dorky protagonist. Other movies on the far left include *Duck Soup, Blazing Saddles,* and *Austin Powers: International*

Man of Mystery. These movies are just plain silly. On the far right side, you'll find dark or heavy movies like *Schindler's List,* which portrays the Holocaust in all its harrowing detail. Other movies on that side include *Taxi Driver, Apocalypse Now,* and *Requiem for a Dream.*

Most movies, however, don't fall all the way to the left or right, but somewhere in between. On your stereo system, volume, bass, and treble aren't on/off switches but dials that allow for variable settings. From 1 to 10 perhaps. (If your dial goes up to 11, rock on, *Spinal Tap* fan). Imagine you have a dial on your screenplay that lets you adjust gradations of light/dark. For example, *Tootsie* is mostly a laugh riot but as it has some moments of tenderness, it would be pretty far, but not all the way, to the left. Whereas *Sideways,* which is really a comedy/drama, is pretty close to the center.

Even two very similar stories can have differing tones. Take, for example, *Rocky* and *Million Dollar Baby,* both dramas about the rise of an unknown boxer. Both of these dramas fall on the right side, but *Million Dollar Baby,* being darker, falls farther right than *Rocky.* Rocky stays on his feet and is the subject of endless sequels; the fighter in *Million Dollar Baby* . . . let's just say it's not likely to produce sequels.

Probably the most complicated mix of light/dark is found in black comedies, in which a serious topic is handled in a comic way. For example, *Dr. Strangelove* deals with a heavy subject, nuclear war, but the characters in this movie are nutty. One of them, a general Jack D. Ripper, is a kook who not only believes that fluoridation of drinking water is a Commie conspiracy to sap Americans of their precious bodily fluids, but gets the plot rolling by initiating nuclear war with Russia in order to bring about peace on earth. Other black comedies would include *Harold and Maude, Prizzi's Honor,* and *Heathers.*

Where does your story fall on the light/dark spectrum? It's a good idea to check out some movies that you think have a degree of light and dark similar to the script you're writing. This will help you get a firmer grip on your screenplay's tone.

World

The tone is also influenced by the world the characters live in. First, this applies to the setting of the movie—the time and place. In *Casablanca*, the city is a route of escape from the Nazis during World War II and so this time and place creates a sense of secrecy, paranoia, and desperation. Suspicious glances lurk around every corner. *American Graffiti* takes place in small-town California at the end of summer, 1962, when teenagers entertained themselves with making out, drag racing, and rock-and-roll. It's a world of youthful exuberance and pre–Vietnam War innocence.

It's not, however, only a matter of letting your setting influence the tone. You can manipulate your setting to match the tone that works best for your story. Both Monet and Van Gogh painted haystacks, but the difference in their styles resulted in very different haystacks. The gritty, dirty, violent New York City of *Taxi Driver* contrasts sharply with the beautiful, sentimental, romantic view of the city in *Manhattan*. Or think about the two versions of small-town America presented in *It's a Wonderful Life*. With George Bailey around, Bedford Falls is a quaint, friendly, nice place to live. But we also see what the town would be like if George had not been born—Pottersville, a gritty, dirty, violent town, one where Travis Bickle, and not Ernie, should be driving the cab.

You might even choose a setting specifically for the way it will enhance your desired tone. *Body Heat* is a tale of sexual obsession, so the screenwriter chose a setting as sultry and delirious as possible—south Florida during a heat wave. The whole movie is permeated with sweat and heat and distraction in a way that reflects the psychology that would drive a man to murder for the chance to keep sleeping with a certain impossibly sexy woman. The place can even be *the* major thing that affects tone. This is true in *The Shawshank Redemption,* which is dominated emotionally by that cold, bleak, unforgiving, gray prison.

The world of a movie also extends beyond the literal time and place. When we speak of the world, we also need to consider how real the world is. As you may have noticed, Some movies are more realistic than others. Popeye Doyle of *The French Connection* and Spider-Man are both crime fighters who reside in contemporary New York City, but they don't live in the same world. One lives in a world that is meant to mirror ours with a great amount of verisimilitude. The other inhabits a world that is far removed from reality, where a young man who has absorbed the genes of a spider can zip around skyscrapers by spinning webs.

Here, let me use another spectrum:

Real_____Surreal

At the far left, you have movies like *The French Connection,* that are meant to resemble real life. This would include such movies as *On the Waterfront, Ordinary People,* and *The Verdict.* At the far right, along with *Spider-Man,* you'll find movies like *Men in Black, Beetlejuice,* and *Who Framed Roger Rabbit?* These are worlds in which the fantastical, supernatural, or just plain weird abound.

But most movies fall somewhere in between, so imagine you have another dial on your screenplay that lets you adjust gradations of "real" and "surreal." Some movies are set in fairly realistic worlds but there is some surreal little thing is going on, as in *The Sixth Sense* and *The Usual Suspects.* These movies are on the right, but not all the way over. Then there are many movies, perhaps most movies, where nothing surreal happens but they aren't completely realistic either. *Die Hard,* for example, would fall on the left side of the spectrum, but not too far left. It is set in a recognizably real world, where people work in offices and have holiday parties and deal with marital problems, like everybody else. But this world is unreal enough to let us accept such improbabilities as McClane surviving a leap off the roof of a skyscraper while tethered to nothing but a fire hose.

In *Thelma & Louise*, the waitress and the housewife get to play around at being action heroes, but they're not as invincible as Mc-Clane because this is a fairly realistic movie, most of the way over to the left. *Sideways* is even more realistic, all the way over to the left. This movie feels very much like real life. Miles in *Sideways* would not fool many people by wearing a dress and heels, not because he is less feminine than Michael Dorsey but because *Tootsie* lies somewhere on the right of the spectrum, set in a world where it's believable that a man can dupe all of America into thinking he's a woman.

At first glance, *Shawshank* might look extremely realistic with its gang rapes and lye dousings. But that's not exactly the case. Andy is a little too good and patient to be true, and the warden and Hadley are slight exaggerations of villainy. This is because *Shawshank* is meant to evoke a sense of myth or tall tale, and not be too realistic.

How real or surreal is the world of your movie? It's important to know this because it will determine the kinds of events that happen in your story, and what will be believable within the context of your world.

How do you find out where your movie falls on the reality spectrum? Well, it's simple, you give the characters the ol' frying-pan test. It goes like this. Imagine you're in the world of, say, *Ace Ventura, Pet Detective*. Ace lives in Miami and it seems like it's the Miami we know. But how real is this world? Let's find out. Pick up a cast-iron frying pan. Now get a good grip on the handle and hit Ace in the face. Hit him hard.

Now, how's Ace doing? He's probably hurt. Probably holding his nose. But do we need to rush him to the emergency room? Not likely. This isn't the real world. Ace is okay. Ace Ventura is living in a world that lies on the far right on our spectrum of reality.

Let's apply the frying-pan test to the following movies:

Sideways: Well, we pretty much know what would happen here. A frying pan is roughly as bad as the motorcycle helmet with which Stephanie attacks Jack. Jack would be hurt and have to go to the hospital. But because it's a comedy we'd see a big, funny bandage on Jack's face.

Thelma & Louise: What if Louise banged that rapist on the head with the pan instead of putting a bullet through him? He would go down with some serious pain, perhaps even pass out. Of course, if this happened, the rest of the movie would be about two ladies on a fishing trip.

The Shawshank Redemption: Hell, the pan could easily kill someone in this place. If Hadley hit Andy with the pan, Andy would, at the very least, end up in the infirmary for a while. Of course, in the mythically bad world of Shawshank, Hadley wouldn't stop at just one hit.

Die Hard: What if Karl lost his machine gun and had to settle for clobbering McClane with the pan? McClane would be hurt. He'd even bleed, But he wouldn't go down, not like you or me. He'd somehow wrestle the pan from Karl and come right back at him, saying something like, "Let's iron out our differences, pal."

Tootsie: What if Dorothy thwacked the lecherous Dr. Brewster with the pan instead of her prop clipboard? He'd be stunned. But not too much pain; certainly no blood. Then he'd probably grab Dorothy and try to kiss her. And he'd probably get the pan again.

Guess what? You can also use the frying-pan test to see where your movie falls on the light/dark spectrum. Just hit one of your characters with that frying pan and ask yourself how funny or un-funny it ought to be.

Consistency

The tone must stay consistent throughout the movie. If you've written a comedy in a very light tone and then, and well into the script, something extremely dark happens, the reader or viewer will be jolted out of your story. You must establish the tone early and stick to it. When you establish the tone early, you're essentially setting the parameters of your movie's world, and if you break the rules you establish, readers will lose faith in the credibility of the world. Imagine that Julie killed herself after Michael reveals his true identity. Would that seem sad but okay? No. It would be very wrong. We'd feel as if a promise had been broken. *Tootsie* starts out as a whimsical comedy, and it must stay that way until the end.

Consistency doesn't mean that every scene of the movie must have the same tone, or that the movie can't shift between light and dark, or grow progressively darker or lighter. But the *dominant* tone must remain the same. This dominant tone has room for variation within it. As in music, there is a dominant chord. Many other chords are used but there is one holding everything together. The movie, or music, can darken and deepen and do all kinds of shifting without dropping its dominant tone. The tone of most movies of any depth offers some variation. *Tootsie* never gets too heavy but has moments of poignancy, mostly later on when Dorothy grows close to Julie and her baby. *The Shawshank Redemption* is grim throughout but lightens during that last sun-drenched scene on the beach in Mexico. Variation within a dominant tone is perfectly fine, but you have to set the dial correctly at the outset.

Take *Thelma & Louise*. This movie takes a risky tack. It feels humorous at the start, with funny stuff as they're packing and driving. And then something really dark happens at the end of Act I— Louise murders Harlan. It's a sharp turn, but it doesn't come out of nowhere. Clues are laid to pave the way, to prepare us for the shift, even though we may not be aware of them. We see that Louise and Thelma are genuinely unhappy in their lives. Then the gun is introduced. Then we see Louise's anxiousness when Harlan approaches her. The seeds of darkness are planted before the murder. After that, the movie maintains a delicate balance of humor and seriousness. Sometimes the women have a great ol' time as outlaws, sometimes they realize they are staring death in the face, and it all works together in harmony.

Communicating Tone

Yes, it's true that when you see a movie, the cinematography and music are especially helpful for establishing tone, and that it's also influenced by the direction, acting, editing, and design. But the screenwriter does not deal with these things. The screenwriter deals with words, what's on the page. Screenwriters communicate tone by what the characters do and say, their actions and dialogue, as well as with their details and description. And the vast majority of this is right there in the screenplay, in black words on white paper. When someone reads a good screenplay, the tone is made apparent from the get-go.

In the opening moments of *Sideways*, Miles is awakened from a dead sleep and told he needs to move his car because it's blocking some workers. Let's take a look at this passage:

```
EXT. HIDEOUS APARTMENT COMPLEX - DAY

Wearing only underwear, a bathrobe, and clogs,
MILES RAYMOND comes out of his unit and heads to-
ward the street. He passes some SIX MEXICANS,
ready to work.

He climbs into his twelve-year-old Saab convert-
ible, parked far from the curb and blocking part
of the driveway. The car starts fitfully.
```

Did you pick up on the tone? Look at the clues. The scene header tells us that the apartment complex is "hideous." It's a little humorous. What's Miles wearing? Underwear, bathrobe, and clogs. That's a funny thing to wear. Even funnier when you pass six laborers who are waiting for you. Notice the car is parked far from the curb, which suggests, in a humorous way, that Miles parked while under the influence. Then the twelve-year-old car starts fitfully, which is also funny. See, a sense of comedy is being established. Notice that the humor is not coming from jokes or cute phrases. There is a hint of wit in the word choices—"hideous," "fitfully"—but the humor mostly stems from the reporting of what we're seeing, the actions and details.

The script continues with:

```
EXT. STREET - DAY

Miles rounds the corner and finds a new parking
spot.

INT. CAR - CONTINUOUS

He cuts the engine, exhales a long breath and
brings his hands to his head in a gesture of
headache pain or just plain anguish. He leans back
in his seat, closes his eyes, and NODS OFF.
```

Is it a comic hangover Miles suffers or is it something more serious, some deeper emotional torment? Both, actually. The hangover seems both funny and a little pathetic. *Sideways* is really a comedy/drama and an underscore of sadness is being injected, some darkness mixed in with the light.

Look at what we're learning about the world. A depressing place, not a tenement but not the home of someone with money to burn. The car's not so new either. We're also seeing that this is an intensely realistic world, one in which people are awakened to find they must move their car, the everyday world that most of us live in.

The tone is further established by what comes next, Miles' dialogue and actions.

```
INT. MILES'S APARTMENT - DAY
ON THE PHONE -

Miles hurriedly throws clothes into a suitcase.

                    MILES
          Yeah, no, I know I said I'd
          be there by noon, but
          there's been all this work
          going on at my building, and
          it's like a total nightmare,
          and I had a bunch of stuff
          to deal with this morning.
          But I'm on my way. I'm out
          the door right this second.
          It's going to be great.
          Yeah. Bye.

INT. MILES'S BATHROOM - DAY
ON THE TOILET -

Miles has a BOOK propped open on his knees. He
turns a page, lost in his reading.
```

Another laugh, a bigger one, comes with the classic ironic cut. Miles is obviously late to meet someone, tells this person on the phone, that he's "out the door right this second," and then they cut to Miles on the can, reading a book.

The tone of the movie is already perfectly established. We expect this movie to be funny, and it is, wildly so at times. But we're also prepared for some not so funny things, like the agonizing moment at the end when Miles learns that his ex-wife is pregnant by her new husband and that he has nothing. Also notice that the script provides those people who make the movie—director, director of photography, editor, composer—with plenty of clues as to how put this movie together, tonally.

Let's take a look at another script that opens with a scene of a guy in a car, namely, Andy in the beginning of *The Shawshank Redemption*. See if you pick up a different tone here.

> He is disheveled, unshaven, and very drunk. A cig-
> arette smolders in his mouth. His eyes, flinty and
> hard, are riveted to the bungalow up the path.
>
> He can hear them fucking from here.
>
> He raises a bottle of bourbon and knocks it back.
> The radio plays softly, painfully romantic, taunt-
> ing him:
>
> > You stepped out of a
> >   dream . . .
> > You are too wonderful . . .
> > To be what you seem . . .
>
> He opens the glove compartment, pulls out an ob-
> ject wrapped in a rag.
>
> He lays it in his lap and unwraps it carefully -
> revealing a .38 revolver. Oily, black, evil.

Notice how unrelentingly dark this is. Here's the situation: a guy waiting in a car, with a gun, while someone we presume is a spouse or lover is screwing someone else nearby. The dark situation is re-inforced by the details and description. His eyes are "flinty and hard," the song is "painfully romantic." The word "fucking" certainly makes a statement, as does the description of the gun, "Oily, black, evil."

But here's the thing about tone. You can relate, say, dark events and put a humorous spin on them by careful selection of what you show and how you relate it. What if we kept the same situation but altered the opening of *Shawshank* to look like this?

> Andy, wearing only underwear, a bathrobe, and
> clogs sits in his car, asleep. He's a mess. The

man seems to have forgotten he owns a razor. He
wakes with a jolt.

He rubs his temples. Looks toward the bungalow up
the path where all the monkey business is going on.

He can hear them getting down. He hears her orgas-
mic moans, yep from all the way over here, despite
being in the car with radio playing.

The song is taunting him:

> Clang-clang-clang went the
>   trolley
> Ding-ding-ding went the bell
> Zing-zing-zing went my
>   heartstrings
> From the moment I saw him I
>   fell.

Different, huh? So you see, tone is not something screenwriters
should leave up to the director to communicate. With your words,
you can control the tone of your screenplay, the way a painter con-
trols his palette.

Theme

Let me tell you about another of my favorite movies, Alfred Hitchcock's *Rear Window* (written by John Michael Hayes).

You might know this classic starring Jimmy Stewart as Jeff, a
photojournalist laid up with a broken leg who passes the time spy-
ing on the neighbors who live in the apartment building across the
way. The objects of his interest include a sexy dancer, a lonely lady,
a couple of newlyweds, a middle-aged couple, a struggling song-
writer, and one or two others. Soon Jeff begins to suspect that one
of the neighbors, Mr. Thorwald, a costume jewelry salesman, has

murdered his wife, chopped up her body, and disposed of the parts. Having nothing else to do, Jeff determines to prove that a murder has been committed.

This is a movie about romantic love. So that my tone is clear: I am not being sarcastic. How is this so? How could this voyeuristic suspense thriller possibly be about love? The answer: theme.

If you look closely at *Rear Window*, you'll see that the idea of romantic love is everywhere. Each apartment across the way dramatizes romantic love in one form or another—the good, the bad, and the ugly—from the happy Newlyweds busy doing what newlyweds do, to Miss Torso, the sexy dancer who has many gentlemen callers, to the Music Man who is trying to compose a great love song, to poor Miss Lonelyhearts who pines for a love of her own, to the recently (perhaps self-made) widower, Mr. Thorwald.

Then there's the subplot, in which Jeff's girlfriend Lisa does everything she can to convince Jeff that she's the woman he should marry. (A little far-fetched, I know, considering Lisa is played by Grace Kelly.) But Jeff is a globe-trotting guy who doesn't see how Manhattan socialite Lisa could make it in his adventurous world. And then . . . Lisa tries to help prove Thorwald's guilt when she climbs up and into his apartment and finds Mrs. Thorwald's wedding ring, something any married woman would be wearing, were she alive, that is. As Jeff watches the action in Thorwald's apartment through binoculars, Lisa puts the ring on her finger, showing Jeff several things at once: Thorwald's guilty, I am adventurous, and this is what I want you to give me—love.

The movie mogul Samuel Goldwyn once said, "If you want to send a message, call Western Union." (Today he'd say, "If you want to send a message, e-mail it.") Goldwyn had a point. The first priority of any good storyteller is to entertain. If you don't keep the audience entertained you won't have an audience for very long. There's a reason why they don't sell popcorn, soda, and Goobers at church, which is the same reason I don't go to church. Well, that and the fact I'm Jewish.

Theme, however, can actually enrich the entertainment value of a movie. Although the audience shouldn't be thinking about the theme, it's there beneath the surface, unseen but making us experience the movie all the more deeply. Earlier in this book, you learned about subtext in scenes and dialogue. Theme is like the subtext for the entire movie—that submerged layer that adds a little something extra to the experience. That's why theme is an underlay.

Theme Unearthed

Most people think of theme as a moral or message. That's fine if you're a preacher or a student forced to write an essay, but it's not what theme means in terms of a good story. What screenwriters mean by theme is simply an underlying idea. Just an idea, any kind of idea. Very possibly, the theme will *not* be a moral, *not* be a message. It'll be . . . something else.

Let me go out on a limb and say that *all* good movies have themes. It probably wouldn't surprise you in the least to hear that such movies as *A Clockwork Orange, Midnight Cowboy, One Flew Over the Cuckoo's Nest, The Seventh Seal,* and *Les Enfants du Paradis* have themes. But let's put my claim to the test with a "popcorn" movie like *Die Hard.* Probably not the first movie that comes to mind when you think about theme. Let's face it, *Die Hard* is primarily an entertaining action flick about Bruce Willis kicking butt. Nothing wrong with that. And that's all it needs to be, entertaining. Okay, so what's the theme of *Die Hard?*

Die Hard is about *the triumph of the little guy.* That's the underlying idea. John McClane isn't physically little—he's got more muscles than me, to be sure—but he is presented as something of a little guy. McClane's just an honest, hardworking New York City cop with street smarts who seems small and out of place in the tall office tower and the glitzy world of the Nakatomi Corporation. He's

competing for survival against chic, well-financed, European terrorists who smoke European cigarettes. He's up against the big
guns of the LAPD and FBI. And he's one man against all of this,
which makes him a little guy. And who are his two allies in the
movie? The street cop, Powell. Little guy. Argyle, the limo driver
on his first run. Little guy. McClane's even something of a little guy
against his wife, who has been promoted to a big-shot position in
her company.

Subplots are good for supporting the theme of a movie, and
the bond between McClane and Powell, both regular-joe cops, is
where the theme comes through especially strong. And you know
that at the end, when Karl gets blown away and we see that it's Powell who shot him—the man who's been afraid to pick up a gun
ever since he mistakenly shot a kid. That's a great moment, got a
big cheer in the theater. What's that moment about? Triumph of
the little guy.

A theme is something that we can all identify with, even if our
life is nothing like what's portrayed in the story. Theme helps connect the movie to the audience. We've all felt like the little guy at
one time or another. Perhaps you were the new kid at school? Perhaps you found out that your ex was dating someone richer, pret
tier, or younger (or all three—yikes)? Perhaps the sports team you
root for is always the underdog. I know for a fact that you know
what it's like to feel like the little guy—you're hoping to break into
the movie business for crying out loud!

Now, if somebody asks you what *Die Hard* is about, it would be
preposterous to say, "Oh, it's about the triumph of the little guy."
You'd only know that if you were out to unearth the theme, which
you wouldn't do unless you were a screenwriter or film studies
professor. It's actually not the least bit important that the audience leave the multiplex saying, "Wow, that movie had such a
great theme!" If they're thinking of a movie's theme, it usually
means they're not involved in the story and characters. It usually
means it's a bad movie. The theme of a movie is there to be

absorbed subliminally. Felt. So if someone asks you what *Die Hard* is about, you tell them, "It's about Bruce Willis kicking butt." But, take my word for it, *Die Hard* is a better kick-butt movie because of its theme.

Now I realize that "triumph of the little guy" isn't an especially unique theme. We could probably think of a bunch of other movies that use that exact same theme. But uniqueness isn't really what counts. What counts is how well that theme is dramatized in the story. In fact, the most powerful themes are often the ones that are the most universal.

The theme of *Thelma & Louise* could be stated as: *It's a male-dominated world, and men don't always treat women very well.* Not an especially unique theme. But *Thelma & Louise* tells a unique story, and the movie illustrates its theme in a unique, not to mention powerful, way. What about *Tootsie*? What's the theme there? You could make a case that it has the exact same theme as *Thelma & Louise.* It's true; think about it. Yet look at how different these two movies are.

What about *Sideways*? Hmm, this isn't always so easy, but if you press me I'd have to say that the theme of *Sideways* is: S*top worrying so much and just live your life.*

See, a theme can come in many forms:

- A concept: Triumph of the little guy; romantic love.

- A truism: It's a male-dominated world, and men don't always treat women very well.

- Advice: Stop worrying so much and just live your life.

A theme can even come in the form of some odd or provocative theory or conundrum that the movie explores. Here, let me open my *Bartlett's Familiar Quotations*:

The only way to get rid of temptation is to yield to it.
—*Oscar Wilde*

You can't always get what you want / But if you try
sometimes / You just might find / You get what you need.
—*The Rolling Stones*

I'm fairly certain that you, or someone else, could write a fascinating movie using either of those themes.

Let me point out that you may not agree with some of my thematic interpretations, and that's fine. Plot is concrete and on the surface. We can't miss it. Theme should be abstract and way below the surface. Theme shouldn't be as easy for the audience to identify as the plot, or even the tone. It is important, however, for the writer to understand the theme of a story being created, even if no one else gets it or agrees with it.

Can a movie have more than one theme? Yes, but you'll be better off thinking about your movie having one dominant theme. As with tone, one dominant theme keeps your movie consistent while allowing for variations that support the main thread. And although the dominant theme of *Tootsie* is about men not treating women well, I also see a sub-theme about identity, hiding from yourself and then learning who you are.

Working with Theme

If you're like me, you don't just do things because others say it's good for you, so don't agonize over theme just because some guy in a book told you to. Here's another reason to think about theme, perhaps a better one. Not only does a theme make a movie more powerful, it makes it easier to write. With all those scenes and characters and events, it may be hard to know which ones you really need and how to slant them. Your theme will help you make those choices, and will help tie together your dozens of scenes, your cast of characters, the main storyline, the subplots, and everything else. The more unified the movie, the better.

This brings up the question of how to go about working with

theme. I don't believe there should be strict rules on how you develop your screenplay. My experience in writing and teaching, however, has shown me time and again that developing a screenplay to demonstrate a theme often, if not always, proves disastrous. Theme is best handled loosely at first and move tightly later on.

Start with your story—the characters and the action. After you've got a good handle on those things, consider the theme of your movie. And even then you shouldn't worry about it too much until you're in the revision stage. Better that you let the theme emerge naturally from the story you are trying to tell. Theme is there to enrich the story, not the other way around.

Let's say that I am writing *The Shawshank Redemption* (oh, wish I had!) and let's say it's an original story, not one based on a novella by Stephen King. My story conferences with myself might go something like this:

Ah, yes, I have an idea for a movie: A hero tries to maintain hope despite overwhelming obstacles. No, that's no good. It's a theme. Forget about theme for now.

Okay, think story. What's the story? It's about a guy in prison serving a life sentence who survives for years but ends up making a big escape. Maybe the movie is about him organizing and planning the escape. Nah, that worked in *The Great Escape* but I like the idea of him being quieter about it, operating solo.

Let's make him a quiet type, someone you don't expect to do well inside, but he does. Then maybe he becomes a hero to all the other guys and eventually he feels like they're worshipping him too much. Nah, that worked in *Cool Hand Luke* but this guy is quieter than that. Not a showboat.

Maybe he tunnels all these years and no one knows. That's better. And maybe we don't even let the audience know. So then what do we see him doing? He likes to help others, and this also helps him sustain his spirits. He builds a library, teaches a guy how to read.

And then I go to work on my script, maybe even hammer out a

rough draft. Afterward, I go back and look at what the characters do and say, digging deeper now for some possible (not definite) meaning. It may go like this:

Let's see what I've got. I see a man tunneling, slowly, out of prison. I see a man building a library for his fellow inmates. I see a man making the prison a better place, filling it with Mozart's music. I hear a man telling others not to give up hope, despite how hopeless things might appear. Wait a second, that strikes a chord. The man is tunneling out, hoping to escape. The library gives hope by allowing prisoners to read books and escape the prison via their imagination. The Mozart brings hope that the impossible is possible and that there are some things the warden can't take away from them.

Interesting, it all connects. It all has something to do with hope. He's maintaining his sense of hope. That's what he's doing. That's what the movie is really about. That hope is what'll keep him alive, and that's what'll give him the courage to keep tunneling. Maybe the theme is: *Hope will set you free.*

Yes, good theme. I like it. Like it a lot. You don't have to be a prisoner to identify with that. We all feel trapped by something. And it works perfectly with the story I'm writing.

That's how I may have arrived at my theme, letting it come from the story itself. I may have even changed my mind about the theme a few times before settling on what I wanted it to be. Then, once you do settle on a theme, you start making the theme inform your story from its underground reservoir. Ideally, the theme will end up influencing almost everything in the movie. But the principle of "show, don't tell" applies to theme in a major way. Remember, you don't want to preach your theme. It's fine if no one but you knows what it is. All that you're doing here is making your story better and tighter by keeping it focused on a unifying idea.

So, you create new scenes or tweak scenes to make them illustrate your theme. Andy doesn't just build the library, he spends years writing endless letters to get the funding for it, never giving up. After Andy plays the Mozart, we see him in the hole for a long stretch and he's okay, because the Mozart is in his head and heart, giving him hope.

Find images that echo the theme. Shawshank is a stone place. We see Andy carve his name in stone with a little rock hammer. Red assumes he's not trying to break out because it would take "six hundred years" with that hammer; in other words, it would be "hopeless." But whether Red or the audience knows it or not, this little hammer symbolizes hope. And then almost twenty years later, we see Andy has tunneled through the stone, and then we see him free, arms outstretched in the pouring rain. The whole motif of chipping stone is a perfect illustration of *hope will set you free.*

Subplots can help support the theme because they don't have the burden of carrying the main action. Shawshank makes ample use of two thematic subplots. Brooks is released but he's still not free, lacks hope, hangs himself. Later, Red goes down the same road but the thought of meeting Andy gives him hope.

Should you ever come right out and just state your theme? Actually there's no pressing need to do so. When theme is dramatized well, there is no need to state it. Do you remember any scene in *Die Hard* in which McClane said something like, "You know, I may be just a little guy but us little guys can make a difference in the world. Know what I mean, Al?" Not only is there no need to state the theme but if you do it like this it will sound incredibly ham-handed.

You can, however, state the theme, or something very close to it, if you slip it in gently, naturally. Something like this happens at the very end of *Shawshank,* when Red travels to meet Andy in Mexico.

```
A  gorgeous  New  England  landscape  whizzes  by,
fields  and  trees  a  blur  of  motion.  ANGLE  SHIFTS  to
reveal  a  Greyhound  Sceni-Cruiser  barreling  up  the
road,  pulling  abreast  of  us.  CAMERA  TRAVELS  from
window  to  window,  passing  faces.  We  finally  come
to  Red  gazing  out  at  the  passing  landscape.
```

>   RED (V.O.)
>   I find I am so excited I can
>   barely sit still or hold a
>   thought in my head. I think
>   it is the excitement only a
>   free man can feel, a free
>   man at the start of a long
>   journey whose conclusion is
>   uncertain . . .

THE BUS ROARS past camera, dwindling to a mere
speck on the horizon.

>   RED (V.O.)
>   I hope I can make it across
>   the border. I hope to see my
>   friend and shake his hand. I
>   hope the Pacific is as blue
>   as it has been in my dreams.
>   (beat)
>   I hope.

And right then we see panoramic view of the ocean, a visual of
limitless freedom.

Take a Shot

Watch a movie, any movie. How would you describe the tone, using three
to five words and/or phrases? Aside from photography and music, what
are some of the things that convey the tone? How would you define the
movie's theme? What moment in the movie conveys the theme most
strongly? (You can test yourself against our answers if you use one of the
movies listed at www.WritingMovies.info.)

Stepping-Stone: Tone/Theme

Try to capture the tone of your movie in three to five words and/or phrases.

Take a stab at defining the theme of your movie in a word, phrase, or sentence.

CHAPTER 10

Revision: From Rough to Ready

BY AMY FOX

In *State and Main* (written and directed by David Mamet), a film crew invades a bucolic Vermont town to make a movie. Joe, the nervous first-time screenwriter, is called in to the director's office and asked to do a rewrite when the film crew learns that a key location is not available. "We can't shoot the old mill," the director tells him.

The mill, it seems, burned down years ago. There is no money left to build a new old mill, and the old mill the crew built for their previous location is being held hostage by the New Hampshire town from which the film crew has been banished. "What would they have used, instead of an old mill?" the director asks sharply. "I need it tonight."

Joe goes pale. And we catch a glimpse of the film's title on the script's cover: *The Old Mill*.

Joe is going to have to do some serious revision under serious pressure. But that's the game. Every writer understands sooner or later that revision is a fundamental part of the writing process. You've probably heard the phrase "writing is rewriting." Sometimes it's fixing minor matters, like sharpening dialogue or shortening a scene, and sometimes it's a major overhaul, like removing the old mill from *The Old Mill*. But remember, you simply can't write a terrific script without plenty of revision.

We've all heard stories of someone who punched out their first draft in three weeks and sold it the next day. I've never met this person. I have my doubts that this person actually exists. The writers I know do lots of drafts. Even if they suspect that someone in Hollywood will rewrite the script later on, they go through many drafts to get to the point where their script might actually sell.

The ability to revise is an essential skill for your development and success as a screenwriter. Revision will not only make your script better, it will make you a better writer. Being able to identify and fix problems in a script will inform the way you approach your next project. There are a surprising number of people walking around out there with a good story to tell, but far fewer people know how to fix a script that has problems, and can get that good story to stop tripping over itself and achieve its potential.

Often I am asked how many drafts it takes to fully revise a screenplay. People look especially nervous when they ask this question. They want me to say two, or maybe four. I tell them that by the time I'm sending my scripts out, the file is usually labeled something like *Heights*-15 on my computer. Their faces fall. I explain that some of these drafts contain rather minor revisions, but that usually, in my experience, a script goes through four or five drafts with major revisions. Obviously the number of drafts varies from project to project, writer to writer. The point is, though, that it takes numerous drafts to make a great screenplay.

The more you work with your script, however, the more you recapture the energy and feeling of inspiration that motivated your first draft. Bit by bit, you will feel your script getting better. And that's a good feeling, good enough to make you want to sit down at your computer for as long as it takes for your story to evolve from rough to ready.

The First Draft

Before you can even think about revising, you have to get your first draft down on paper. Filling 120 or so blank pages can be intimidating. You can make the first draft easier by starting off with some kind of outline. You might even revise your outline several times before you actually dive into that first draft. Working on profiles of your characters at the outset might also prove helpful.

Depending on your subject matter, it can also be useful to research your story before beginning your first draft. Maybe you are writing a period piece or a script based on true events, or maybe you need only a few facts to get started. Research helps bring you into the world of your story. Just don't get so caught up in your research that you never start writing. Visiting the library or surfing the Internet can easily become a way of procrastinating. If you find yourself delaying your first draft until you become an expert on your subject matter, ask yourself what kind of information you really need to know before getting started. Remember, you can always do more research along the way.

Sooner or later, though, it's time to start that first draft. When you are writing a first draft, you have one fundamental task that trumps all others: Build momentum. One of my teachers, the playwright Connie Congden, once told me that if you are writing a story about five brothers, and you realize on page 85 that there are only two brothers, you still go forward. You go forward with two brothers, as if they were the only ones that ever existed, and you write their ending. Then, you go back to the beginning and kill off the extraneous brothers so that your ending fits.

I've met lots of people who have never completed a draft, but have a suitcase full of half-written screenplays. Sometimes they simply ran out of steam or enthusiasm. Sometimes it was because they got sucked into the cycle of rewriting too early. Maybe they showed their first ten pages to a friend, got some feedback, and set out trying to fix the problems. Then they showed the revised ten pages to a different friend, got some new feedback, and went back to page 1. They refuse to continue writing the rest of the screenplay until those first ten pages are perfect. What they may not realize is that once they reach page 95, it's possible that those first ten pages will turn out to have nothing to do with this screenplay. Even the most polished opening will need an overhaul once you have a sense of the whole movie.

Revising as you go not only slows you down, it suggests the false and dangerous notion that you are writing a perfect script. You are not writing a perfect script. You may not even be writing a good script. You have to give yourself permission to write some pretty terrible material in your first draft. You have to try things out, and you can't be afraid of taking a wrong turn. There will be time to revise your script later, to bring it up to your highest standards, but don't let those standards squelch your momentum as you get the first version of this story onto paper.

Preparing to Revise

All right, let's say you've done it. You've written a first draft, you've followed your characters on a journey, you've figured out your ending, and you've even written those two wonderful words: Fade Out. Pour some champagne, dance on the table. But whatever you do, don't FedEx your script to your cousin who knows an agent. Not yet. You still have a lot of work to do.

The first thing you want to do is get perspective. Take a break from your script. Don't study it, don't read it over the phone to your friends, don't tell everybody about the movie you just finished writing. You want to give yourself a clean slate. I recommend taking at least two weeks off. Sometimes people need longer.

When you feel refreshed and ready, sit down with a hard copy of your script. Allow yourself enough time so that you can read the whole thing from beginning to end without interruption. Read the script relatively quickly, to simulate the experience of an audience watching a film. You can make a list as you go, and mark questions and places you want to return to, but don't start rewriting or fixing problems as you read. What you want is a sense of the whole.

Then it's time to start revising. This can be daunting. For one thing, you've already spent the initial burst of energy that made you sit down to tell the story in the first place. People rarely feel *inspired* to begin a revision. Discipline is often required. Also you have to turn back on that critical voice that you may have managed to turn off while you wrote your first draft. *I'll fix that later,* you may have said, plunging forward to the next part of your story. When you sit down to revise, "later" is now.

As you prepare to enter the stages of revision, there is a fundamental question you must ask yourself. What is the one thing in this screenplay that you, the writer, must preserve, no matter how many other elements you change. It could be anything—a character, a central idea, the tone. It usually has something to do with why you wrote the script in the first place. You have to identify what is most essential to your vision of this project. If somebody recommends cutting your five brothers down to two brothers, and your screenplay is fundamentally an exploration of sibling rivalry, that might still work. But if you wrote the screenplay to dramatize the dynamics of large families, that revision probably isn't the best idea. This may sound obvious, but it's dangerous to begin a revision without knowing what must be preserved in order for this story to still have backbone and legs to stand on.

When I was working on my screenplay *Heights,* I was told by the producers that a character's conflicted sexuality was no longer an interesting theme these days. Apparently all that gay stuff had been worked out in the '90s. The producers asked me if I could give my character "another kind of secret" to hide from his fiancée. I had made a lot of changes to this script, and was extremely open to the revision process, but I knew that if I made that change, I would lose what the story was fundamentally about. I was writing about people who follow their passions, even while they try desperately to keep up public appearances. And, like it or not,

I had built an entire drama around a man desperate to avoid facing his sexuality. Without that element my screenplay would collapse like a house of cards. I wouldn't be able to defend any part of the story. So I told the producers I couldn't do it, not out of principle but out of honesty; I could not do a decent job with that kind of revision. Luckily, they changed their minds, and the character's conflicted sexuality remained intact.

The Process

So what do you tackle first? It's practically impossible to revise a script all in one fell swoop. A screenplay is a big, unwieldy product, and our minds tackle it best in steps and stages. The concept of separate drafts is key to maintaining your sanity as you revise. Without it, revision becomes an endless and ongoing process, in which you find yourself constantly tinkering with your material, unsure whether you are making it better or worse. For each draft, you should determine your priorities from the outset. For example, in one draft you will cut out the extraneous brothers and focus on strengthening the relationship of those remaining. This way you won't get distracted by minor things in the script or end up with a muddle of old and new material. Each draft should strengthen a particular aspect of your script, and each draft should take you closer to your finished product.

Usually the revision process breaks down into early drafts, middle drafts, and late drafts. In early drafts, it's important to keep two things in mind: Focus on the big picture; and be open to change, no matter how major. In an early draft, for instance, you may find that the protagonist is someone other than who you imagined, or that the story should go in a direction you did not envision. If this happens, don't think of that first draft as wasted time. Sometimes it takes a draft or two to find the best way to tell your story. M. Night Shamalyan, the writer-director of *The Sixth Sense*, has remarked that it took five drafts for him to figure out the major plot twist in the story—the one that made this movie so unforgettable—and another five to execute what he was trying to do. His openness to change paid off, in a major way.

When you are certain about the fundamentals of your story, you move into middle drafts. Here you are improving the execution of that story. Look at your script from the perspective of the audience. What is their experience of this story the way you have written it? What information do they have? What are they paying attention to? What are they feeling? Middle drafts are also a good time to focus on subplots and secondary characters that may have gotten short shrift in earlier stages. It's also important to start cutting and compressing at this point.

Late drafts are versions that you go over with the eagle eye of an informed craftsperson. You tighten every moment of every scene, you rework transitions, you sharpen the dialogue and description. You clean up every typo, and you use every tool in your kit to prepare your baby for the harsh world.

What about feedback? You probably want some feedback on your script along the way. Feedback will help you get perspective and prioritize what are the most critical issues and questions to address in your revisions. People usually ask two big questions about feedback: When should I let people read my script, and whom should I ask? These are important queries, because although feedback is extremely helpful, it can also be damaging.

The general rule is to write as much as you can without asking for feedback. Trust yourself and your instincts, particularly in the middle of a draft. It's much better to show someone a complete story than a fragment that is not complete or out of context. You want to figure out your own agenda for the story before worrying too much about other people's ideas. You're probably best off not showing your script to anyone until after you've hammered out a few drafts. Many writers prefer not to show their work at all until it's in its final stages. (The process works differently, of course, if you're in a screenwriting class, where ongoing feedback is solicited and given.)

Be selective about whom you ask. It's best not to solicit opinion from someone who will be either too easy (your mother) or unnecessarily harsh (wounded exes, especially if they recognize something familiar in the material). You should also avoid showing your early work to any contacts you may have in the industry because they should see only the most polished version possible. But if someone is at hand who knows a little about screenwriting or storytelling, give it to that person. If not, at least seek out someone who is genuinely interested in movies and in taking a look at your work. When your script is nearing completion, you might want to ask three or four people for feedback at the same time. That way you can begin to determine whether similar trends are appearing in people's responses. In this way, you avoid getting a critique based on one person's very subjective reading.

When you are given feedback, make sure you filter it. You don't have to follow every piece of advice. Which opinions resonate for you? How can you *improve* your story, not change it into the story someone else wishes you were telling? I'm not suggesting that you be defensive when people tell you what they think. It's not a question of right or wrong. It's about making your script better. The comments will either be useful or they won't. You decide. But first listen with an open mind, and let other people's advice help you see your own work from a different perspective.

Take a Shot

Think of something you have recently experienced or seen or heard about that might be fabricated into an interesting three-minute movie. Write a first draft of the mini-movie very quickly. Then write two more drafts of the movie, improving it substantially with each draft. This will give you a crash course in the entire process.

Things to Consider

I won't attempt to recap everything that has been covered in this book, but rather let me highlight some of the major issues that you should consider as you rewrite. After years of advising my students on their revisions, and struggling through my own drafts, certain challenges come up again and again.

The Protagonist's Journey

Your first priority is to make sure the protagonist's journey remains on track. Everything will hinge on this.

Always refer back to your major dramatic question. Even in the early drafts, you should know what it is, but things change or get clarified along the way. Is the protagonist's goal working? Is it strong and specific enough to sustain the movie? Are there enough obstacles to the goal, both external and internal, to keep the story riveting all the way through? Are hard choices required in pursuit of the goal? Do the obstacles build to a climax where this character is forced to make a difficult choice or survive overwhelming obstacles to reach the goal? And keep an eye on the protagonist's arc: Is the protagonist changing as the journey intensifies?

You also want to ensure that the protagonist's journey fits well within the three-act structure. It's not necessarily as important for you to follow all the classic rules of plotting as it is for your story to progress as powerfully as it should. If you're breaking with the norms, make sure it's for a good reason.

Also, keep your protagonist front and center. This may sound obvious, but a surprising number of writers reach the end of their first draft having lost clarity about which character is really driving the action. Remember that a protagonist is the most active character, the one who makes the most difficult choices, and undergoes the most changes over the course of a film. If you have inadvertently allowed other characters to overshadow your protagonist, this is the time to pull back on some of them and make your protagonist more central and dynamic.

Often you will find your protagonist can be the driving force behind scenes, choices, and conflicts that already exist in the script but currently spotlight other characters. Your secondary characters can still be fascinating people, and have their own motivations and arcs, but not at the expense of constructing a dramatic journey for your protagonist. Your protagonist does not have to be in every scene, but he or she shouldn't disappear for a large chunk of story time.

If you are writing a script that has two protagonists, then this is the time to ascertain that the balance between the lead characters is working. Do your two protagonists both remain active and central throughout the script? For example, in a romantic comedy, be careful that one of the protagonists doesn't run away with the film for too long.

You also have to pay attention to balance in a multi-plot script. In my multiplot film, *Heights,* I considered each of my characters separately, and took care to identify a goal, conflict, and obstacles for each independent story. When I wove them all together, I found a handy visual tool for checking how I was balancing these plot lines. I printed out a list of every scene in the script, and color-coded it according to which character the scene was focused on. The color chart gave me a quick way to determine whether certain parts of the script were more heavily weighted on behalf of certain characters. If a certain sequence included only green and yellow, I knew my blue character should make an appearance.

Impact

It may seem as if the easiest way to make sure that your audience understands the protagonist's journey (or anything else) is simply to tell them. Your little girl shows up on page 1 and announces that she wants to join the circus. Now that the goal has been established, you can check that off your list, right? Not really. Because the easiest way is not always the best way. You are not simply trying to transmit information about your story to your audience. You want that information to have impact. You want your audience to feel invested in the characters; to care whether they succeed; to squirm in their seats when the obstacles crop up. How do you do that? You show us. Do we see that girl in the audience, loving every moment of the circus? Is that enough? Most kids love the circus. Do we see her going back every night, attending every single performance? Do we see her sadly watching the circus performers pack up their belongings and take down the tent? Do we see the obstacles she faces, and feel her desperation to overcome those obstacles?

As you revise your script, think about how to create maximum impact from each scene in your screenplay. If you are soliciting feedback, pay attention to whether more than one reader seems to be missing important aspects of your story. They may ask you what the character really wants, or why they act a certain way. You may find yourself flipping to the page in your script where you clearly told us the answers to these questions. But instead of arguing that the answer is "right there on the page," consider the impact of the information. Is there a more dramatic way to show us what we are missing?

Stakes

The best way to keep an audience on the edge of their seats is to make sure the stakes are high enough. Stakes are best defined as how much a character stands to gain or lose at any moment.

Take a simple scene in which a man asks a woman out. If your main character is a smooth, charming, ladies' man, then this scene will not necessarily have high stakes. If your main character is a shy recluse who has never dated anyone, suddenly there's a lot at stake in the scene. What does Don Juan have to lose if the woman says no? Not much. He will probably take it in stride, move on to the next bird. The shy recluse has much more to lose; he may never ask out another woman. And if she says yes, this unlikely, awkward man may actually find true love, whereas the charmer probably wouldn't take this relationship all that seriously.

This is not to say that you can't create higher stakes for the ladies' man. You have to ask yourself what he could gain or lose from this situation. Is this woman different from all the rest? Is she his chance at redemption? How does the audience know that? Or maybe he's married, and this woman works with his wife. There are all kinds of creative ways to heighten the stakes for your characters. How can you tweak the scene so there is even more to be gained or lost at this moment?

Sure, the climax is a high-stakes moment. But it's important to look at the rest of the script so that dramatic consequences are at stake throughout. The actions in your script should always feel risky; moment by moment you want us to feel that something wonderful or terrible could result.

Picture an audience member who has to go to the bathroom, but doesn't want to get up and leave the theater because she might miss something. When should she go? Ideally, there should be enough at stake in every scene to make that audience member want to stay in her seat to see what happens next. And when she does finally make her trip out to the lobby, she absolutely should miss something.

Cutting and Compressing

If your screenplay exceeds 120 pages, you already know that you have to do some cutting. Nobody in the movie industry likes to receive a script longer than 120 pages. Even if you have written the next *Lawrence of Arabia,* your reader will assume that you have not learned the skill of compression. But even if your script comes in under 120, you are not off the hook. Because cutting is not only about length. It is about making sure that every bit of that script is working double duty to achieve as much as possible in a short space of time. That's the art of screenwriting.

Cutting and compressing is an essential part of the revision process. Not only will you tighten your existing material, but you will also create space for any new material which may strengthen your script. To cut your script so you can add to it may sound contradictory, but in doing so you are creating room to fix problems identified during revision. Chances are, the new material will have a clear purpose and will serve you better than the material you cut. It's like cleaning out your closet so you can buy the outfits you really want to wear.

One helpful exercise is to go through a hard copy of your script and cross out everything you suspect you don't need. Be ruthless. You don't have room for small talk, hellos, or moments when people tell us things we already know. See if you can cut scenes in half while retaining their essential function. Take comfort knowing you can always put something back (but usually you won't need to).

Instead of putting things back, however, see if you can maximize the impact of every line of dialogue and description. Every moment, every word should do something significant, whether it moves your story forward, reveals character, increases conflict, or simply adds atmosphere.

Supporting Characters

Supporting characters are not usually fully fleshed out in a first draft. This is a good thing. It means you have focused on your protagonist. As you revise, however, turn your attention to developing these other characters. You might even want to do a separate draft for each significant character, focusing only on that one character as you revise.

I sometimes imagine my screenplay as an office where I have been hired as a consultant. If the office is full of laconic people who don't know why they are there or don't perform the jobs they are supposed to do, the office needs help. Imagine how much better the office will function if you cut that staff down to a core group in which every employee fills a very specific and essential job. In other words, it's time to consider whether you can cut any extraneous characters, and whether the characters that remain are really doing their best job. The good news is you don't have to hurt anyone's feelings or lay off a father of six. At least, nobody who is real.

Subplots

Many writers find that their main plot and subplots are so intertwined in their first draft, that they've lost track of which is which. Is your movie a love story in which a guy also happens to find a career, or is it a story about a guy finding success in his career, while he also happens to fall in love? Your main story is the one linked to your protagonist's *primary* goal. The protagonist may have other goals as well—he's always wanted to ride horses, he wouldn't say no to true love, and he certainly wouldn't mind patching things up with his estranged sister. But unless these are what your protagonist wants *most*, they are subplot. And if they are subplot, they should also get trumped by the needs of your main plot. If you need to make a change in your main plot and your subplot is compromised, so be it.

In early drafts, you may want to reduce your subplots to their function in your big picture. Ask yourself: What do you need from this subplot in order for your main plot to succeed best? In later drafts you can go back to these subplots, to give them more depth and specificity. Just as you might want to spend a draft focusing on each of your major characters, you might want to devote a draft on each subplot. Now that you know how your subplot fits your big picture, you can isolate your subplot from the rest of the script and look at its scenes back to back. You can revise it as if it were a short film—more compressed than your feature story, but populated by interesting characters battling conflict while on journeys of their own.

Make It Visual

A major goal of revision is to look for opportunities to make your script more visual. Is there dialogue that can be replaced by an image? Are there places where people are talking about something that can be shown instead of discussed? A character shouldn't tell us they have nightmares. They should wake up shaking and drenched in sweat. A character shouldn't tell his friend how he got stood up last night. We should watch him drinking glass after glass of wine alone at the bar. In the scene from *State and Main* mentioned earlier, the joke is a visual one. The first-time screenwriter doesn't tell us, "But that's the title of the script." It's much funnier to let us *see* the title on the cover page.

A screenplay should be a mix of action and dialogue. If your pages contain only dialogue, you are not visualizing your story enough. This is not a simple matter of adding a line of action such as "he leans forward" to break up the dialogue. It's a matter of watching your story unfold in front of a camera and staying aware of the essential physicality of the scenes.

Watch the first ten minutes of *The Triplets of Belleville*, an animated movie that contains essentially no dialogue. We learn that the main character is an orphaned boy living with his grandmother in a small town in France that has been left behind by industrial development. We see this boy's melancholy, his desperate desire for a bicycle, his relationship with his dog and grandmother, and the routine nature of their lives. Every bit of emotion and information we receive is transmitted visually. You don't have to create a movie without dialogue, but you want to treat dialogue as a valuable privilege you have been granted to *help* you tell a story, a story that *could* be told solely through images.

Logic

Someone will notice your script's gaps in logic. We all know that guy. We've all gone to the movies with him. The guy who wants to know how they flew the plane to Alaska without refueling, or how that woman had time to change her outfit. That guy who keeps pointing out all the little gaps in logic throughout the film. Usually we remind that guy that this is a movie—a certain suspension of disbelief is called for. And this is true, to some degree. But how much should an audience be asked to forgive? As little as possible. It is our job, as writers, to create and sustain the logic of a story. An audience will believe anything if you do your job right.

If you're working in a surreal world, as found in many sci-fi, horror, and fantasy stories, then you need to work overtime on your logic. In a movie like *The Matrix*, for example, numerous questions of logic arise. How and why did the AI machines create a world where humans live in a virtual simulation? How do the rebels manage to evade the machines? What happens when a human is pulled into his true consciousness? How does what happens in the virtual world affect the humans in the real world?

Some movies, like thrillers, have lots of surprising twists and turns, and each of them has to make sense. Why would the smart woman marry a man who is secretly a psychopathic killer? How does he manage to change his identity so handily? How is she able to obtain police reports in Kansas City without special access? You need to find answers to such questions. This takes work, experimentation, and mapping things out.

Logic is also important in more realistic movies. Most likely your plot will contain a set of extreme circumstances occurring a condensed period of time. These circumstances may not seem very probable, but they should seem possible. In *Thelma & Louise*, for example, two perfectly nice women turn into outlaws in a matter of days, and yet the writer has worked out the logic well enough for us to understand why Louise murders Harlan, why Thelma robs a store, and why the women run for Mexico rather than turn themselves in. The writer has established motivations and chosen the best catalyst for each new development, so it all feels plausible.

It's best to avoid coincidences. They defy logic and make us question the believability of the story. Whenever possible, find a logical reason for something to happen rather than relying on coincidence. In *Heights,* two major characters, Diana and Alec, meet early in the film. Alec is noticeably nervous about the encounter. Much later, we discover the reason for this—Alec is having an illicit affair with someone very close to Diana. But how can we believe that these two characters might cross paths early on? If they happen to meet at a party, or sit next to each other on the train, that's coincidence. But they meet when Alec, a struggling actor, auditions for a play Diana is directing. If you ask anyone familiar with the small world of New York theater, it is entirely plausible that they would meet under these circumstances. (More than once I've been surprised to find an ex-boyfriend showing up to audition for one of my plays.)

If you must use a coincidence, use only one. If you're lucky, the audience will forgive you that one time.

Setup—Payoff and Foreshadowing

Usually, major developments in your story will be more believable and dramatically satisfying if they have been carefully set up. Toward the end of *The Shawshank Redemption* Andy not only makes a spectacular escape but he arranges things so he can withdraw a vast sum of money from a bank, on which he will live for the rest of his life. It's fairly improbable, but we buy it because it's been well set up. We learn that Andy is a banker and that he's very smart—he curries favors with the guards by giving them tax advice. Soon the warden uses Andy's expertise in an elaborate money-laundering scheme in which funds are channeled into the account of a phantom person named Randall Stevens. When Andy escapes, he knows exactly how to access the money by pretending to be Stevens. The payoff works.

Sometimes, it's a matter of finding out what the plot needs—in this case, Andy needs a large sum of money to live on—and then working backwards to figure out the steps that would make it possible. It's then a matter of figuring out how to parcel out the information throughout the screenplay. If you drop in these big things all at once, without adequate setup, it won't be believable. You have to pave the way for the payoff.

Foreshadowing is a type of setup and payoff, but it speaks more to emotion or tone than plot detail. Foreshadowing prepares an audience psychologically for what's coming (without telling them what it is) and also builds a sense of suspense.

Thelma & Louise, for example, gets off to a light, comical start, but there are a few hints of the darkness to come. Most notably, Thelma brings a gun on the trip in case they encounter "psycho killers." The introduction of the gun is humorous but, all the same, we register that a gun is present. It's a moment of foreshadowing. The playwright Anton Chekhov said that if you introduce a gun in the first act, it must go off at some point, and *Thelma & Louise* follows this advice. (The point is that if you set something up, you are obligated to pay it off.)

Body Heat tells the story of a lawyer who has a torrid romance with a femme fatale that leads to the two of them plotting the murder of her wealthy husband. We don't know where things are leading but numerous moments of foreshadowing infuse the movie with a sense of doom. A hotel in flames viewed from a distance. A clown driving down a street in a red car. A lawyer visiting a client in jail and wincing at the clang of a cell door. These moments have nothing to do with the plot, but they guide the viewer slowly but surely in the right pyschological direction.

Titles

Your title sets up an expectation on the cover page, before we even open the script. A great title will whet your reader's appetite. (It will also help when it comes time to pitch your story.) Imagine yourself calling a friend on a Friday night: "Hey, you want to go see _____?" How does your title sound when it fills that blank? *Moonstruck* was originally titled *The Bride and the Wolf.* Opinions about titles might be subjective, but in this instance the writer obviously did himself a big favor by rethinking his choice.

There's no rule about titles, except they should feel right for the movie. *Die Hard* signals heart-pumping action. *Tootsie* signals light-hearted comedy. *Thelma & Louise* tells us that this is the story of two women, and their names speak to their background. We have no idea what *Sideways* means but there's something quirky about it, which is true of the movie. *The Shawshank Redemption* is by most accounts a terrible title, but since when did that movie follow the rules?

Seek out a title that is catchy and easy to remember. Also intriguing and evocative. Some of my favorites? *Vertigo, Good Night, and Good Luck, Being John Malkovich, The Player, Scream, Witness, The Insider, Raging Bull, Bullets Over Broadway, Wall Street, Raising Arizona, The Incredibles, Dirty Pretty Things.*

Evolution at Work

Let me show you how the process of revision can improve a script by revealing the process I'm going through on a screenplay of my own, *Stuyvesant Town.* The story is set in New York City, just after World War II. In the first act, one of my goals is to portray the transition from wartime to peacetime, particularly for women who had been working on the homefront and were then expected to go back to being housewives. My protagonist, Edith, is having a difficult time making this transition. During the war years, she worked in a radio factory and liked the job, but now she knows she won't be able to stay there.

Here is a very rough first version of one scene:

EXT. BUS STOP. DAY

Edith and her neighbor, Ann, are waiting for the bus on a busy New York street.

                    ANN
          Where are you headed?

                    EDITH
          Going to work.

                    ANN
          Really? You're still
          working?

                    EDITH
          Just for a little while
          longer. I'm going to give
          notice, but I keep putting
          it off.   .

                    ANN
          I left the factory months
          ago. As soon as Richard came
          home. What are you doing?

                    EDITH
          Fixing radios.

                    ANN
          I'm sure they don't need as
          many radios now that the
          war's over —

                         EDITH
          Yeah, it's not so much for
          the Army anymore. I guess
          mostly it's families that
          want to sit around and
          listen to the news.

                          ANN
          You know, there's a whole
          lot of men who came back
          from overseas and need their
          jobs back. Like my brother
          Jack . . .

                         EDITH
          I know.

                          ANN
          And there are the widows of
          course, who have to keep
          working . . . I mean,
          they're the breadwinners
          now.

                         EDITH
          I know. We're lucky to have
          the choice.

                          ANN
          My brother says they're
          keeping the women on because
          they can pay them less.

                         EDITH
          I don't know if that's true.
          I do a good job.

                         ANN
              Well, that's what he says.

                         EDITH
              I'm going to give notice.
              Maybe today even. It's just
              that I've liked working.
              It's always a new challenge.
              And I liked being part of
              something. You know what
              I mean? Feeling like I'm
              really making a difference.
              I guess I'll miss that.

The bus pulls up.

                         EDITH
                    (continuing)
              Do you take this one?

                         ANN
              Oh no, it's the other one.
              I'm going to pick my daughter
              up from school. Who's picking
              up your daughter?

                         EDITH
              A friend. She's been very
              helpful.

                         ANN
              Well. Good luck.

                         EDITH
              You too.

Edith gets on the bus.

Obviously this scene needs work. It's slow and boring and not very visual. It feels like it's only purpose is to give us exposition. There is a subtle conflict between the women, but their dialogue is stilted and too on the nose. Here is a revised (and somewhat better) version of the scene:

```
EXT. BUS STOP — DAY

Edith and her neighbor, Ann, are waiting for the
bus amid the typical chaos of a New York street.
Ann leans in to see what Edith is reading. Edith
shows her the cover: a manual on radio repair.

                    ANN
          You're not still working,
          are you?

                    EDITH
          For now.

                    ANN
          I left the factory months
          ago. As soon as Richard came
          home. There's so many men
          who need their jobs back.
          Like my brother Jack . . .

                    EDITH
          I know that. But —

                    ANN
          And there are the widows, of
          course, I mean, they're the
          breadwinners now.

                    EDITH
          I know. We're . . . lucky.
```

                              ANN
                    My brother says they're
                    keeping the women on because
                    they can pay them less.

                              EDITH
                    I can fix a radio faster
                    than anyone in the shop.

                              ANN
                    Well, that's what he says.

          Edith shuts the manual.

                              EDITH
                    I'm going to give notice.
                    But I just liked being part
                    of something, you know?

          The bus rumbles up.

                              ANN
                    I take the other one. To
                    pick my daughter up from
                    school. I guess you leave
                    that to somebody else?

                              EDITH
                    Some of my friends have been
                    very helpful. And Barbara
                    understands. Or she will
                    someday.

          Edith gladly boards the bus.

          As the bus rumbles away, Edith watches Ann get
          smaller and smaller in the distance.

     In this version, I tightened the material, cutting out most of the
extraneous dialogue, creating more subtext and conflict. I also

tried to add some visual detail. But this scene still doesn't dramatize the situation as fully as I want it to. So I decided to take a whole
new tack on the scene. Here is what I came up with:

```
EXT. RADIO REPAIR SHOP — DAY

Edith sits at a worktable, focused on an intricate
tangle of wires and radio parts. Most of the other
worktables are now empty and the few workers pres-
ent are men.

GEORGE, a red-faced bruiser, sets up at the next
table.

                    GEORGE
               (teasing)
          How did I know you'd be here?

                    EDITH
          I just want to get this one
          working.

                    GEORGE
          And then you're quitting.

                    EDITH
          And then I'm quitting.

                    GEORGE
          You know, there's a whole
          lot of men who need their
          jobs back. My brother
          Jack . . .

     Edith remains focused on the radio, determined.

                    EDITH
          George — I don't need to
          hear this from you . . .
```

George gestures toward management offices.

> GEORGE
> Just 'cause these guys can
> save some money keeping you
> on instead, doesn't mean
> it's right.

> EDITH
> That's not why they've kept
> me on.

> GEORGE
> Oh yeah?

> EDITH
> I'm good. And I'm fast. Can
> your brother fix a radio as
> fast as I can?

> GEORGE
> Probably not. And he won't
> look as pretty trying.

Edith ignores this and continues fiddling with the radio.

> GEORGE
> (continuing)
> And you're not a widow—
> Someone like Mary has to
> stay on—You're lucky—

> EDITH
> I know. But I liked this. I
> was part of something.

She tests the radio. Static, more static, then . . . music. A burst of Vivaldi. Edith sets the radio upright, momentarily triumphant.

> Eyeing George, she turns off the radio.
>
> She glances toward the management offices, takes a deep breath, then marches in that direction.

Using the workplace setting is a much more visual way to convey the type of work Edith is doing, as well as the fact that she is good at her job and enjoys it. Instead of simply talking about her work, we actually see her working, stubbornly fixated on the radio until she manages to fix it.

The neighbor has been replaced with a male coworker, George, which gives us more tension. It's one thing for another woman to question Edith's choices, but there is more conflict if she is arguing with a man at the factory who suggests that she quit. Also this creates an opportunity to show the sexism of the working environment.

I also decided to set the scene in the moments before Edith quits. This raises the stakes, so that we see what Edith is giving up, rather than simply hearing a vague discussion of what she is thinking about. Lastly, I compressed the scene, using the setting and visuals and tighter dialogue to convey everything we need to know.

I can probably still make the scene better, and I may. But guess what? Now, I'm wondering whether this scene is absolutely vital to my screenplay. It may disappear altogether. And that's the way the process goes.

When Is It Done?

The revision process should not go on forever. A script can always be improved, but there is a point at which you need to settle on a final draft to send out into the world. Knowing when you have reached this point is largely instinctive. One of my teachers, Caryl Phillips, says it's when you start putting back in the commas you took out the day before. Feedback can also be a helpful way to gauge whether your script is ready. As your readers suggest fewer and fewer changes, and as their comments start to focus on smaller and very subjective matters, you know you've gotten very close.

It is possible to burn out on a script. And if that happens, it's usually a good idea to set it aside. You may come back to it later, after you've written other scripts and learned more about the craft and about yourself as a writer. Or you may decide that that script was a stepping-stone in your development as a writer. I have at least three scripts that taught me a great deal but will probably never leave my desk drawer.

So, know when to quit. But never quit too easily. Good writers are obsessive rewriters. The best of them have a little Cheech in them. Cheech is a tough-guy bodyguard in Woody Allen's *Bullets Over Broadway*. He's watching rehearsals for a Broadway play so he can keep an eye on one of the actresses, the girlfriend of a Mafia boss. Turns out, Cheech has a flair for the dramatic and he starts giving bits of advice to the playwright. Realizing that Cheech's ideas are good, that Cheech might even be more talented than he is, the playwright begins incorporating Cheech's suggestions. The cast falls in love with the rewrites without realizing who is doing most of the work. Cheech comes to care passionately about the project, and won't settle for any of it being less than perfect. He spends every moment thinking up revisions. He becomes so ruthless about improving the play that he bumps off his boss's girlfriend, whom he feels is ruining the production. When his boss finds about this, he has Cheech shot in a backstage alley during a performance.

Even in his dying moments, Cheech is trying to make the play better. Just before he collapses, he whispers one last rewrite to the playwright: "At the end of the play, tell Sylvia Poston to say she's pregnant. It will be a perfect finish."

Stepping-Stone: Write the Script

This is not a quickie. Not by a longshot. In terms of writing a screenplay, however, this is the most essential series of steps. Write the entire first draft of your screenplay. Then revise the entire screenplay numerous times, until you can make it no better.

CHAPTER 11

The Business: Slipping Past the Velvet Rope

BY CHRISTOPHER MOMENEE

Here's the scene: An aspiring screenwriter is printing out a script in a crowded NYU computer lab (thanks to the bogus validation sticker he's glued on to his old student ID). Someone enters, calls out his name—mispronouncing it as everyone does—declaring that there is an urgent phone call for him. Fearing a family emergency, he rushes to the phone. It's his writing partner on the other line. "Get home now!" he shouts. "This thing is going down! Disney wants to buy *Kid*!"

The writer runs the six blocks to his apartment in the East Village of New York City, visions of a sugarplum deal dancing in his head. He imagines attending the premiere of *Kid* at Mann's Chinese Theater on Hollywood Boulevard, doing the red carpet crawl with a budding starlet he'd met in the lounge of the Four Seasons the night before, pausing for flash-bulb-popping paparazzi, and sure, what the hell, maybe a few words for *Entertainment Tonight*. His heart pounding, the writer charges up the three flights of steps, fumbles for his keys, bursts through the door and gets on the phone with his writing partner in Jersey and their entertainment lawyer in midtown.

"Hey, guys, we have a good news–bad news situation on our hands," the lawyer says. "Good news is, Disney really likes your script."

The writer flashes on Elijah Wood for their main character.

Wait, he may be too old already. What about Haley Joel Osment? Too young?

"In fact," the lawyer continues. "They want to buy it . . . for mid-six figures."

Holy shit! This is like Lotto money. More money than he's ever dreamed of making in one fell swoop.

"What's the bad news?" the two writers ask, wondering what could possibly be bad news after that.

"Well," the lawyer says with some reluctance. "They want to bury it."

The writer's mouth falls open. Wha . . . ?

This is a true story. It happened not so long ago to my writing partner and me. *Kid* was my very first script sale, a family action/adventure about a young boy who befriends a King Kong–size "kid" gorilla. Basically E.T. in a gorilla suit. At the time, as it turned out, Disney was developing a remake of the 1949 movie *Mighty Joe Young*—also featuring a gargantuan gorilla—and wanted to make a "defensive purchase" that would take our competing script off the market. (For what it's worth, word leaked out that some executives liked our script better.) Right then and there, with the lawyer on the phone, we had to decide whether to accept the deal Disney had put on the table, or take our chances and hope that another studio would make an offer, and then make our movie. So we did what most fledgling writers would do in our position—we took the money and ran like hell.

The sale was never posted in *Variety* or the *Hollywood Reporter* with their patented industry-speak that makes you feel oddly legit, like DISNEY GOES BANANAS FOR "KID" SPEC or MOUSE NETS APE. There was no mention anywhere. Nada. The sale was buried like our script. It was as if we'd been paid with hush money. As we soon learned, a defensive purchase is standard practice in Hollywood. The studios spend millions every year on scripts they don't necessarily intend to make, often just to prevent another studio from potentially spinning them into box office gold.

It's a mad, mad, mad, mad business. You hear about the producer with a hair-trigger temper who throws phones at his assistants; the starlet who locks herself in her trailer after discovering a pimple on her chin; the screenwriter who comes onboard a project after eleven before him have been dismissed. With so much money riding on every project, so many egos vying for power and control, so much paranoia and glamour and hype in the mix, madness seems a prerequisite. Is there any other business, besides maybe gambling, where fortunes are made or lost in the span of a single weekend? Careers launched or grounded by a single project? And while a critically acclaimed film may bomb at the box office, a brainless teen movie might stay number one for five weeks in a row. It's inexplicable. It's mad. It's a world where, as the master screenwriter William Goldman so famously proclaimed, "No one knows anything."

It's also a world that is extremely difficult to enter. Think of it as an ultra-exclusive nightclub decked out with palm trees, lily ponds, and maybe a few exotic women swinging from trapezes. You saunter up to the entrance, but are quickly stopped by the 300-pound bouncer standing guard at the velvet rope. You look past him and see all these clubbers having a great time inside— dancing, laughing, sipping cocktails. But unless someone on the inside has put your name on the list, you don't have a snowball's chance in hell of getting in. That's what it's like being a new screenwriter. Standing in front of an exclusive club, proudly clutching your new spec script, hoping that someone has put your name on the list. Odds are, your name's not there. You may have to wait a long, long time. You and the hundreds of other screenwriters standing in line with you.

But while it may be tough getting into that club, it's not impossible. This writer did it and I assure you he's just an ordinary guy from Toledo, Ohio, home of Jeep, the Mud Hens and the Maumee River. So why don't I tell you what I know about slipping past that velvet rope.

Preparing the Script

You might be thinking, Why should I waste all my time and talent writing an entire script when I can just come up with an irresistible idea? Isn't that what they want anyway? A pitch for a potentially huge hit? Or maybe a pitch for a breakaway indie that could capture lots of awards? No. Not now, anyway. Almost never will the decision-makers in the business indulge a pitch—without a script—from an unestablished writer. Great ideas in Hollywood are like brass fasteners. Everyone has hundreds of them. You have to show them that you can write, that you can make that great idea come alive in a fully developed, winning script.

Let's say you found your great idea. Or it found you. You outlined it, wrote that sloppy first draft, and now, some thirteen drafts later, you have a killer spec on your hands. Yep, it's all there; it moves and is moving. It's a movie. You've given birth to your bouncing million-dollar baby.

So, with the creative work done, it's time to concentrate on the business side of this endeavor. You're essentially changing hats from Writer to Salesman, viewing the spec not as your "baby" anymore, but as your widget—a product you would now like to put on the market where it becomes the object of a bidding war, finally bought by a major studio for a small fortune, and ultimately made into a hit movie for all to see.

If your widget's a winner, you have to make sure it looks like one. That old proverb, "Don't judge a book by its cover" doesn't apply to screenplays. Remember, this is Hollywood. Looks count. Don't give them a reason to dump your script in the trash before even turning to the first page.

So, first, let's get physical:

- Use the correct format. There's screenwriting software that translates your text into the industry-standard format. If you're serious about screenwriting, you should spring for the software.

- Check for typos and spelling/grammatical errors. Sloppy script=sloppy story. Don't be sloppy in any aspect of this process.

- Keep your script between 90 and 120 pages. Don't cheat with the "tightening" features on your software. People in the industry have a built-in detector for that.

- Use a title page that states the title, your name, and your contact information. Period. Don't include any mention of your script being legally protected. This comes off as amateurish.

- Use three-hole-punch paper, bound with two 1 ¼-inch brass fasteners, leaving the middle hole open. Use only solid brass fasteners, not the flimsy ones. (Most professionals use Acco Brass Fasteners #5R.)

- Print your script on a good printer.

- Don't include pictures or photos or illustrations of any kind.

- Use a plain card-stock cover (available at any office supply store). Any color is fine, but don't choose glossy or fluorescent. And do not adorn your cover with any kind of info or decoration.

Follow each of these rules to the letter. Any deviation will brand you as unprofessional.

Next, your script needs legal protection; otherwise, you may worry about someone coming along with a wodget that looks just like your widget. While the chances of this happening are fairly small, it's best to err on the side of caution.

One way to cover yourself is to register your script with the Writers Guild of America (WGA)—www.wga.org. For a modest price, your script is protected for ten years. Another option is to copyright your script through the U.S. Copyright Office. Go to www.copyright.gov and click on PERFORMING ARTS, as you're protecting a piece of dramatic work. For a fee, your script is protected until you die, plus an additional seventy years after your death. Most screenwriters only register their script with the WGA, as the paperwork is processed more quickly. However, a copyright is more binding in court and lasts much longer. You may want to do both.

With your script ready to go, set it aside. Now, you've got to pitch it.

The Pitch

Wait a second, you're thinking. You just told me I couldn't pitch these people an idea by itself. So I went off and wrote a whole script. Can't I go ahead now and mail it off to an agent? A producer? A star who's perfect for the leading role? I'll even enclose a little cast list of whom I think would be right for each part and we'll discuss it in the limo ride from LAX.

Sorry, it just doesn't work that way. People in the industry have enough solicited material to wade through on any given day without troubling themselves with an unsolicited script unless they have some inkling that it has promise. And that's exactly the purpose of the pitch. To give them that inkling, that promise.

And *then* they'll want to read your script.

What's the key to a killer pitch? Think of the whisper game. You tell someone a story; that person turns to then neighbor and repeats it; the neighbor turns to someone else and repeats it and so on. Ideally your pitch will undergo an industry version of the whisper game. An assistant tells your pitch to the agent who tells it to a producer who tells it to a studio executive who tells it to the studio head. In order for the pitch to be great, capable of reaching the most important ears in the industry, it must be clear, concise and, above all, intriguing.

You'll actually need to create three different versions of your pitch—a logline, a one-paragraph pitch, and a brief synopsis. Somewhere along the way, each of these three versions comes into play. Crafting the perfect pitch is a lot of work, but you need to take the time and effort to get good at this. So much in the movie business revolves around pitching.

The Logline

A logline is a one- or two-sentence encapsulation of your story. The story in a nutshell. It's basically the same thing as a premise, but while a premise conveys the story idea in a few sentences, a logline conveys it in only one or two. With the logline, pay close attention to the wording, making the summary as compact and compelling as possible.

For example, the premise of *Die Hard* would go something like:

> A New York cop visits L.A. for the Christmas holiday to patch things up with his estranged wife. A party in the corporate tower where his wife works is interrupted by high-tech terrorists who take everyone hostage in a ruthless scheme to crack the company's vault. The cop is the only one who has a shot at stopping them.

A logline of *Die Hard* would look more like this:

> A New York cop visiting L.A. is the only one who can stop the terrorists who have invaded a high-rise and taken the people inside hostage—including the cop's wife.

The logline is the quickest kind of pitch, which makes it extremely valuable in the movie business, where everyone is always pressed for time. A story is often pitched for the first time as a logline—over the phone, on Web sites, poolside at a party. Think of it as a literal pitch, a fastball into the strike zone. (Be careful not to confuse a logline with a "one-sheet." A one-sheet is the sexy ad slogan used on the movie's poster and promotional materials. For *Die Hard*, it was: "40 stories of sheer adventure!" While a one-sheet may titillate, it doesn't tell us much about the story.)

The logline usually contains the following:

- A glimpse of the protagonist

- The basic story idea, usually including the goal and major obstacle

- A sense of the genre

You also want the logline to have some kind of "hook" to it, something that grabs attention because it's so fresh or surprising or provocative or dramatic. In the *Die Hard* logline, for example, the hook has three prongs: It's not enough that the off-duty cop *has to battle terrorists*. Hell, that's ho-hum. In this story he has to do it *alone*. And not only that, he has to do it in an *L.A. high-rise*. But wait, there's more. There are *hostages to be rescued—among them his wife!*

Here are loglines that would work for our other four movies:

Tootsie
    A struggling actor becomes a soap opera star by disguising himself as a woman, only to fall in love with the leading lady.

Thelma & Louise
    Two southern women—a no-nonsense waitress and a sheltered housewife—turn into outlaws when a weekend away spins out of control. Running for their lives, they find their souls.

The Shawshank Redemption
    A mild-mannered banker must find an endless reserve of strength while serving a life sentence for murder inside the menacing Shawshank Prison.

Sideways

   An insecure novelist and his womanizing friend learn
hard lessons about love, cheating, and Pinot Noir through a
series of misadventures on a weeklong road trip through the
California wine country.

High-concept stories like *Die Hard, Tootsie,* and *Thelma & Louise*
can usually be nailed in just one or two sentences. The idea alone
is a grabber. Low-concept ideas like *The Shawshank Redemption* and
Sideways are more challenging to pin down in a logline because
the focus is more on character. While these kinds of stories aren't
expected to have as much flash, you still want to make them sound
as intriguing as possible.

The One-Paragraph Pitch

The one-paragraph pitch stretches the logline to include a few
more details about the protagonist and story. Like the logline, the
one-paragraph pitch should be carefully crafted so that you build
excitement in very concise language. Try to keep it under 125
words.

   The one-paragraph pitch for *Die Hard* might go something like
this:

> John McClane, a wisecracking New York City cop, comes to
> L.A. to save his failing marriage. Yet everything comes to a
> crashing halt when a band of terrorists invade a high-rise of-
> fice building and take the people inside hostage—including
> McClane's wife. The terrorists seal off the building electroni-
> cally and keep the authorities at bay with missiles. Once they
> crack a computerized code protecting millions in bonds, they
> plan to blow the building, killing the hostages and masking
> their escape. McClane, lurking in the building, unseen and
> armed with just his wits, is the only one who can stop them.

The Synopsis

The synopsis is the longest version of your pitch. You're laying out the major plot points here, giving a fuller sense of how the movie will unfold. The synopsis, however, should run no longer than 500 words (one single-spaced page).

To see a synopsis of *Die Hard*, go to www.WritingMovies.info.

Take a Shot

Pick a favorite movie. Pretend you wrote the screenplay and are now trying to sell it. Write a logline for the movie, using only one or two sentences. Make it as concise and compelling as possible. (You can test yourself against our answers by using one of the movies listed at www.WritingMovies.info.)

The Players

Now that you have your script and pitches ready to go, let's briefly meet the various people you'll want to get to, those already mingling and mixing beyond the velvet rope. The players.

The Movie Makers

Ruling over the kingdom are the studios—behemoth companies that oversee every aspect of a movie's production, including development, financing, marketing, and distribution. At present, there are six: Warner Bros., Fox, Disney, Sony, Paramount, and Universal. All six are based in or just outside of L.A. and each has a multitude of projects continually in development. Studios tend to favor the big-budget Hollywood-type movie, though most of them have smaller offshoot companies, such as Universal's Focus or Fox's Searchlight, that make indie-style movies. Then there are big production companies, often called the "mini-majors," that do all of this on a slightly reduced scale.

The top decision-makers in these companies are the executives, or "the suits." They go by all kinds of titles (usually prefaced by "vice president") and they are the ones who decide where the money goes and what projects are granted the power of a "green light."

Then there are the hundreds of smaller independent production companies known as "indies." There are actually two distinct kinds of indies: those that make primarily Hollywood-style films that are financed by the studios (many have their offices right on the lot). And then there are the truly indie indies that make films without any outside interference. They lean toward lower budgets and the offbeat style that's become the trademark of the indie film. These companies too, however, often turn to the studios for help with financing, marketing, and distribution. That's why when you watch the opening credits of a movie, you often see the banner of a production company (sometimes several) in addition to the studio banner. While many indies are in the L.A. area, they're also based in places like New York, San Francisco, Chicago, and Miami.

Producers run these production companies. They oversee all the various elements of a movie's production, from financing to casting to arranging that the crew has enough to eat. There are no set requirements to be a producer. While one producer might have a shelf full of Oscars and a parking space on the studio lot, another producer may be running his fledgling outfit out of his basement. All it really takes to call yourself a producer is a phone and some stationary with a letterhead.

Studios and most of the larger production companies have development departments. The heads of development determine the potential of incoming scripts and actively pursue other, adaptable material such as novels, plays, comic books, and magazine stories. You don't hear much about the development people, but they are a significant part of the process, especially where the writer is concerned.

Only the smallest and newest production companies will consider material from someone unknown to them. If you're a newcomer, you won't convince the studios or most production companies to look at your script. They won't even look at your pitch. They don't have time to sift through this material and they are paranoid about being sued should they produce something similar to your project. You will need help getting your material before their eyes.

The Talent

Talent refers to the actors and directors. They're the most famous players, certainly the most visible. Should one of them, especially one with any box office clout or star caché, take an interest in your script, the chances of it selling go way up. You may have someone in mind who would be "perfect" for your project and feel you absolutely have to get your script to that person. But talent is no more likely to consider your material than the studios, for pretty much the same reasons. And, look, if talent were open to considering anyone's script, writers would simply hand them their scripts as they stepped out of their limos and Hummers. "My number's on the cover. It's got Oscar written all over it." Ain't gonna happen. Actors and directors safeguard themselves from such intrusions.

Of course, there are exceptions to the rule. A first-time writer-director, Dylan Kidd, hit the jackpot when he approached the actor Campbell Scott in a Manhattan café and asked if he would read his script *Rodger Dodger* (which he carried around with him at all times). Scott accepted the script, liked it, and got it made into a movie starring himself. Bear in mind, however, that Scott is a minor star, who also produces low-budget films. Approaching A-list talent, on the other hand, will most likely lead to an unfavorable result, especially when there are bodyguards present. Once again, you'll need some help getting your material past the bouncer and into the club. You'll need some representation.

The Reps

Representation is invaluable. The reps introduce writers and their material to the moviemakers (and sometimes to the talent). More than anyone else in the industry, they're the ones who can get your name on the list. A great rep will even personally usher you past the bouncer and straight into the club. Through phone calls, lunches, and parties, the reps stay on top of what producers are looking for and attempt to get you work on rewrites whenever they see a good fit. Having a rep gives you instant credibility and connections. While obtaining one isn't the easiest thing, it's an almost essential step for the writer trying to break in.

A writer can be represented by an agent, a manager, an entertainment lawyer—or by all three at the same time.

First, agents. To take on a new client, an agent must truly like the writer's work and/or believe the work is marketable. Naturally, agents prefer to represent clients who generate saleable scripts on a semiregular basis rather than one-script wonders. Should a studio or production company show interest in a client's script, the agent will negotiate the best possible deal for the client, and if more than one company should want the script, the agent will put the script up for "auction" (a writer's dream) and let the companies bid against each other, driving up the price. For negotiating the deal, refining the terms of the contract, giving advice on scripts, agents do not directly charge the client. Instead, they take 10 percent of everything the writer makes from the material represented by the agent.

Agencies come in three sizes: big, medium, and small. The so-called Big Five—CAA, ICM, UTA, William Morris, and Endeavor—are also the most powerful, devoting their services largely to heavyweight writers and talent. The medium-size agencies usually have four to ten in-house agents, while the small agencies have only a few agents, sometimes only one. In the medium and large agencies, you will find a hierarchy of agents. Sometimes the levels are designated by the terms "senior agents" and "junior agents." As you might expect, the senior agents have much more experience and clout than their lower-level counterparts.

Managers are similar to agents but they are not regulated by the Writers' Guild of America, as agents are. In fact, managers are not regulated by anyone. This means that they cannot finalize contracts (an entertainment lawyer or agent would have to do this). Like agents, managers take their pay out of the client's gross, but there is not a set percentage. They usually charge from 5 to 15 percent.

As managers tend to have fewer clients, they can offer the writer more time and attention than an agent can. For example, while an agent may not call a writer for weeks on end, a good manager will stay in regular touch with a client, providing in-depth notes on a script and/or just offering encouragement. There are many managers who function almost as partners and will participate in their clients' projects as a producer. Some managers work with well-established companies, or with a stable of colleagues, while others operate entirely on their own, often working out of their home or rented office space.

Some writers have both an agent and a manager. This may seem extreme as it requires paying off a lot of money in percentages, but given the highly competitive nature of the business, even for those already inside the club, some writers figure they can use all the help they can get.

There are also entertainment lawyers. Like agents and managers, the better entertainment lawyers in L.A. are very plugged into the movie scene. They can get scripts read by key people and finesse the finer points of a contract. For these reasons, many screenwriters work with a lawyer in addition to an agent and/or manager. An entertainment lawyer usually takes 5 percent of any sale made through his assistance.

Last, there are the swindlers. When anyone in the business, be it ABC Agency or XYZ Management Firm, asks you for money, he might as well have "swindler" scrolling like a Times Square ticker across his forehead. The most common con is their request that you pay a "reading fee" to make a critical assessment of your script. This practice is shady. Legitimate agents and managers make money only when you make money. If an agent or manager asks you for money, stay away. They make their money from these bogus fees, not by selling scripts.

Targeting

If you have a script, you need a rep. But with thousands of reps out there, not to mention the different kinds—agents, managers, entertainment lawyers—which one should you go after? Who will best serve your needs as a screenwriter? It's a hard thing to determine and often it's hit-or-miss. Sometimes you just have to go with your gut. But the bottom line is that any representation is better than no representation. Now it's time to do a little homework. You'll need to find the most current and correct information to enable you to create a list of viable reps whom you can contact.

First, you'll need specific names. Never cold-call an agency to say, "Hey, I've just written a blockbuster and am looking for a good agent to rep me. Any ideas?" You'll be summarily dismissed. You need to target specific reps.

The most reliable resource for contact information is the *Hollywood Creative Directory*, AKA the HCD, AKA the phone book of the entertainment industry. There are actually several volumes of the HCD that deal with different aspects of the business. The volume most helpful to you as a screenwriter is the *Hollywood Representation Directory*, or HRD, which lists thousands of literary agents, managers, and entertainment lawyers, under the names of their respective companies or agencies. (The volume called *Hollywood Creative Directory* lists studios and production companies.) The HRD comes out twice a year, as the players tend to move around a lot. Be sure to consult the most current edition so that you're using the most up-to-date info. Unfortunately, this directory isn't cheap; you might want to track one down in a bookstore, where you can browse through it for free. You can also subscribe to the HCD Web site, where you receive a continually updated version of the HRD, in addition to some other directories. The subscription for this is on the steep side, too, but if you drank one less mocha latte per day, you could probably afford it.

Because you're starting out, don't think you have to target only the smaller agencies or management firms. Query every kind—small, medium, and large. The biggies will be less likely to consider you, but the more reps you query, the more chances for a positive response. No pain, no representation. In the end, the best agent/manager is the one who believes in your talent and works hard to get your material out there.

There are also numerous other resources to aid you in your targeting research. On the Internet you'll find dozens of Web sites devoted to screenwriting and the movie business. There are two trade papers for the entertainment industry, *Daily Variety* and the *Hollywood Reporter*. Again, no need to buy them; just flip through them at a large newsstand or bookstore. Inside their pages you'll read about films in production, script sales, company shake-ups, "anklings" (resignations), agent hirings, and promotions.

Zeroing In

Now it's time to narrow down your list of reps to those that might make a little more sense to contact than others. Some ideas:

1. Connections. As in most careers, if you know someone who knows someone who knows someone, you'll have a

"friendly" target on the inside. It behooves you to take advantage of the fewer degrees of separation—whether it's a relative, friend of a sister-in-law, an old classmate. Any connection you have is the obvious and best place to start.

2. If the shoe fits. If you have no connections, the best approach is to pinpoint agents and managers who represent material that seems to be in the same vein as your own. Think of recent movies, especially successful ones, that have a style and sensibility similar to your script. Find out who the writer is and who reps them by calling the Agency department of the WGA, or by searching their Web site. Also, check out the script-sale news in the trade journals or movie-business Web sites. If the script seems to fall within the same ballpark as yours— zany teen comedy, slasher, biopic, psychological thriller— note the agent and agency that made the sale.

3. Ear to the ground. While you're trawling the trades and Web sites, take special note of the insider news. For example, you might come across a small item about an agent who's broken away from Agency M to start up his own agency. Given that he's breaking new ground, he just might be open to taking on new clients. Or you may read that a producer is looking to do a movie about Exactly What You've Written. Get his name and info from the HCD.

Other factors to consider as you zero in:

Los Angeles: You want an agent or manager who is located in the greater L.A. area. Only the ones who drive on the 405 are truly plugged into the movie scene. (Granted, there are several exceptions among New York agents and managers.)

WGA signatory: For agents, you need one who is a signatory of the WGA. Only these agents have the legal right to negotiate contracts with studios and production companies that are also WGA signatories (all the significant ones are). WGA affiliation does not apply to managers.

Literary, Film: Make sure you're tracking "literary" agents, who rep writers, as opposed to "talent" agents, who rep directors, actors, or other performers. And you'll find some names that specialize in either film or TV.

Do what you have to do: In these directories or elsewhere, you'll often come across stipulations such as "no unsolicited submissions" or "by referral only." Truth is, most of the significant companies and agencies post these barriers. You can heed these warnings and move on to the next listing, or, if it's someone you feel strongly that you should contact— say, an agent who sells your kind of comedy—then by all means ignore the warning and make the attempt. No industry police will come knocking on your door to confiscate your screenwriting software.

Finally, keep in mind that the same strategy you've employed to target reps can also be applied to targeting smaller production companies. If you're having no luck securing a rep, it's worth a try.

All in all, how many reps should you target? Obviously you can't contact everyone, nor should you. But obviously, the more pitches you make, the more chances you'll get. Shoot for a hundred reps as your max, but send out your letters and make your phone calls in waves of twenty-five. That is, do the first wave, wait a month or two, then do the next wave of twenty-five. It will make the process saner and much more manageable. Start with your top choices, those that seem like the best fit. As you do this, be sure to keep careful track of the process: Record all the reps that you contact, the date you contact them, the response (if any) that you receive. This is your business now. You have to stay on top of it.

Making Contact

As you now know, you can't just send your screenplay to those reps you've targeted. It's not how it's done. First you'll need to contact them and ask if they would be willing to look at your screenplay. Your pitch is what will entice them. And once enticed, they'll want to take a look at the script.

Should you send a query letter or simply call them on the phone? Opinions vary on this. Some argue that no one in the industry bothers with letters anymore; it's all done on the phone. Others believe that making a cold call is bad form; you're just going to tie up phone lines and make people resentful.

So try both ways. And if a phone call fails, write a letter. If a letter fails, call.

Let's take a look at each approach.

The Phone Call

The phone call is more direct and aggressive than the letter, and that's not necessarily a bad thing. So learn to get your phone game on. Sound smart, professional, and confident without ever being rude or pushy.

The call will probably go something like this:

1. You call the person you've targeted from your research. Ask the "gatekeeper"—a receptionist or assistant—to speak to that person.

2. The assistant will toe the agency line and tell you something like, "We don't consider unrepresented material."

At this point, you can either:

3a. Thank them anyway, hang up, and move on to the next target.

Or:

3b. Try to edge past the agency's protocol by mentioning
that you've written a comedy (or whatever your genre)
that you believe Agent Q could really get behind.
Then, if you don't get an immediate protest, go right
into your logline. If they seem a tad interested, you
might even go into a verbal version of your one-
paragraph pitch. Why not? These people often have
the ear of their superiors. At this point, the person on
the line will either be impressed by your pitch and
request the script, or they'll simply repeat the "no
unrepresented material" line. If that's the case,
don't bother leaving a message with them. It won't
be returned. Just remain gracious and say thanks
anyway.

Regardless of what happens, always treat the person who answers the phone with courtesy and respect. Don't view them as obstacles, but as potential allies. You need them. If they hear a smart,
winning personality on the other end of the line, they will be
much more inclined to hear your pitch and relay your script to
their boss. If you're pushy or demanding, you've pretty much
wasted an opportunity. Also, you never know where these people
might end up; invariably they are grooming to be players themselves.

Whenever the phone route fails, write the target rep a query letter. This is the game. You have nothing to lose. No pain, no representation.

The Query Letter

If you're nervous or uncomfortable pitching on the phone, the
better way to go is to write a query letter. While some industry in-
siders consider it a waste of time and postage—many query letters

do get tossed out with the junk mail—there are some letters that get noticed.

A winning query letter will be brief, but impressive. A half page is ideal, never more than one page. Use decent paper and proper business format. These should never be handwritten. Always address a specific person. If you find yourself writing "Dear William Morris Agent" or "To Whom It May Concern," you might as well be writing "Dear Dumpster."

There is no standard template for a query but it usually consists of these parts:

> Reason for contact: State the reason you are contacting this specific person. If you have any connection to this person, say so up front. If not, say something else, such as mentioning you're aware that he or she represents a writer you admire and feel a kinship with.

> Pitch: Pitch your story, using the one-paragraph version. This, of course, is the part that really counts. Don't brag about how good your script is. Show them by giving a killer pitch.

> Who you are: Say a few words about yourself, especially as a way of demonstrating your ability to have written a great script. If you're a graduate of a screenwriting/playwriting/ creative writing program, or if you have something published or produced, include that here. This shows that writing isn't just a hobby you've been tinkering with down in your basement. Also, any personal experience that relates to your story might be worth mentioning.

And then sign off by saying you hope they'll request the script.

Here's pretty good example of a query letter:

Samantha Waters
The SWE Agency
1234 Rodeo Drive
Hollywood, CA 90210

Dear Ms. Waters:

I'm aware that you currently represent Meredith Harmon, who wrote *The Middle Man*. I'm a huge fan of that film, one of the most original comedies to come along in quite some time. I've written something with a unique edge of its own—a dark romantic comedy called *Noir*.

Noir is the story of Frank Merchant, a hard-boiled detective who—after chasing a suspected serial killer down an abandoned subway tunnel—enters this world, the real world, where he discovers that he's just a character in a crime novel series. When he learns that his maker, the author, plans to kill him off in the series' final installment, Frank must convince Maggie Turnbull, his biggest fan, to talk the author out of it and thus save Frank's "life."

While I was a creative writing major at Oberlin College, I always ended up steering my short stories into screenplays. Finally I just gave in to my cinematic desires. After completing *Noir*, my third feature-length screenplay, I feel both ready and confident to be seeking representation at this time.

Thanks for your time, and may I possibly send you my screenplay?

Sincerely,
Michael Cortez

Take the time to write an excellent letter. Any information that you can learn about your target rep (i.e., news items from the trades, an interview in a magazine) will be useful to add a customized touch and make your query stand out from the scores of others these folks receive. Don't get too cute or flashy. Just be yourself, on a good day. You want to come off as smart, likable, and professional. Be extra attentive to your spelling and grammar.

Finally, be sure to include an SASE (self-addressed stamped envelope) or it's highly unlikely you'll get a response. Send your query by regular mail, via the U.S. Postal Service. No need to use FedEx. Avoid faxing your letter, unless someone has specifically requested that you do so.

Sad to say, but most of the people you send query letters to will not respond. That's just the way it is. The rules of courtesy as we know them do not apply in the movie business. Silence usually means "no," and it's nothing personal. But if you have a killer pitch and you send it to enough of the right people, someone will eventually request your script.

And then there's e-mail. This is the twenty-first century after all, and more and more places are accepting it. But send your letter as an e-mail only if you know for sure that you're welcome to do so, and this will require having the e-mail address of the specific person you've targeted. When sending an e-mail query, you should observe the same professional care as you would with a conventional letter. Don't start sentences with lower-case letters, and by all means no :). As for the subject heading of your message, be simple and clear, like so: Query letter—Noir.

Getting Read

If it all goes well, the target person may ask for the script, the synopsis, or both. The person will send you a standard release form and you'll sign it, waiving your rights to sue should they represent or produce a movie that bears any resemblance, striking or otherwise, to your story. (Remember, they're all paranoid about getting sued.) You'll sign the release because, at the end of the day, what's the alternative? You send your script to *no one*. Just take a deep breath and have a little faith. Almost never do true professionals steal ideas. If they do, and your script is protected, you still have some legal recourse.

Send the script right away before you are forgotten. Enclose with it a brief letter, reminding them that they requested the script and refreshing their memory with the logline. Use Priority Mail through the U.S. Postal Service this time, and be sure to write in bold print AS REQUESTED on the envelope to prevent it from getting tossed in the slush pile, which is what happens to unrequested material. Send it via FedEx or e-mail only if they've specifically requested it to be sent as such.

So, now they finally read it, right? Right . . . ? Well, not exactly. Virtually all players—agents, managers, producers, studio execs, development people—rely on "readers" to give scripts a first screening. The larger outfits keep a stable of readers on staff, while the smaller ones commonly use interns, freelancers, or office assistants. Despite their low place on the totem pole, readers wield considerable power as far as you are concerned. They are the ones who decide if your script moves forward or stops at their desk.

After readers read your script, they write an assessment report, known as "coverage." Coverage comprises a synopsis and a one- or two-page critique of the script's merits and flaws. There will also be a kind of scorecard that looks something like this:

	Excellent	Good	Fair	Poor
Premise/Concept	X			
Storyline		X		
Structure			X	
Characterization			X	
Dialogue				X

Finally, and most significantly, the reader renders a verdict of "Pass," "Consider," or "Recommend." This verdict carries a lot of weight. When a player reviews coverage, their eyes will naturally go straight to the verdict. If, like most scripts, yours receives a "Pass," it's pretty much game-over, with this particular outfit anyway. Should a script earn a "Consider," then the odds are good that a superior will at least give it a look. Should a script merit a "Recommend," then it is almost certain to be read by the higher-ups. Readers rarely "Recommend" anything, however; if their boss reads the script and disagrees, the reader's judgment will henceforth be questioned. So even if the readers love your script, chances are they will play it safe and give it a "Consider."

The Sale or Option

Let's say your script has passed the first test. The reader gave it enough kudos to make an agent or manager want to rep you, meaning he or she will send your script around town to those producers and studio executives he feels would make for a good fit. These producers and executives, in turn, will give the script to their own readers for a second opinion. The process never ends. But the good news is, your name is getting out there. Your script is being talked about by industry people.

And then, let's say, in the best of all possible worlds, your script has impressed other readers and maybe a few suits along the way. There's been talk of actors who would be perfect for the lead. The heat and buzz intensify. A production company or studio is interested. Very interested. Your phone will ring. They want your script. What will they do to get it?

The interested party will do one of two things:

1. They will buy it.
Woo-hoo! This is what you've been waiting for. This is why you've holed up in your apartment and ignored your friends and family over these past months. The payday can be phenomenal, depending on how much a studio or

producer wants it (or how badly they want to bury it). The amount can be anywhere from $100,000 to more than a million. At the least, if you're dealing with a company that is a signatory of the WGA, there is a minimum they are required to pay you for a spec sale, which, at this writing, is in the mid–five figures. With a non-signatory company (usually a smaller production company), the money can be much lower.

Or . . .

2. They will option it.
An option is not the same as a sale. Think of it more as a rental. An option means they are purchasing the right for sole and exclusive access to your script for a set amount of time, usually six to eighteen months. When the option expires, the producer or studio will either renew the option for another six to eighteen months, or the script goes back to you. If and when shooting starts, known as "commencement of principal photography," an option turns into a sale and the purchase price goes into effect.

As a rule of thumb, a standard option with a studio or larger production company is 10 percent of the purchase price, which is how much they'll pay to buy your script should they decide to move forward and make a movie from it. So the terms of an option agreement might be $10,000 against a purchase price of $100,000. But if you're dealing with a small production company, they might pay you considerably less, or nothing more than a contract that promises monetary compensation only if the project goes into production.

An option, while not an outright sale, is still good news. It's a major vote of confidence to have a producer or studio interested in your script. Your name still gets out there and if you're lucky, you may get a little money to boot.

Development Hell

After your screenplay is sold or optioned, it goes into development. Rarely, if ever, does a writer's original script experience an immaculate conception—getting shot as is. Many of the players involved feel compelled to throw in their creative two cents on the script (usually worth much less than that) before any production checks are written. Except in the case of some low-budget indies, scripts are "developed," or reworked further. They are often developed to death. So much so that the process of developing a script is often known as "development hell." If you're lucky, you will be kept on to do at least the first couple of rewrites, per notes from one or· more of the studio executives and/or the producer attached to the project. If you're not so lucky, your script will be given to someone else to rewrite. It's not unusual for a script to be worked on by numerous writers.

Here's a fairly typical example. My writing partner, Gary Nadeau, and I wrote a spec script called *Godspeed, Lawrence Mann*, about a thirtysomething Mercury astronaut who returns to Earth after being lost in space for forty years. MGM optioned it and, about a week later, our agent at William Morris revealed that Michael Douglas was interested in playing the lead role. Our reaction was less than ecstatic as Douglas at the time was about twenty years too old for the role. All the same, Douglas was an A-list actor with Oscars for both acting and producing. Who the hell were we to snub Michael Douglas?

So, in our first rewrite, my partner and I had to make adjustments to accommodate the character's older age but, hey, we had Douglas attached and we were now part of what appeared to be a go project. Until, that is, we were taken off the project in favor of an A-list writer. When that writer turned in a disappointing rewrite, we were brought back on and wrote umpteen more drafts, only to be replaced yet again by another A-list writer, who turned in another disappointing rewrite. Eventually the project ran out of steam because the producers could not agree on the direction the script should take.

The script currently resides in development "limbo"—floating out there in space like our hero—although one of the two producers (the other being Douglas) has recently taken sole control of it and intends to get it back up and running.

That's development.

The Professional Screenwriter

Most working screenwriters don't make a living by selling their own scripts. Most working screenwriters make their living by rewriting other writers' scripts. Or by writing scripts based on ideas or properties (books, comic books, articles, plays) owned or generated by executives and producers. It's "work for hire," but it can be very lucrative. The two A-list writers who did rewrites on *Godspeed, Lawrence Mann,* for example, made ten times more than we were paid for all of our writing services on the script that got everyone interested in the first place. You would think that the creator of the original story would be the one rewarded most. Unfortunately it rarely works that way, at least not in this particular club. (And, in yet another aspect of the Hollywood madness, many incredibly successful screenwriters have never had their original material produced.)

To get these rewrite jobs, you have to go up for them, much like an actor must audition for a part. Your agent and/or manager will have the most current listing of "open" writing assignments, which could be either a rewrite or developing a concept from the ground up. Ideally you'll zero in on two or three of these projects, the ones that speak not only to your personal taste but also to your strengths as a screenwriter. Your rep will set things up. Then you'll carefully craft a pitch for each one—your take on the project, how you would rewrite/develop the script/idea. You'll deliver each pitch either as a 20-minute in-person presentation or as a 10- to 15-page treatment (a prose version of the story), or both.

If you're able to consistently deliver on these jobs, work will come your way on a regular basis. In addition, you'll get the chance to pitch your own ideas—without necessarily having written the scripts—and possibly get offered a contract based solely on that pitch. Pitching your own ideas, as well as your takes on rewrites, is akin to doing stand-up. There's no question it can be nerve-racking. Before the meeting, you sit outside the office, like a comic waiting in the green room to go on. You sip on the Evian or coffee the assistant offers, as you flip through the day's trade journals on the glass coffee table. And then the door opens, the producer or studio executive appears and lets you in. Showtime.

By the time you reach this point, you have essentially established yourself as a damn good screenwriter. The players in the industry will not only know your name, they'll put your name on the list. By now, you have not only made it past the velvet rope, you've made it onto the dance floor.

The Velvet Rope-a-Dope

Let's not lose sight of the facts: Every year about 80,000 new specs try to enter the market, or the "Big Lottery," as some writers call it. Every year about a thousand scripts are bought or commissioned, but only fewer than 10 percent of those sales are specs, meaning less than a hundred specs are purchased per year. These are very rough (and unreliable) stats, but you get the idea. The odds just aren't good for selling a spec script. The odds go up a smidge for an option but not much. You might actually be better off if you write your story as a novel, publish it, then try to sell the film rights. But that can be a tough route, too.

With the odds stacked so high against you, what can you do to beat them? Here are a few suggestions and strategies.

Write a fantastic script

I know, I know. Easier said than done. It's like saying, to win the game you have to go up to the plate and hit a grand slam. But truth is, if you don't swing for the fences, your script will not make the necessary impact. It will be just one of the countless decent scripts that flood the offices of producers and studio execs every day and ultimately slip into oblivion. But write a fantastic script and people in the industry will sit up and take notice. Even if they're unable, for whatever reason, to buy or produce or represent your script, they won't forget you. They may ask what other projects you have in the works, or they may offer you the chance to come up with a take on an in-house project they're looking to develop or rewrite. A fantastic script is the best possible calling card. If you have more than one, even better.

The fact is, breaking in is more about marketing yourself as a writer than about marketing any one script. That's why it's so crucial that you write scripts you feel passionately about, rather than to merely write what you think is saleable. Passion will bring out your best talent as a writer and storyteller and that talent will become the real ticket that gets you in the door.

Connections

While it's true that a great script will sometimes speak for itself, even the masterpieces, more often than not, need help from the inside. Without it, getting your script into the right hands, while not impossible, is a tricky proposition that requires luck and pluck.

It's extremely helpful to have an "in." A viable connection. Ideally, you have a friend in the business. Or you know someone who knows someone. But, hell, you've been holed up in the back booth of the Night Owl Café in Toledo writing your damn script for the past year and a half. When have you had time to hobnob

with anyone but Dolores, the waitress? Who you gonna meet in
Toledo?

Consider everyone you know and have ever met in your lifetime. And everyone means everyone. What about that guy who
used to live down the hall from you your freshman year in college?
You used to cram for biology exams together. Didn't you recently
read in the alumni magazine that he's working now as junior agent
in L.A.? Or even Dolores, the waitress. Didn't she mention that her
younger brother's married to a woman who works for a producer
in New York?

If you don't have any connections, what then? Make some. It's
not that hard. Especially if you have a great script to show.

To live and write in L.A.

If you're truly committed to breaking into this business, you
should consider moving to L.A. Simply put, it's where the action
is—the studios, the major production companies, the players, the
deals. You might bump into a producer at the gym, for example,
and be able to pitch her your killer logline while sweating side by
side on the treadmill. A friend of mine met his ICM agent in an
L.A. pool hall.

That said, L.A. can also put a crimp in your creativity, if not your
soul. You're sitting in a café in West Hollywood. Three guys in the
back are clacking away on their laptops, writing screenplays. The
woman sitting next to you is on her cell complaining to her agent
about the studio script notes she just received, and the pair next to
you are actually having a creative meeting. L.A. can be angst in-
ducing as the industry chatter buzzes around you like flies. You
start to fret about your own project, or wonder why your agent
hasn't called you back. Writing takes a back seat to worrying.

A compromise is to simply hang out in L.A. for a few weeks
every year, especially if you have a great script to unleash. If you've
managed to make favorable contact with some people out there,
you might be able to set up meetings. That's the way I've done it

thus far. But then I live in New York, which is the second best place to be.

Get a job in the biz

There's no better way to meet players than to work in their offices. Get a low-level job working for an agent or producer, perhaps even working as an intern. You'll see firsthand how things operate and you'll find a chance to slip someone your work. My first break in this business came when I interned for a producer while I was still a student at NYU. I would give him scripts of mine to read on the plane to L.A. He wound up optioning one of them. Of course, most of these jobs are in L.A. or New York.

Attend film festivals

They're everywhere these days, from Seattle to Sydney. Hell, by now Toledo might even have one. While some of the larger film festivals preview films that are soon to be released, most festivals showcase indie movies that are still looking for a distributor. Movie biz folk are usually in attendance and this is a good place to hobnob with them—at the theaters, bars, after-parties, restrooms.

Take writing classes

There are many good screenwriting classes that can help you fine-tune your screenwriting craft. In addition, you'll get feedback and support from your teacher and classmates, not to mention the structure and deadlines that many of us need to stay disciplined. You're also getting to know others interested in screenwriting with whom you can share information, which counts as a kind of networking. If it's within the realm of possibility, consider entering a graduate program at a reputable film school. The best of these—UCLA, USC, AFI, NYU, and Columbia—can be especially helpful to emerging writers. Also know that there are many script consultants available for private consultation on scripts, some working independently, others with teaching organizations. Classes and consultations cost money, of course, so make sure you're handing it over to a reliable place.

Join a writing group

A writing group is simply a group of writers meeting on a regular basis, reading and critiquing each other's work. Like a writing class, they can provide support, camaraderie, and those deadlines that don't let you slack off. Join a group or form one of your own, but make sure that all participants are responsible and serious about their work. This isn't like a knitting club; it's your career. If everyone stays on task, good work—and sometimes good networking—can come out of it.

Enter screenwriting contests

There are well over a hundred screenwriting contests out there, offering prizes that may include free script software, meetings with agencies for possible representation, or a nice chunk of change. You should be aware there is a ladder of prestige among contests, ranging from the elite to those no one in the business has ever heard of. Each one requires an entry fee, so choose your contests carefully or you'll blow a fortune.

Can taking a top prize in a contest get you noticed by people who count? For most of them, probably not. But there are a few top-tier contests that the players keep an eye on, requesting scripts from those who place very high. Conduct research to find which contests truly count.

Try online script marketing

Dozens of Web sites offer to post screenplays on their sites and market them to a subscriber base of film industry professionals, including agents, managers, producers, and executives. It's basically an online version of the open-air bazaar where pros trawl for product they can develop. Different sites work in different ways. For example, at some sites the pros surf the loglines, selecting those scripts they will go on to actually read. Other sites provide coverage of your script, passing along the ones marked "Recommend" to the participating pros.

Do people actually break in this way? The online brokers all boast success stories, and they claim that their service will revolutionize the spec market, becoming the primary way entertainment professionals look for fresh writers and stories. This may or may not be true. Some people, however, have managed to hook up through these sites.

There is also an in-person method of pitching for a fee, known as the pitch-fest. A group of industry types gather in a convention-like atmosphere and listen to verbal pitches from the participants. Between the two, you are probably less likely to see significant players at a pitch-fest than on the better online marketing sites.

All of these places charge a fee, of course, so check out any outfit you're considering. Look for the ones that seem the most reputable.

Produce something yourself

If you've written something that can be made on a low budget, you just might want to produce it yourself, perhaps shooting digitally, which is much cheaper than filmstock. An even more realistic option is to write and produce a short film, which you can then show as a sample of your work. It's easier to get folks in the business to watch a short film than read a long screenplay. If you're not a director, go to a film festival and find one.

You Are the Protagonist

You, as a screenwriter, are the protagonist in your own story. You weren't satisfied with your ordinary world of corralling runaway shopping carts in the A&P parking lot or fetching romance novels for the purple-haired ladies at the local library. You were reluctant, at first, to pull yourself out of that safe and familiar setting, but you finally listened to the voice inside your head (or maybe gut) and answered the call to be a screenwriter.

In the tradition of all heroes, you'll encounter obstacles on the path to your first break. Plenty of them. A demanding full-time job that leaves you little time to write. A computer virus. Acid reflux from all that coffee. A reader who gives you a "Pass" because he had a fight with his girlfriend the night before he read your script. Pressure from your parents/spouse/friends to give up. You'll encounter even more dangerous obstacles of the internal kind. Procrastination. Laziness. Writer's block. Insecurity. Fear of failure. Self-doubt.

And then there's your nemesis, Rejection. One of the fiercest villains you'll ever encounter, Rejection can sucker-punch you with a dismissive form letter or blindside you with scathing criticism. He can also deliver his most dastardly blow of all: silence. Rejection will seem, at times, invincible.

But lest ye forget, you have allies: the manager's assistant who said she liked your story idea; your high school English teacher who always encouraged you to do something with your writing; and let's not forget Dolores at the diner, who comes over to refill your coffee mug whenever she sees your eyes starting to droop while you clack away on your laptop.

You also have discipline on your side. As Woody Allen said, "Eighty percent of success is showing up." You show up at the café or your desk or wherever you prefer to work every single day. No matter what. Because the more you write, the more skilled and confident you'll become. Your voice will get stronger and more original, and as a result, your screenplays will get better and better.

And, most important of all, you have the one secret weapon that rivals the Excalibur of King Arthur, the .44 magnum of Dirty Harry, and the light-saber of Luke Skywalker. You have Perseverance. All heroes and successful screenwriters possess Perseverance. They stay the course and soldier on through the gauntlet of grueling tests and trials. They try every path and backalley in their quest because they never know which one will lead to that magic moment when they finally manage to slip past the velvet rope and enter the realm of Moviedom.

So how will your story end? You are the protagonist. The outcome is in your hands.

Stepping-Stone: The Pitches

Write a killer logline for your own movie. (You get only one or two sentences.)

Write a killer one-paragraph pitch for your movie. (You get no more than 125 words.)

Write a killer one-page synopsis of your movie. (You get no more than 500 words.)

SAMPLE SCREENPLAY TITLE PAGE

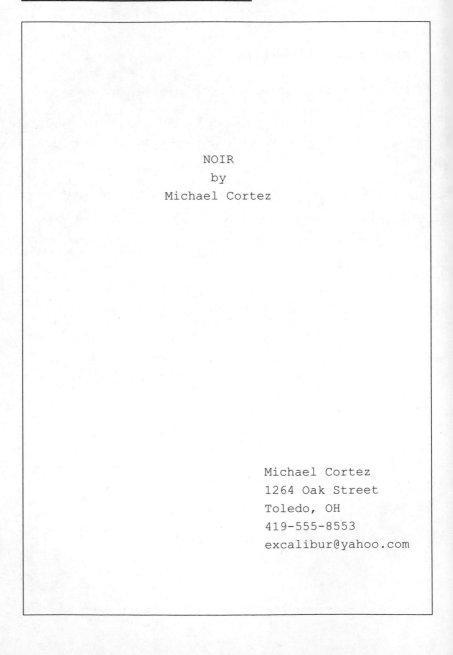

```
                    NOIR
                     by
                Michael Cortez




                        Michael Cortez
                        1264 Oak Street
                        Toledo, OH
                        419-555-8553
                        excalibur@yahoo.com
```

SAMPLE SCREENPLAY PAGE

FADE IN:

EXT. DESOLATE STREET — NIGHT

Fog. A diner. A Dumpster. Way past the hour when anyone should be out and about, at least for this neighborhood.

A man turns a corner and strolls onto the street. This is FRANK MERCHANT. A fedora shadows his face but we can tell that's he's tough. He'll remind you of Sam Spade, perhaps a little nicer and slightly dumber.

He stops, checks his watch, then takes a look at the faded sign on the diner's exterior — Nite Owl Café. This is the right place.

Merchant taps his foot, waiting, maybe a little on edge.

He reaches inside his trench coat, pulling something out. A stick of gum. He unwraps it, slips it in his mouth.

A sound. He turns. A rat scurries under the Dumpster.

But wait, that wasn't it. From somewhere comes a muffled moan.

Merchant strides to the Dumpster, opens it.

Inside lies an elderly man, elegant in a white suit, bound and gagged. This is PROFESSOR VLADIMIR STANISLAV.

Merchant removes the gag.

                    STANISLAV
                (thick Russian accent)
          It's a trap, Frank.

Eyeballing the man. Is he speaking the truth? Merchant hoists Stanislav out of the Dumpster, removing the binding.

                    STANISLAV (CONT'D)
          Hey, Frank, might you have a
          cigarette I can borrow?

                    FRANK
          Sorry, Professor, I'm trying to
          quit.

Format Guide

Screenplays should be formatted according to industry standards. Scriptwriting software will make these adjustments for you automatically, or you can set the proper tabs with your word-processing software.

The measurements given below will vary among screenplays (and scriptwriting software) but these measurements are acceptable norms. There are some minor variations in format between spec screenplays and shooting scripts. The following guidelines apply to specs.

General Layout

Font

12-point Courier only

Pages

A page number appears on the upper-right-hand corner of every page (except the first).

Each page represents approximately one minute of screen time. This is the reason your screenplay should run between 90 and 120 pages.

Page margins

Top: 1"

Bottom: 1"

Left: 1.5" (the extra width allows room for binding)

Right: 1"

Spacing

Everything is single-spaced.

Always insert a blank space between paragraphs or when you switch from scene heading to description or from description to dialogue.

Scene Headings

Each scene begins with a *scene heading*, also known as a "scene header" or "slugline." The scene heading indicates the time and place of each scene. Whenever either the time or place changes, by even a little bit, this constitutes a new scene.

The scene heading contains three pieces of information:

• Interior or exterior (INT., EXT.)

• Place: where, in a general sense, the scene occurs

• Time: when, in a general sense, the scene occurs, usually DAY or NIGHT

Scene headings start on the left margin. They are spelled in CAPS. Insert one space between the end of the previous scene and the scene heading. Before the time designation, you can use a dash, double dash, or just a space. A scene heading looks like this:

```
EXT. THELMA'S HOUSE — DAY
```

If it's essential that the scene take place at DAWN, MORNING, DUSK, EARLY EVENING, then you can use those terms. If it's essential that the scene take place at an exact time, then you can state the time, such as 4:00 A.M.

If a scene occurs shortly after the previous scene in the same location, then you can indicate the time with LATER, or some variation thereof, like so:

```
INT. INTERROGATION ROOM — MOMENTS LATER
```

When the action moves from one place to another without a break in time—say, following a character who is walking through a building, then you can indicate the time with CONTINUOUS, like so:

```
INT. HALLWAY — CONTINUOUS
```

Scene Description

Scene description, also known as "action" or "direction," conveys what happens: physical actions, character and setting description, sounds, etc.

All description starts at the left margin and runs straight across to the right margin, and looks like this:

```
Louise drives through the desert back toward the
road, past the burning debris of the truck. As she
gets to the road she stops. Thelma climbs into the
front seat.
```

Dialogue

The words spoken by the characters are *dialogue*.

Dialogue is always preceded by a *character name*, also known as a "character cue," which gives the name of the character speaking in

CAPS. If the character is very minor, you might use a designation, such as WAITRESS or OLD MAN.

The character name starts 4" from the left of the page.

The dialogue itself starts 2.5" from the left of the page. It should run no farther than 2.5" from the right of the page, and looks like this:

```
                    LOUISE
          Why don't you ditch that
          loser husband of yours?
```

Parentheticals

A parenthetical, also known as a "line action," is a brief description inserted within dialogue and surrounded by parentheses. A parenthetical will indicate how a line is said, or indicate a minor action done by a character while speaking.

A parenthetical is inserted into the dialogue section, but on a line of its own. It starts 3" from the left of the page. It should run no further than 3.5" from the right of the page, and looks like this:

```
                    LOUISE
                (wistful)

          I wonder if
          Jimmy's gotten back.
```

V.O./O.S.

When a character speaks in narration (or speaks without being in the scene) it is referred to as *voice-over*. Voice-over is indicated by placing V.O. beside the speaker's name, like so:

```
              THELMA (V.O.)
     Alright, ladies and
     gentlemen, let's see who'll
     win the prize for keepin'
     their cool.
```

When a character speaks from nearby but is *off screen*, this is indicated by placing O.S. beside the speaker's name. For example, if a character is calling from a neighboring room, O.S. might be used, like so:

```
              J. D. (O.S.)
          (through the door)
     Thelma? It's me.
```

Transitions

Some screenplays indicate the transition from scene to scene with this:

```
                    CUT TO:
```

The words begin 5.5" from the left of the page.

As there's no real need to use CUT TO after every scene, you can just skip it. You may wish to use it if you want to indicate an especially fast or dramatic transition from one scene to the next.

If you want a transition that is really fast or shocking, then you may use this:

```
              SMASH CUT TO:
```

If you want a transition that is especially slow, then you may use this:

```
              DISSOLVE TO:
```

It's optional, but a screenplay may start with:

                        FADE IN:

And end with:

                        FADE OUT.

Continued

If a character's speech is cut off at the page break, then you continue the speech on the following page. You indicate it is a *continued* speech with CONT'D (although some scripts don't capitalize "cont'd"), like so:

                    LOUISE (CONT'D)
            I don't want to see any more
            beef jerky. It's drivin' me
            crazy. The whole car smells
            like it.

You may also use this technique when a character's speech is interrupted by action, but it's not essential. Like so:

                    THELMA
            And smooth, boy, are you
            smooth.

They kiss passionately.

                    THELMA (CONT'D)
            You're kinda the best thing
            that's happened to me in a
            long time.

In a shooting script, CONTINUED (or MORE) is sometimes used on the bottom and top of pages where a scene continues from one page to the next, but this isn't necessary for a spec script.

Other Capitalization

Capitalize each letter of a character's name the first time that character appears in the script, like so:

```
DARRYL comes trotting down the stairs.
```

In a shooting script, sound effects are capitalized. You may also do this in a spec script, but it's not essential. It works like so:

```
As they speed out of the parking lot back to the
road, we hear MUSIC blaring from the nightclub.
They hit the main road with tires SQUEALING.
```

Camera Directions

Spec screenplays should include few or no *camera directions*, but if it's crucial to indicate what the camera should show, you can indicate it, like so:

```
Hal goes over a list of every registered green
T-Bird in the state.

COMPUTER MONITOR

Names are scrolling by as Hal stares blankly at
the screen.
```

Occasionally, you can use actual camera terms, if you must. The most common types of camera directions are CLOSE ON,

CLOSEUP, EXTREME CLOSEUP. If the camera is close, indicate it like so:

```
EXTREME CLOSEUP of Darryl's face.
```

The terms ANGLE, and ANGLE ON designate where the camera is focused, like so:

```
ANGLE ON THELMA

She has her finger on the lever.
```

When a character's name is preceded or followed by POV, this means we are seeing something from that character's point of view. Like so:

```
LOUISE'S POV OF THE SPEEDOMETER AT 100mph.
```

Notice that all explicit camera directions are spelled in CAPS.

Montage

When a series of scenes or shots is shown in quick succession, this is called a *montage*. A montage may forgo scene headings and appear like so:

```
MONTAGE

1.Early-morning staff.
2.A truck driver climbing into his cab with a sil-
  ver thermos.
3.Squirrels hopping around on the ground.
```

You can skip the numbers if you like. Or you can use letters. Or you can go as simple as this:

```
MONTAGE of early-morning staff, a truck driver
climbing into his cab with a silver thermos,
squirrels hopping around on the ground.
```

Glossary

Screenwriting terms are not standardized; various people use different terms, or use different meanings for the same terms. The following terms are defined the way they are used in this book. (Format terms are defined in the format guide.)

Action What characters do

Acts The major sections of the story, three acts being the norm—Act I, Act II, Act III

Antagonist The character or force that provides the primary obstacle to the protagonist

Arc A character's progression, usually including an internal change

Beat sheet An outline that shows every event of the movie

Climax A major event occurring near the end of the story, usually a showdown between the protagonist and his or her primary obstacle that will determine the answer of the major dramatic question

Deeper desire A desire underlying a goal, often something internal and abstract

Goal The primary objective that a protagonist (or another character) pursues throughout the bulk of the story, usually something tangible and specific

Inciting incident A major event occurring early in Act I that sets the story in motion

Lead-in The start of the story up to the inciting incident

Logline A one- or two-sentence encapsulation of the story, used to help sell the script

Main relationship character The character with whom the protagonist has the most significant relationship

Major dramatic question The question around which the story is centered, usually involving the protagonist and his or her goal

Marker 1 and 2 Significant events that, along with the midpoint, break Act II into quadrants

Midpoint A major event occurring in the middle of Act II that sends the story in a new direction or brings about a new vibe

Objective Whatever a character is trying to do or obtain in a scene

Obstacle Whatever is blocking a character from achieving a goal or objective

Plot point 1 A major event occurring at the end of Act I that creates or solidifies the major dramatic question

Plot point 2 A major event occurring at the end of Act II that propels the story toward its climax

Plot strand An aspect of the plot with its own progression, that is too connected to the main plot to be considered a subplot

Premise An encapsulation of the story, of no more than three sentences, used to help plan the story

Protagonist The main character, usually associated with a goal and an arc

Resolution A brief section after the climax where loose ends are tied up and a hint of the aftermath is shown

Scene A segment of the story occurring in a single time and place

Sequence A series of linked scenes that tell a mini-story

Story map An outline that shows the major events of the movie

Subplot A storyline that is somewhat separated from the main plot

Subtext The meaning beneath what is seen or heard on the surface

Treatment A prose version of a movie, used for planning or communicating the story

Cheat Sheet

Premise

- Can you focus your story into a premise of no more than three sentences?

- Does your premise have appeal?

- Do you have a sense of the type of movie you're writing? High/low concept? Hollywood/indie? Can you pinpoint the genre?

Plot

- Do you have a major dramatic question?

- Do you have a protagonist with a strong goal that is specific and tangible?

- Does your protagonist have plenty of obstacles? Both external and internal obstacles?

- Does your story have three acts? Are the proportions of the three acts about right?

- Do you have an inciting incident, a plot point 1, a midpoint, a plot point 2, and a climax?

- Are the events of your story linked by cause and effect?

- Does your lead-in set up the story quickly and effectively?

- Do you have enough conflict to sustain Act II? Does the conflict escalate? Do you raise the stakes effectively?

- Does your story swing between highs and lows?

- Do you have a strong enough climax? Does the protagonist take a final action against his or her biggest obstacle? Does it lead to an answer to the major dramatic question?

- If you are bending or breaking the standard "rules" of plot, are you doing it for a good reason?

Character

- Is your protagonist active? Does he or she have an arc? Appeal?

- Do you have other major characters that are compelling? Are the minor characters interesting enough?

- Do you have the right number of characters? Too many? Too few? Have you orchestrated the cast well?

- Do all your characters have desires?

- Do your major characters have contrasting traits that make them complex?

- Do you know your characters well enough?

- Have you given your characters the right names?

- Are you showing your characters through their actions?

The Pages

- Is your screenplay formatted properly?

- Do your descriptions convey only what is seen and heard? Do they do it clearly and vividly?

- Are your descriptions economical? Do they have a vertical flow? Are they a pleasure to read? Are you using strong verbs?

- Have you found a compelling voice?

Scenes

- Are your scenes relevant? Do they contain conflict? Do they have a beginning, middle, and end?

- Are you using enough sequences?

- Are you showing, not telling? Using strong visuals?

- Do you have the right settings?

- Do your scenes contain subtext?

- Are the scenes focused enough? Are you entering late, getting out early?

- Are your transitions effective? Is there "space" between your scenes?

- Do you have the right scenes? Are they in the right place?

Dialogue

- Does your dialogue sound real yet also get to the point quickly?

- Do your characters sound distinctive from each other and appropriate to who they are?

- Is there anywhere your dialogue can be improved by using subtext?

- Are you letting actions and visuals enhance (or replace) your dialogue?

- Are you saving exposition for the right places? Does it feel natural?

Subplots

- Have you found one or more subplots?

- Do your subplots enhance the story through character, plot, or theme?

- Do your subplots have a beginning, middle, and end?

- Are your subplots interwoven effectively with the main plot?

- Do you have too many subplots? Do any of them overshadow the main plot?

Tone/Theme

- Have you zeroed in on the tone of your story? Are you conveying it consistently and well?

- Have you identified a theme for your story?

- Are you showing your theme, rather than telling it?

Revision

- Have you gotten enough distance from your story to begin the revision process?

- Have you considered re-envisioning your story?

- Have you looked through a magnifying glass at all the "Big Things" in your story?

- Have you looked through a microscope at all the "Little Things" in your story?

- Have you cut and sharpened as much as you possibly can?

Acknowledgments

Much like an actual movie, *Writing Movies* emerged from the efforts of many people.

The studio, so to speak, is Bloomsbury USA, and there does not exist a more legendary group of moguls than Colin Dickerman, Sabrina Farber, Peter Janssen, Sara Mercurio, Greg Villepique, and Miles Doyle.

The producers are the founders of Gotham Writers' Workshop, Jeff Fligelman and David Grae, and the president of Gotham, Andre Becker, who declared at the outset, "Make it better than *Lawrence of Arabia* and never mind about the cost."

The stars are the Gotham screenwriting teachers who contributed the chapters to this book. Each of them did their own stunts and none demanded a bigger trailer.

The agent is, well, the agent, Faith Hamlin of Sanford Greenburger Associates.

The director is Alexander Steele, a man who makes Erich von Stroheim seem tame.

Then there's the invaluable crew, consisting of the Gotham office staff—Joel Mellin, Dana Miller, Linda Novak, Betsey Odell, Stacey Panousopoulos, Charlie Shehadi—and a long scroll of Gotham teachers. None of these people has ever taken a day off.

And let us not forget the audience, which consists of all the Gotham students who have taught us how to teach over the years, and you—the readers who make this book spring to life through the sheer act of reading it.

Contributors

MICHAEL ELDRIDGE cowrote the feature film *Beauty Remains* (Emerging Pictures) and has optioned and developed screenplays for numerous independent production companies. With Barataria Productions he produces feature films, documentaries, and theater. He lives in New York City.

AMY FOX wrote the feature film *Heights* (Merchant Ivory Productions), which is adapted from her play. Her plays have been widely produced and she has developed screenplays for numerous independent production companies. She lives in New York City.

JOHN GLENN has written screenplays and TV scripts that have been sold to or developed for Sony, Warner Bros., Paramount, Disney, Fox, Touchstone/ABC, Bruckheimer Films, Revolution, and DreamWorks. He lives in Los Angeles.

JASON GREIFF has developed screenplays and TV scripts for Universal and Touchstone/ABC, and his screenplays have won contests sponsored by the Writers Guild of America and NYU. He lives in New York City.

TOMMY JENKINS wrote and directed the short films *Obit* and *Come Back to the Five and Dime Buster Keaton, Buster Keaton*. He has published sports articles and short fiction, and *Movie Trivia Quiz Book* and *TV Trivia Quiz Book*. He lives in Raleigh, North Carolina.

HELEN KAPLAN wrote and directed the award-winning short film, *Return to Sender*, served as associate producer on the PBS documentary *New York*, and has worked as a film editor on projects for ABC and PBS. She lives in New York City.

TAL MCTHENIA wrote the independent films *Clear Out* (Dalzell Productions) and *Shift* (ITVS), and has developed screenplays for numerous independent production companies. He served as associate producer on the documentaries *Every Mother's Son* and *Out at Work*. He lives in New York City.

CHRISTOPHER MOMENEE has sold or optioned feature screenplays to Disney, MGM, Columbia, and numerous independent production companies. He lives in New York City.

DANIEL NOAH wrote and directed the feature film *Twelve* (Emerging Pictures), and has developed screenplays and TV scripts for Warner Bros., Fox, Dimension, Imagine, and NBC. He lives in Los Angeles.

ALEXANDER STEELE serves as dean of faculty of Gotham Writer's Workshop. He has edited the books *Writing Fiction* and *Fiction Gallery*, and written plays, screenplays, nonfiction pieces, and books for children. He lives in New York City.

PAUL ZIMMERMAN wrote the feature film *A Modern Affair* (Tribe Productions). His plays have been widely produced and he has developed screenplays for numerous independent production companies. He lives in New York City.

Index